The Parsi Theatre

SEAGULL
BOOKS
•
CELEBRATING
40 YEARS

THE INDIA LIST

The Parsi Theatre

Its Origins and Development

SOMNATH GUPT

EDITED AND TRANSLATED BY

Kathryn Hansen

LONDON NEW YORK CALCUTTA

Seagull Books, 2023

Originally published in Hindi as Somnath Gupt, *Parsi Thiyetar: Udbhav aur Vikas*
by Lokbharati Prakashan, Allahabad, India, 1981
© Rajkamal Prakashan, 2022

First published in English translation by Seagull Books, 2005
English translation, forewords, and annotation © Kathryn Hansen, 2005, 2023

Images © Individual agencies, networks, archives

ISBN 978 1 8030 9 200 3

British Library Cataloguing-in-Publication Data
A catalogue record for this book is available from the British Library

Typeset by Seagull Books, Calcutta, India
Printed and bound by WordsWorth India, New Delhi, India

Contents

Illustrations

Foreword to the Second Edition

It gives me great pleasure to join in the celebration of 'Seagull at 40' by presenting this new edition of the classic study of the Parsi theatre. In the history of popular entertainment, the Parsi theatre holds its own with vaudeville in America and music hall in Britain. Its imprint on Indian theatre has been immense. Habib Tanvir (1923–2009) and Girish Karnad (1938–2019), dramatists who crafted the most creative expressions of Indian modernity, grew up with Parsi theatre spectacles and were powerfully affected by their childhood experiences. Parsi theatre's impact on India's popular cinema is legendary. From the music-and-dance format to the mythological genre and domestic socials, Parsi theatre paradigms vied with Hollywood influences to shape the talkies. Outside of India, touring troupes led by adventurous Parsi entrepreneurs sparked the creation of new dramatic styles across Southeast Asia and beyond.

Fascination with Parsi theatre has long inspired my scholarship. But as a field of study, it was barely recognized a decade or two ago. Since then, research in Parsi theatre has flourished on multiple fronts. Parsi theatre now features as a necessary chapter in surveys of Indian theatre and performance. In the perennially popular area of Indian Shakespeare Studies, Parsi theatre adaptations are recognized as central. The turn towards images over texts in the study of visual culture has highlighted the connections among media, linking Parsi theatre's penchant for melodrama with other genres. Parsi theatre in consort with chromolithographs ('god posters'), Marathi musical theatre, and Dadasaheb Phalke's silent films produced the resurgence in the nationalist era of 'mythologicals'—dramatized epic tales—with enduring consequences for popular culture and politics.

Gender theory has also cast a new light on Parsi theatre, a personal interest of mine. Novel interpretations of the practice of female impersonation and scrutiny of the life narratives of female impersonators have been my focus for long. My 2011 book, *Stages of Life: Indian Theatre Autobiographies,* was the outcome of this exploration. Another bonanza for Parsi theatre scholarship was the arrival of 'connected' and global history approaches. Article after article have sketched the routes of Parsi companies' travels on mental maps, linking Bombay to Aden, London, Nepal, Sri Lanka, Burma and Indonesia. The discoveries are ongoing.

Somnath Gupt's *Parsi Theatre* is cited as a vital source of information in every scholarly treatment of the subject. The translated, annotated edition of 2005 is an essential text for researchers and students alike. A quick Google search shows that university syllabi all across India list Gupt/Hansen as required reading—as do many North American and European courses on South Asian theatre and cinema studies. Yet the book has become more and more difficult to obtain. It is clear that its reissue is long overdue. I applaud the initiative to bring this core document back into circulation and make it available in print and ebook formats.

With fulsome thanks to Bishan Samaddar and the team at Seagull who have facilitated this effort, let me send my earnest congratulations to Naveen Kishore, Seagull Books' founder, on this very special occasion. Naveen's personal passion for contemporary Indian theatre, fiction and poetry in translation, and critical theory gave Seagull its distinctive stamp from the start. Under his guidance, the press became internationally recognized as a discerning publisher of the best in world literature. I felt privileged to publish with Seagull Books in 2005, and I am proud to be able to contribute to the festivities in its honour in 2022–23.

Kathryn Hansen
Austin, Texas, USA
May 2022

FIGURE 1. Fida Husain, the last legendary actor of the Parsi theatre, who died in 2001. Courtesy: Natya Shodh Sansthan.

Foreword to the First Edition

Beginning in 1853, the Parsi theatre rapidly developed into a mobile, company-based entertainment that reached across colonial and princely India and extended overseas into Southeast Asia. It arose at approximately the same time as the modern Bengali and Marathi theatres, and, like them, employed the prevailing local languages: Gujarati, Urdu and Hindi. All three Indian-language theatres shared the use of the European-style proscenium with richly painted backdrop curtains and trick stage effects. Like the English stage of the period, they depended on spectacle and melodrama to create audience appeal. Simultaneously, these emerging theatres ushered in the conventions and techniques of realism, marking the transition from stylized open-air presentations to a new urban drama. Although largely displaced by motion pictures after the advent of sound in the 1930s, the Parsi theatre remains significant for its long-term impact on diverse regional theatrical styles and on the popular cinema.

At present the Parsi theatre is a source of fascination to theatre practitioners, scholars of visual culture and the cinema, and students of media and popular culture. At the National School of Drama in New Delhi, veteran performers like the late Master Fida Husain have been tapped to reconstruct the art of the Parsi theatre for budding actors and metropolitan audiences. Film studies scholars likewise are investigating the record to discover the relationship between the theatrical legacy and the genres of popular Indian film. Others are fascinated by the songs, dances, and musical repertoire associated with the Parsi theatre and are attempting to preserve them archivally before it is too late. Cultural historians of western India have also begun to re-evaluate this once hidden chapter of the collective Parsi past.[1]

Indeed, the Parsi theatre is a vital component of India's cultural heritage, but one that has often been dismissed and misunderstood. In this context there is a great need for reliable information in English that would shed light on the history and practice of this important theatrical form. Early in the twentieth century, contemporary observers like A. Yusuf Ali, Ram Babu Saksena, and R. K. Yajnik provided documentation that is still of value.[2] Critical research on the subject, however, is scant until a new crop of academic explorations emerged in the 1990s. For their investigations, Anuradha Kapur, David Willmer, and the translator/editor of the present volume are all indebted to a common source.[3] That source is a Hindi book that appeared in 1981, Somnath Gupt's *Parsi Thiyetar*. Simply stated, Gupt's book is the best single reference for the early period of Parsi theatre history. It covers the antecedent phase of English theatre in eighteenth-century Bombay and extends through the end of the nineteenth century.

Gupt's full title is *Parsi Thiyetar: Udbhav aur Vikas* (Parsi Theatre: Its Origins and Development). The book was published in Allahabad by Lokbharati Prakashan in 1981. The work apparently grew out of Gupt's earlier book, *Hindi Natak Sahitya ka Itihas* (History of Hindi Dramatic Literature), published in Jalandhar in 1949 and in Allahabad by Hindi Bhavan in 1958. Gupt may have finished *Parsi Thiyetar* by 1969, judging by the date of its foreword ('Do Shabd'). A professor in the Hindi Department of Rajasthan University at Jaipur, Gupt also published *Ashtachhap Padavali* (1940), *Alochana ke Siddhant* (1952), *Purv-Bharatendu Natak Sahitya* (1958), and several other books.

Two things make Gupt's book stand out among the various Hindi monographs on the subject.[4] First, Gupt consulted a range of source materials in several Indian languages as well as in English. These are acknowledged in his footnotes and preface. The references point to a dense layer of primary evidence consulted by Gupt himself or cited from the secondary literature. The type of material is diverse, including advertisements, reviews, and letters from the English newspapers, *The Bombay Times* and *The Bombay Courier and Telegraph*, and the Gujarati newspapers, *Rast Goftar* and *Kaiser-e Hind*; early autobiographies and memoirs, like Jahangir Khambata's work, *Maro Nataki Anubhav* (My Experiences in the Theatre); and compendia of theatre lore published in Gujarati and Urdu, such as those by Dhanjibhai Patel (*Parsi Natak Takhtani Tavarikh* or The History of the Parsi Theatre) and Abdul Alim Nami (*Urdu Thetar*).

Second, Gupt's interpretive apparatus is relatively free of the bias that pervades most of the Indian-language writing on the Parsi theatre.[5] Closely correlated to the specific language in which it was composed—Urdu, Gujarati, or Hindi—this literature often reveals a preference for one particular group or community over another. Typically, Urdu-language histories of the Parsi theatre laud the Urdu playwrights' contributions but barely recognize the existence of Gujarati and Hindi playwrights. In similar fashion, the accounts in Hindi and Gujarati denigrate the Urdu *munshis* (staff writers) as hacks or do not even mention them. Yet as Gupt himself states, it was 'Parsis, non-Parsis, Hindus, Muslims, and Christians who spread the art of theatre by founding theatrical companies, who built playhouses and encouraged drama, who became actors and popularized the art of acting, who composed innumerable dramas in Gujarati, Hindi, and Urdu, who composed songs and defended classical music, and who wrote descriptions of the Parsi stage and related matters.'[6] The Parsi theatre in the nineteenth century was quite free of communal antagonisms. It is, rather, literary history written in the twentieth century that has compartmentalized its development and divided it along linguistic, ethnic, and religious lines.

For these reasons, Gupt's *Parsi Thiyetar* is a worthy source whose English translation is long overdue. As one who has consulted the book repeatedly over a period of years, I have come to both appreciate it and to recognize its limitations. Its omissions and commissions now require some mention, in that my editorial strategies are intimately connected with them. Although Gupt was successful in locating a number of significant sources, he was unable to consult the records of the British Museum and India Office Library, where many of the old printed play texts are housed. Gupt therefore perpetuates the belief that Parsi theatre play texts were not published or are unavailable, and his bibliographic details are accordingly incomplete. Wherever possible, I have supplied the missing information, drawing on my numerous research visits to the archives in India, the United States, and England. All of my editorial additions are indicated by square brackets in the endnotes.

My thorough familiarity with the Parsi theatre literature has also enabled me to identify the extent of Gupt's dependence upon previously published (and unpublished) works for major sections of his book. These include Mehta's English-language dissertation on the eighteenth- and nineteenth-century English stage in Bombay, Patel's and Sharof's Gujarati works on the history of the Parsi theatre, and Nami's multi-volume *Urdu Thetar*.[7] Because of Gupt's rather minimal use of citations, the large measure of his reliance upon these authors is not clearly visible. As editor, I have compared Gupt's text with these sources and amplified the footnotes wherever necessary. I have also corrected the errors that have crept in during the process of transliterating from one Indian script to another, as well as when copying English-language passages. What has not been possible is to resolve the discrepancies contained within and among these multiple sources. Numerous inconsistencies and fragmented bits of information remain in this translation. Many of these stem from the works that Gupt consulted. However, Gupt himself made mistakes and allowed contradictions to stand. This translation represents a corrected version of Gupt's original text, but its level of accuracy is still probably somewhat below desirable standards for scholarly research today.

Another difficulty posed for the English reader is the variation in the spelling of Indian proper names. Public personages of the period often spelled their names in English one way, and in Gujarati or other Indian languages quite another way. Even within a single language or writing system, numerous variations occur. The Parsi predilection for attaching the honorific suffix '–ji' to the elements of a name adds to the possibilities. Thus Kaikhushro Navrojji Kabraji is referred to as Kabraji, K. N. Kabraji, K. N. Kabra, Kaikhushro Navrojji Kabra, and Kaikhushro Kabra, to say nothing of the occasional Kaikhusro, Kekhusro, Navroz and Nauroz. For this edition, a standard form of each name has been adopted; the same principle has been extended to the names of dramas and theatrical companies. Generally speaking, titles and honorifics such as Dr, Seth, Miyan, Pandit, Master, Dadi, Dadabhai and –ji have been deleted to aid in name recognition.

Gupt's expository style is rather prolix and repetitious, although no more so than comparable Hindi literary studies. Since the value of Gupt's book lies in the information it contains rather than its prose per se, I have taken the liberty of tightening the syntax and removing redundancies. Another characteristic is the descriptive rather than analytical nature of the treatment. Although it supplies much valuable detail, the book carries no central argument. Often the amassing of evidence is not well organized. The result is a certain tedium for the reader, who must sort through an excess of fact without a strong supporting framework.

To overcome these obstacles and make the book more accessible, several years ago I published an abridged version of the translation in three instalments in *Sangeet Natak*, the journal of India's national academy of the performing arts, the Sangeet Natak Akademi.[8] The response to these excerpts was enthusiastic. Several prominent theatre practitioners and scholars encouraged me to publish the entire volume as soon as possible. It is now my good fortune to be working with Seagull Books, the pre-eminent publisher in the field of Indian theatre and performing arts, and Gupt's original text has been transformed into a beautifully produced book. The text as translated appears here in a slightly abridged form. Only one of the three appendices has been included in this edition, and several repetitious lists have been compressed. However, all of Gupt's introductory matter, chapters, and footnotes have been reproduced.

Another major enhancement is the inclusion of a number of illustrations collected during the course of my research. Gupt's original text included fourteen photographs without attribution, printed rather poorly in an appendix. For this edition, I have selected about twice that number of historic photographs of old playhouses, actors, and scenes on-stage. Permission to publish certain of these illustrations has been generously granted by the Natya Shodh Sansthan, Kolkata, the Indira Gandhi National Centre for the Arts, New Delhi, and the British Library. I also include a smaller number of photographs taken by myself in the theatre districts of present-day Mumbai. The remainder are from printed books no longer under copyright.

During the years when I worked on this translation, I was fortunate to receive funding in the form of research fellowships from the American Council for Learned Societies, the National Endowment for the Humanities, the American Institute of Indian Studies, and the USIA Fulbright Senior Scholar Program. The generosity of all of these agencies is gratefully acknowledged. Their role in enabling me to travel to India for the collection of primary sources and photographs was particularly critical to the success of this work.

Many individuals have also supported and assisted me, among whom I particularly wish to thank Abhijit Chatterjee, Sushma Merh-Ashraf, Samira Sheikh, and Karline McLain. As editor of *Sangeet Natak*, Abhijit carefully went through my drafts, and encouraged me in preparing the abridged translation for the select readership of his journal. Sushma served as patient translator from the Gujarati of Dhanjibhai Patel's history; her readings have helped to clarify a number of points in Gupt's text. Samira's assistance in translating the Gujarati *dibachos* of early Parsi playwrights has been invaluable not only for this project but for other articles I have written. Karline's close scrutiny of the manuscript in its near-final stage was of great help in standardizing spellings and producing internal consistency. All of their efforts to bring this project to completion are sincerely appreciated.

Finally, I wish to express my deep gratitude to the University of Texas at Austin for the University Cooperative Society Subvention Grant which has helped underwrite the costs of publication.

Through the acts of translation, edition, and annotation, I have sought to make Gupt's *Parsi Thiyetar* a useful source of information for the general reader and the theatre specialist. This translation will not put to rest the controversies surrounding the Parsi theatre and its significance to the cultural history of South Asia. However, it will make available in English one of the most frequently consulted studies of this seminal theatre form, thus opening the door to further research.

Kathryn Hansen
2005

Notes

1 Gopal Shastri, 'The Contribution Made by the Parsis to Gujarati Theatre', and Sharatchandra Vishnu Gokhale, 'Indian Music among the Parsis', both in Nawaz B. Mody, ed., *The Parsis in Western India: 1818 to 1920* (Bombay: Allied Publishers, 1998), pp. 221–34, 235–49.

2 A. Yusuf Ali, 'The Modern Hindustani Drama', *Transactions of the Royal Society of Literature*, 2nd ser. 35 (1917), pp. 79–99; Ram Babu Saksena, *A History of Urdu Literature*, 2nd ed. (Allahabad: Ram Narain Lal, 1940, orig. 1924); Y. K. Yajnik, *The Indian Theatre* (London: George Allen and Unwin, 1933).

3 Kathryn Hansen, *Grounds for Play: The Nautanki Theatre of North India* (Berkeley: University of California Press, 1992/Delhi: Manohar Publications, 1993); Kathryn Hansen, 'Making Women Visible: Gender and Race Cross-Dressing in the Parsi Theatre', *Theatre Journal* 51 (1999); Anuradha Kapur, 'The Representation of Gods and Heroes in the Parsi Mythological Drama', in Vasudha Dalmia and H. von Stietencron, eds., *Representing Hinduism: The Construction of Religious Traditions and National Identity* (Delhi: Sage, 1995), pp. 401–19; David Willmer, 'Theatricality, Mediation and Public Space: The Legacy of Parsi Theatre in South Asian Cultural History' (PhD dissertation, University of Melbourne, 1999).

4 These include Lakshmi Narayan Lal, *Parsi-Hindi Rangmanch* (Delhi: Rajpal and Sons, 1973); Devesh Sharma, *Hindi Rangmanch ke Vikas men Bambai ka Yog* (Bombay: Bambai Hindi Vidyapith, 1987); Vidyavati Lakshmanrao Namra, *Hindi Rangmanch aur Pandit Narayanprasad Betab* (Varanasi: Vishvavidyayalay Prakashan, 1972); and Ranvir Singh, *Parsi Thiyetar* (Jodhpur Rajasthan Sangit Natak Akademi, 1990).

5 For a detailed exposition, see Kathryn Hansen, 'Parsi Theatre, Urdu Drama, and the Communalization of Knowledge: A Bibliographic Essay', *Annual of Urdu Studies*, vol. 16, no. 1 (2001), pp. 43–63.

6 See dedication on the facing page.

7 Kumudini A. Mehta, 'English Drama on the Bombay Stage in the Late Eighteenth Century and in the Nineteenth Century' (PhD dissertation, University of Bombay, 1960); Dhanjibhai N. Patel, *Parsi Natak Takhtani Tavarikh* (Bombay: Kaiser-e Hind Press, 1931); Darashah Shyavaksha Sharof, *Purano Parsi Natak Takhto* (Bombay: Kaisar-e Hind Press, 1950); Abdul Alim Nami, *Urdu Thetar*, 4 vols. (Karachi: Anjuman-e Taraqqi-e Urdu Pakistan, 1962–75).

8 *Sangeet Natak*, vol. 36, no. 1 (2001), pp. 3–31; *Sangeet Natak*, vol. 36, no. 2 (2001), pp. 3–29; *Sangeet Natak*, vol. 36, nos 3–4 (2001–02), pp. 22–38.

This volume is gratefully dedicated to the sacred memory of all those Parsis, non-Parsis, Hindus, Muslims, and Christians who spread the art of theatre by founding theatrical companies, who built playhouses and encouraged drama, who became actors and popularized the art of acting, who composed innumerable dramas in Gujarati, Hindi, and Urdu, who composed songs and defended classical music, and who wrote descriptions of the Parsi stage and related matters.

A Few Words

In 1947 I wrote the *History of Hindi Dramatic Literature*.[1] Included in that was one chapter, 'The Stage and Stageable Dramas'. Whatever material I had available at the time was described in that chapter. After my book, several dissertations were written on the subject of Hindi dramatic literature, but none shed much light on the untouched subject of performed dramas. One dissertation, 'The Parsi Stage: A Critical Study of Its Dramas and Dramatists', was written by Dr Pavan Kumar Mishra for his PhD; it is still unpublished.[2] Although Dr Mishra calls his thesis original, its basic source is Dr Dhanjibhai N. Patel's Gujarati book, *The History of the Parsi Theatre*.[3] Secondly, he focuses on only three dramatists: Radheshyam Kathavachak, Narayan Prasad Betab, and Agha Hashr. There were other dramatists of the Parsi stage, and they were much earlier than these three. But Mishra did not make an effort to research the Hindi theatre and its plays in the era before the Parsi theatre, nor to see whether there were other playwrights aside from his chosen three or not.

Mr Balwant Gargi in his work *Theatre in India* shed no new light on the earliest Hindi theatre.[4] He also made several historical errors, such as citing 1870 as the date of the founding of the Parsi theatre, or 1865 as the date that Kaikhushro Kabraji established his theatrical company. His predecessor Dr Yajnik in his book, *The Indian Theatre*, did refer to a playhouse called the Bombay Theatre that was extant in 1770.[5]

In reality, the first facts were provided by Dr Nami in his essays and book called *Urdu Theatre*.[6] But his view, that every play written in Hindi or Hindustani falls under the category 'Urdu drama', is highly controversial. Nami considers Bhave's *Gopichand* an Urdu drama, which is completely false. Possibly he never even saw this drama. He may have reached this conclusion by speculation, or perhaps he thought the play was in Urdu from the words 'in Hindustani' printed in the advertisement for the performance.

In the present book there has been an attempt to use authentic documents to describe the foundations of the modern playhouse and the Hindi stage. The sources of the information have been cited in the appropriate places. For the convenience of the readers, necessary quotations have also been provided. I wish to express my gratitude to all of those writers whose work assisted me.

I hope that the material presented here will prove useful to scholars of Hindi theatre. The beginnings of the Parsi theatre in the princely states is itself a topic for research, which will be published in the second volume.

I am especially grateful to the University Grants Commission, Delhi, which gave me a research fellowship and supported this work from an intellectual and economic standpoint.

Somnath Gupt
Jaipur, 1969

Notes

1 [Somnath Gupt, *Hindi Natak Sahitya ka Itihas* (Jalandhar, 1949).]

2 [Pavan Kumar Mishra, 'Parsi Rangmanch: Uske Natak aur Natakkaron ka Alochanatmak Adhyayan' (unpublished PhD dissertation, place and date unknown).]

3   [Dhanjibhai N. Patel, *Parsi Natak Takhtani Tavarikh* (Bombay: Kaisar-e Hind Press, 1931).]

4   [Balwant Gargi, *Theatre in India* (New York: Theatre Arts Books, 1962).]

5   [Y. K. Yajnik, *The Indian Theatre* (London: George Allen and Unwin, 1933).]

6   [Abdul Alim Nami, *Urdu Thetar*, 4 vols. (Karachi: Anjuman-e Taraqqi-e Urdu Pakistan, 1962–75).]

Preface

The view that no one has ever written on the Parsi theatre is incorrect. Undoubtedly the first ones to write on this subject were the Parsi authors themselves. But what they wrote is in itself insufficient, erroneous in places, and occasionally confusing rather than informative.

In the present work, it has been shown that before the founding of the Victoria Theatrical Company, both Parsi and non-Parsi companies were performing plays, but the credit for establishing drama on a firm foundation is due to the Victoria, Elphinstone, and Zoroastrian Theatrical Companies. A certain amount of information on them is contained in the weekly Gujarati newspaper, *Rast Goftar*. Its editor Kaikhushro Kabraji was himself a playwright, director, and actor. The old files of his newspaper contain various items related to drama that provide information about contemporary conditions. The debates published in *Rast Goftar* illuminate a number of issues. Although they do not contain a chronological history, they are important and cannot be overlooked.

The old files of the English newspapers, *The Bombay Times* and *The Bombay Courier and Telegraph*, are full of notices pertaining to drama. The sad thing is that the old files are not well-preserved or available in one place. The material at the Maharashtra Government's Department of Documents and Antiquities is in extremely fragile condition. Sometimes one is even afraid to touch the documents; the paper tears immediately. Pages are stuck together in places and cannot be separated except by the touch of a very gentle artist.

The most important among the newspapers is the Gujarati weekly *Kaisar-e Hind*. Dhanjibhai N. Patel's essays on Parsi theatre were published serially in it. Of these, numbers 27 through 94 were collected as *The History of the Parsi Theatre* and published by Kaisar-e Hind Press in 1931. Mostly these essays discuss Parsi actors. In places, theatrical companies, their owners and directors are also described. This book, which is now unavailable, is thus a very useful and important source for the study of Parsi theatre.[1] As the author says, it contains the memories of approximately fifty years, and although in places there is no sequence, nevertheless in the context of other available sources Dhanjibhai Patel's history is a milestone that cannot be ignored. Doubtless those who claim to have done original work on the Parsi theatre did not hesitate to use Patel's work but have not acknowledged it.

The first twenty-six essays of the above series were also brought out serially in *Kaisar-e Hind*. They contain much beneficial material, but it seems that writers on the Parsi theatre did not take the trouble to search them out and read them. Fortunately I was able to view these files due to the kindness of the current editor of *Kaisar-e Hind*, Mr Hirji Behidin. The files were foul, deteriorated, termite-ridden, and out of order, but nonetheless useful. Both of these parts by Dhanjibhai Patel have proved important to the present work. In fact, most of the material herein is Patel's material. I have translated it into Hindi according to my own design and requirements and linked it to other material. Jahangir Khambata's work, *My Experiences in the Theatre*, has also proved very useful.[2] Various incidents alluded to in Patel's book are clarified in Khambata's. The work is also a collection of Khambata's thoughts on drama and theatre, but even more important are the contextual details. All of the theatrical companies respected Khambata's acting and directorial abilities. The unfortunate thing is that Jahangir Khambata was not able to achieve stability in anything, as a result of which he became adorned with the title, 'wandering soul'.

Parsi Prakash describes the deeds of almost all the influential Parsis. For the history of theatre, its greatest value is in the information on which play was published when. Dates of the Parsi playwrights' works have proved to be very necessary at times. *Parsi Prakash* also contains an abridged history of the Victoria Theatrical Company. The memoirs of some Parsi actors and company owners are also contained in it.

The most useful and authentic documents are the prefaces found at the beginning of certain plays. These prefaces are attached to original playbooks and sometimes to songbooks. They tell us who wrote the drama, for which theatrical company, its date of publication, and the viewpoint of the playwright on questions of theatre. The prefaces of Kaikhushro Kabraji and Rustamji Nanabhai Ranina are especially enlightening.

It is unfortunate that the number of officially published, available dramas is so few. These authentic plays are generally printed in the Gujarati script. The largest number of them were published by the owners of the Victoria group, chiefly Khurshedji Balivala. The other publishers (J. Sant Singh and Sons, Lahore; Upanyas Bahar Office, Banaras; Jamnadas Mehta, Bombay; Bhai Dayal Singh, Lahore) brought out plays that contain numerous impurities. It is difficult to say whether their texts are authentic or not. It was a common procedure to alter the original text slightly in order to evade copyright.

In the present work all of the readily and less readily available material has been used. As far as I am aware there is no other book in Hindi on the Parsi theatre that uses so much material from original sources. The plays by various playwrights chosen for discussion and study are, for the most part, those that Dr Nami left out of his *Urdu Thetar* or dealt with only in passing. As much as possible, the attempt has been made to avoid repetition.

Mrs Kumudini Arvind Mehta's unpublished dissertation on Bombay's theatrical history shows a lot of research and effort in the writing.[3] This is the prehistory of the Parsi theatre. Thanks to Dr Mehta's generosity, I have been able to acquire some photographs, which are introduced into the text. I wish to acknowledge her assistance and her oral permission to use certain portions of her dissertation. This dissertation makes it clear that the Parsi theatre was not the brainchild of the Parsis. The credit for giving theatre a commercial form and bringing it into Urdu and Hindi from English should go to Shankar Seth, Bhau Daji Lad, and others.

Dr Abdul Alim Nami has published three volumes under the title *Urdu Theatre*.[4] I am in disagreement with his nomenclature. First, the rubric 'Urdu theatre' gives the impression that the theatre was only in the Urdu language, which is factually incorrect. The Parsis started the theatre by writing plays in Gujarati. Urdu and Hindi dramas were performed by them afterwards. Then why not term it 'Gujarati theatre'? Second, within the 'Urdu theatre' Dr Nami speaks of, plays were also performed in Gujarati, Marathi, Hindi and Hindustani. To call the Parsi theatre 'Urdu theatre' is thus an indicator of narrow-mindedness and communalism. Third, Dr Nami says that all of the Gujarati plays were translated into Urdu and were then performed on stage. Possibly for this reason he has included the Parsi playwrights within his essay. But he has given no proof of this assertion. Today we have not one of these translations available. From this we can conclude that it is not appropriate to include such Parsi playwrights in the lists of Urdu theatre. Aram was the only Parsi dramatist known to have written original plays in Urdu and also translated plays by Parsi writers into Urdu. It is well-known that the first Urdu play was *Pak Naznin, urf Zar Kharid Khurshed*, which was a translation of Edalji Khori's Gujarati play *Sonani Mulni Khurshed*.[5] Most of the plays written in Urdu were based on Gujarati plays. They were not translations of Gujarati plays. Fourth, whereas such early Urdu playwrights as Talib and Raunaq wrote Urdu plays, they also wrote Hindi plays. On their covers (e.g. Talib's *Harishchandra*) is written: 'in the language of Hindi, in the Gujarati script.' This shows that the playwright was conscious in regard to his language.

For all these reasons, Dr Nami's nomenclature 'Urdu theatre' is undesirable, incorrect, and misleading. I can concede that the majority of plays for the Parsi theatre were written in the Urdu language, but the place of Hindi in them is not negligible. Later on, Agha Hashr, Betab and Radheshyam, recognized playwrights of the Parsi stage, began writing their plays in Hindi also. Their work was modelled on the style of Talib's *Harishchandra* and *Gopichand* or his *Ramlila*.

Therefore less credit cannot be given to non-Parsi playwrights than to Parsi playwrights in the development of the dramatic art. After the Gujarati dramas, the Parsi theatrical companies performed dramas in Hindi and Urdu. This tradition continued through the era of Madan's Corinthian Theatre. The end came with the advent of the talkies. The first motion picture with sound, *Alam Ara*, was a screen version of an Urdu drama. *Khun-e Nahaq* as well was an exact rendering into film of Ahsan's drama.

Notes

1 [Patel's *Parsi Natak Takhtani Tavarikh* is held in the N. M. Wadia Library of Music of the National Centre for the Performing Arts, Mumbai.]

2 [Jahangir Pestanji Khambata, *Maro Nataki Anubhav* (Bombay: The Parsi Limited Press, 1914). The book is held in the library of the University of Bombay, Fort campus.]

3 [Kumudini A. Mehta, 'English Drama on the Bombay Stage in the Late Eighteenth Century and in the Nineteenth Century' (PhD dissertation, University of Bombay, 1960). This dissertation is held in the University of Bombay library, Kalina campus.]

4 [The fourth and final volume of Dr. Nami's *Urdu Thetar* was published in 1975.]

5 [The first Urdu play is cited throughout the rest of Gupt's text as *Sone ki Mul ki Khurshed*. Its Gujarati original has been standardized in this translation as *Sunana Mulni Khurshed*.]

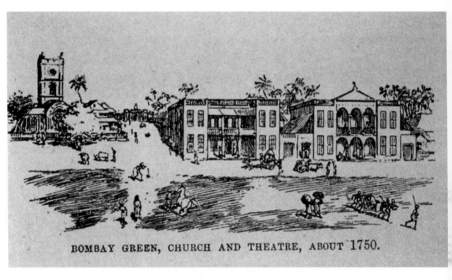

BOMBAY GREEN, CHURCH AND THEATRE, ABOUT 1750.

FIGURE 2. The Bombay Theatre in the eighteenth century. Source: Vidyavati L. Namra, *Hindi Rangmanch aur Pandit Narayanprasad Betab* (1972).

CHAPTER 1

Before the Parsi Theatre[1]

Just as the present is the result of the past, so too the Parsi theatre emerged from a pre-existing form of theatre. Its antecedent was the so-called Bombay Theatre, which available evidence dates to 1776. One of the first references is in an essay by Mr John Forbes, in which he says, 'When I left Bombay, the generality of the public buildings were more useful than elegant, the government-house, custom-house, marine house, barracks, mint, treasury, theatre and prison include the chief of these structures.'[2] Forbes was an employee in the East India Company who retired in 1784. His description proves the existence of the Bombay Theatre.

Another reference to the Bombay Theatre is that of Mr W. Milburn in his memoirs. 'In the centre of the town is a large open space, called the Green . . . : around the Green are many large well-built and handsome houses, the Government House and the church . . . On the right of the church gate is the bazar . . . where the native merchants principally reside; at its commencement stands the theatre, a neat handsome structure.'[3] Milburn's book was published in the same year as Forbes's, 1813.

The absence of the Bombay Theatre before 1776 is deduced from Mr A. Parsons's *Travels in Asia and Africa*, published in 1818. This gentleman arrived in Bombay in 1775, but the Bombay Theatre does not appear in his work. If the theatre had been in existence at that time, surely he would have mentioned it.[4] The second piece of evidence is J. H. Grose's *Voyage to the East Indies*, wherein he describes the place called the Green, 'a spacious area that continues from the fort thereto, and is pleasantly laid out in walks planted with trees, round which are mostly the houses of English inhabitants.'[5] Here too there is no mention of the Bombay Theatre.

No description is available of which plays were performed in the Bombay Theatre or at what times. It appears as though the theatre was on a decline in terms of its finances because in 1833, when it was decided to sell it, there was an investigation into its history. The then Secretary to Government, Mr John Bax, wrote a letter to the Bombay Municipality on 2 August 1833, requesting information on 'the terms on which the Bombay Theatre was originally constructed and has since been held.'[6] In reply the Municipality wrote, 'It is stated in the Plan and Survey of the Revenue Surveyor to belong to the Hon'ble Company, and neither rent nor acknowledgment have consequently ever been received by Government.'[7]

William Newnham's letter to Governor Clare is also important in this connection. He said, 'I have been associated with this Theatre for more than 20 years, as a Manager. It was built, I understood, by sub-scription so far back as 1776, where a Tank of impure water before existed; and was rebuilt in my own time, at the expence of the Community in 1817, on its present extensive scale; and the outlay on that occasion has given it a value it did not previously possess. It may be proper here to state that at the time this great outlay was made by the Community of this Presidency, nothing was known to the Managers of that period whether the ground, (or swamp as before alluded to) was originally the property of Government, or of private individuals, or of any condition being attached to its occupancy, and that it was not till many years after, when filling the office of Chief Secretary to Government, that, on tracing the Records, I discovered, from Proceedings in 1789, that it had been originally occupied with the sanction of Governor Hornby, and its continuance then sanctioned by Governor Meadows but subject to the pleasure of Government.'[8]

In the same document there is a reference to a book that chronicled the complete proceedings beginning in 1776, which was then missing.[9]

Although Mr Newnham's employment lasted for thirty years, he himself never appeared on the stage of the Bombay Theatre.[10] An efficient manager, he carefully recorded the proceedings of the committee's meetings in diaries. When necessary, he also appealed for funds by subscription. He made arrangements for costumes for the actors and took care of their food and drink. In actuality, the theatre became almost his household hobby.

Thus the Bombay Theatre's existence is definitively established in 1776.

The fact is that various groups from Europe came to India to trade, among whom certain traders from time to time remained in Bombay. The Bombay of those days was not like today's city. It was divided into three islands, each with its own importance. Spain, Portugal, France, and England all came to Bombay, but the English finally were the only ones who succeeded in staying on these islands. From the letters and documents of the Belassis family, it is apparent that English society was originally a small military settlement whose means of entertainment were limited. They played cards at home, hunted for rabbits on Malabar Hill, or rode horseback up to Thana.[11] Some individuals must also have got together and built the Bombay Theatre for their amusement.

The history of this theatre is divided into several phases. During the first, from 1776 to 1819, there are few detailed descriptions of the Bombay Theatre. Possibly the earliest notice relating to it appeared in

The Bombay Courier on 27 July 1793. An appeal for the printed book of Sheridan's *The School for Scandal* suggests that the theatre managers wanted to put on the English play but lacked a copy.[12] This indicates the kind of play that was performed in the Bombay Theatre.

The second phase was from 1819 to 1835. In 1818 the theatre was closed for repairs. On 1 January 1819, the renovated theatre reopened with a performance of Holcroft's *The Road to Ruin*. According to *The Bombay Gazette*, 6 January 1819, the audience consisted of 'the whole of our society that were not prevented from attending by ill-health or very urgent business.'[13]

In this period, the Bombay Theatre was greatly encouraged and aided by Bombay's governor, Mountstuart Elphinstone (1 November 1819–November 1827). He gifted a number of comedies and farces to the theatre, himself came to watch the performances, and supported the theatre financially. The theatre mounted a production of *The Rivals* on the occasion of this patron's farewell ceremony.[14]

Elphinstone is considered one of the founders of Bombay. A college, a mill, a bridge, and a street are all named after him. After Elphinstone's departure, dark clouds of neglect and inefficiency settled over the Bombay Theatre, although from the newspapers and journals of the time it appears that the sixteen years passed in great merriment. Meanwhile the debt owed by the theatre kept mounting, and finally it was decided to sell off the building. In October 1835, Jamshedji Jijibhai (Jamsetjee Jejeebhoy) bought it for Rs 50,000. After paying off the loans, a balance of Rs 27,379 remained, which was deposited in a government account.[15]

For ten years the theatre remained closed. Then the people of Bombay again felt the need of a new theatre for their amusement. The public raised a voice, and Bombay's well-known newspapers lent their full support to the movement. Consequently, the government allocated the proceeds from the sale of the old theatre for the

FIGURE 3. Sir Jamsetjee Jejeebhoy, merchant, philanthropist, and theatre patron. Source: H. D. Darukhanawala, *Parsi Lustre on Indian Soil* (1939).

construction of a new one. The question remained as to its location. One of Bombay's leading merchants, Jagannath Shankar Seth (Jugonnath Sunkersett), donated a plot of land situated on Grant Road. The question of location was thereby resolved, and the construction of the new theatre began. The committee formed for the task made sure that the theatre was completed as quickly as possible. The theatrical committee's chairman, Mr H. Fawcett, presented the theatre with a drop scene that had been made in England.[16]

Finally, on 10 February 1846, the Grant Road Theatre was inaugurated. At this point the third phase begins. At first English plays were performed here, although the venue was quite distant from the Bombay Green and Fort area, and the English audience had to surmount numerous obstacles to make the journey. This was the very playhouse in which Parsis, Hindus, and Iranis also began to entertain the public with their own plays.

CHARACTERISTICS OF THE BOMBAY THEATRE[17]

(i) *Building.* The Grant Road Theatre was built after the English fashion, the interior portion being much influenced by the Drury Lane Theatre. Its dress boxes extended around the auditorium and could accommodate seventy-two individuals. The capacity of the pit was sixty-five spectators, and there were 200 seats in the gallery.[18] Thus 337 audience members could be accommodated easily. The acoustics in the auditorium were such that everyone could readily hear the dialogues and songs occurring on stage.[19] In 1847, Lady Falkland wrote that the theatre was 'very pretty', but unfortunately was rarely used and only occasionally filled up.[20]

(ii) *Scenery.* It was minimal. A large sum had been spent for the construction of the building, and no funds were left over for the scenes and scenery. Nevertheless, Mrs Deacle ordered 'a great quantity of new scenery' from England.[21] *The British Indian Gentleman's Gazette* praised its beauty and interest, but other newspapers voiced their displeasure. On one occasion, Prince Waldemar of Prussia was seated in the theatre with his companions. When the drop scene was raised to loud applause, a painted curtain depicting Monsieur Deschappelles's furnished room came into view. Suddenly the rope holding the curtain broke, and the entire scene came crashing to the ground.[22] The audience was outraged, and the newspapers severely criticized the event. These defects were never entirely eliminated.

(iii) *Costumes*. There was a big deficiency in this department also. It was not expected that the costumes correspond to the characters of the drama. None of the newspaper accounts suggest that the costumes were in accordance with the play. One incident was as follows. When Mr Hamilton Jacob inaugurated the theatre with W. H. Wills's play *The Larboard Fin, or The Cornish Wrecker*, he advertised that the play would display 'entirely New Scenery, Dresses, Decorations, etc.,' and announced the names of the designers.[23] But when the play was performed, the audience raised a ruckus about the extravagance and incongruity of the costumes. The Cornish wreckers were dressed in scarlet breeches and white petticoats trimmed with red taffeta.[24] The critics showered curses on the managers, saying that Cornish seamen wore thick broadcloth and detested petticoats. Although the criticism was harsh, attitudes were slow to change. Nonetheless the critique was ultimately beneficial. At least the directors came to realize that the spectators were not fools. They were interested in drama as an art. The latest in stage fittings kept arriving from England, and their influence became visible in Bombay.

(iv) *Lighting*. In the beginning the theatre was lit with oil lamps and candles, but later gas lamps were brought into use. On some occasions gas light alone was employed. In 1847, on the occasion of welcoming the governor's wife, Mrs Reid, the theatre was illuminated with gas lights.[25] Yet a full use of this invention could not always be made, perhaps because the managers were not very familiar with it. In April 1854, *The Bombay Gazette* praised the lighting system, but in December of the same year *The Bombay Telegraph and Courier* called the arrangements 'wretched' and advised that the task be given to another party.[26]

(v) *Management*. When it opened, the Grant Road Theatre was leased to Mrs Deacle rent-free.[27] The managing committee was chaired by one Le Geyt, who was the Revenue Judge and Senior Magistrate of Police. Jagannath Shankar Seth and Khurshedji Jamshedji (Cursetjee Jamsetjee) were the two Indian members.[28] But the committee was not interested in drama. Neither were any of the committee members actors, nor did they stand to gain or lose any money in the theatre. Therefore they did not have as much clout with the government as the officials of the Bombay Theatre had had. The committee only desired that the theatre remain open and not close down. After some days, Mrs Deacle and the committee had a disagreement, and for three years the theatre was rented out. During this period the affairs of the theatre were very disturbed. The rent was not collected. Finally the committee took the management into its own hands. However, financial problems continued, and to reduce the debt, the government was petitioned for aid, which it refused. The committee was reduced to announcing that the theatre building be auctioned off on 29 August 1855.[29] Jagannath Shankar Seth purchased it, and the Grant Road Theatre became his personal property.[30] After he died the theatre passed to his heir, Vinayak Shankar Seth, and then to his widow, Mrs Lakshmibai Vinayak Shankar Seth. In 1885 she sold it to the Western Indian Flour Mills.[31] In 1860 Mrs Deacle returned to England. The round of English plays ceased. Somewhat earlier, plays in Indian languages had started to be performed, and Parsi and Hindu players began to appear on stage.

(vi) *Audience.* As long as it was patronized by the governor and high-level officials, the theatre was frequented by people of good family. Because of the location on Grant Road however, it was a long distance for people who lived in Fort, Malabar Hill, and Colaba. They began to feel inconvenienced, and when their attendance decreased, ordinary people too stopped going to the theatre. Some Christian preachers also opposed the theatre as depraved and immoral. *The Oriental Christian Spectator* was chief among the newspapers writing in opposition to

Hindu drama, especially against Dr Bhau Daji Lad.[32] In consequence, for some time the theatre was attended by sailors from trading ships, soldiers, traders, and others. A low class of public came and made the theatre foul-smelling with their smoking. The performances began to start late, and etiquette deteriorated. Drunken sailors and soldiers behaved rudely with the women. The junior officers began to think that because their superiors were not there, no one was looking after them and no one could control them. It began to be necessary to bring in the police to keep order.[33] Sometimes the spectators shouted out objectionable things, and sometimes there were fisticuffs. One significant point was that some people objected to the tall turbans of the Parsis, because those who sat behind them could not see properly.[34] This audience in later times was inherited by the Parsi theatre.

(vii) *Ticket Prices*. As long as English dramas continued, the prices for admission to the theatre were as follows:[35]

Dress box	Rs 8
Pit	Rs 6
Upper box	Rs 5
Gallery	Rs 3

But sometimes these rates were reduced. In 1825 the dress box ticket was priced at Rs 6. In 1830 the prices were reduced to Rs 6, 5, 3, and 2, respectively. The income from one night was generally between Rs 1,500 and 2,000, and on special occasions Rs 3,000.

The performance usually lasted until 12.30 a.m. No performances were shown for free. The spectators were pleased at seeing their friends perform. Hearing an actor make a lovelorn speech, the young ladies in the audience were delighted by the fancy that the words might be spoken for themselves.[36] In 1821, Indian spectators also began to attend the theatre. On 3 August 1821, Balkrishnanath Shankar Seth (Balcrustnath Sunkerset) purchased a ticket for the dress box.[37] On 13

December 1822, Hormasji Bomanji (Hormusjee Bomanjee) and Sorabji Framji each bought two tickets.[38] A silver piece is preserved in the University of Bombay on which 'Complimentary Season Ticket' is written. This was presented to Manakji Karsetji (Manackjee Cursetjee) by the Bombay Amateur Theatre.[39]

(viii) *Actors*. The actors of the Bombay Amateur Theatre were all non-professionals. They put on plays for their own interest and amusement. However, after the construction of the Grant Road Theatre, the actors usually were professionals. The theatre's lessee, Mrs Deacle, was herself a professional, as was her companion Miss Clara Ellis. They gave solo performances and also appealed to amateur actors to assist them.[40]

Whenever a foreign actor or theatrical company arrived, heading to Calcutta, Australia, or China, they stopped in Bombay for a performance. This pattern continued for many years. Later on, directors like Vishnudas Bhave and their companies began to perform in Bombay while touring various places in India.

(ix) *Audience Taste*. If the taste of the Bombay audiences can be guessed from the dramas performed, then it seems they preferred melodramas and farces. This was the influence of the contemporary English theatre. In London in the mid-nineteenth century, these were the kinds of dramas that were most frequently performed. Although such plays were paltry from a literary standpoint, they were forceful, amusing, and lively.[41] This influence had come to England from Germany. The plays of Lessing, Goethe, and Schiller were influential throughout the European dramatic world. Their dramas contained an excess of sentiment in lieu of logic and thought. They were dominated by medieval ideas and offered comparatively more dramatic scope. Prior to these sentimental musical dramas, mainly literary dramas were written that were meant for reading rather than performing. These dramas were more viewable. The spectator tired from a long day could ease himself, seeing life's romanticism and joys and pleasure. His body and mind received solace. This too was one purpose of drama. Morton's *Speed the Plough* and Bulwer Lytton's *The Lady of Lyons* were favourites at the Grant Road Theatre. They mixed serious comedy and melodrama. At the inauguration of the Grant Road Theatre, Mrs Deacle had said, 'Old wines made mellow and improved by age, / New fruits, but late from the London stage.'[42]

Because of various difficulties, it was often impossible to perform a complete drama, be it a tragedy or a comedy. For this reason, perhaps, Shakespeare was not very popular. Only portions selected from his dramas were performed. To link the different scenes in a sequence, farces, music, and other entertaining fare were inevitably added. The audience liked this. They preferred action and gesticulation to speechifying. They especially liked an abundance of songs, exciting dancing, and clowning. No matter whether the plot was well structured, the characterization interesting, or the stage design appropriate. They wanted spectacle, demanding supernatural scenes and an element of romance even in serious plays. This was more or less the condition of the theatre in England then as well. Literary beauty was lacking, and it was pointless to expect any intellectual satisfaction.

Whenever an actor in a soliloquy made a satirical remark on a contemporary topic or poked fun at an important person or incident, the audience burst out with rounds of laughter. The element of topicality was a necessary part of theatrical representation.

The popular dramas of the time were as follows:[43]

The Lady of Lyons	Edward Bulwer Lytton
Speed the Plough	Thomas Morton
Love, Law and Physic	James Kenney
The School for Scandal	Richard B. Sheridan

She Stoops to Conquer	Oliver Goldsmith
The Castle Spectre	Matthew G. Lewis
The Critic	Gregory V. Buckingham
The Honeymoon	John Tobin
The Heir at Law	George Colman
Rule a Wife and Have a Wife	Francis Beaumont and
	John Fletcher
The Mountaineers	George Colman
Miss in Her Teens	David Garrick

The playhouse system, lack of actresses for female roles, inappropriate costuming, worn-out scenery, middle-class viewership and their taste—all were inherited by the Parsi theatre. The Parsi theatre was grounded in both the accomplishments as well as the deficiencies of the English stage in Bombay. What it did with this inheritance, and how, form the subject of the following chapters.

Notes

1 [Most of this chapter's contents and citations are from Kumudini A. Mehta, 'English Drama on the Bombay Stage in the Late Eighteenth Century and in the Nineteenth Century' (PhD dissertation, University of Bombay, 1960). Gupt's errors have been corrected and English names spelled as in Mehta. Anglicized spellings of Parsi names have been added after the Hindi transliterations as found in Gupt.]

2 John Forbes, *Oriental Memoirs*, 4 vols., London, 1813; Vol. 1, p. 152. [Mehta, p. 5.]

3 W. Milburn, *Oriental Commerce*, 2 vols., London, 1813; Vol. 1, p. 170. [Mehta, p. 6.]

4 [Mehta, p. 5.]

5 J. H. Grose, *Voyage to the East Indies*, 2 vols., 2nd edition, London, 1761. Vol. 1, p. 52. [Mehta, p. 4.]

6   General Department, vol. 38-A/370A for 1836, pp. 13–14. [Mehta, p. 1.]

7   Ibid., p. 15. [Mehta, p. 1.]

8   Ibid., pp. 16–18. [Mehta, pp. 2–3.]

9   Ibid. If this book had been found, numerous errors would have been avoided.

10 [William Newnham served the government for thirty years, first as Secretary to the Governor's Council and later as Chief Secretary. Mehta, p. 49.]

11 [Mehta, pp. 7–8.]

12 [Mehta, pp. 15–16.]

13 [Mehta, p. 32.]

14 [Mehta, pp. 35–36.]

15 [Mehta, pp. 97–98.]

16 [Mehta, pp. 110–13.]

17 [The next six characteristics refer to the Grant Road Theatre of 1846 and thereafter, not the earlier Bombay (Amateur) Theatre.]

18 *The Bombay Courier*, 10 May 1842, and *The Bombay Courier*, 8 May 1845. [Mehta, p. 145.]

19 Vinayakrao Madhavrao Pitale, *Shrimant Namdar Jagannath Shankarset urf Nanashankerset Hyanche Charitra* (Mumbai: Pitale, 1916), p. 316. [Mehta, p. 11, p. 145.]

20 [The Viscountess Falkland, *Chow-Chow: Being Selections from a Journal Kept in India, Egypt and Syria*, 2 vols., London 1857; Vol. 1, p. 52. Mehta, p. 146.]

21 *The British Indian Gentleman's Gazette*, 30 May 1846. [Mehta, p. 147.]

22 *The British Indian Gentleman's Gazette*, 1 May 1846. [Mehta, p. 149.]

23 *The Bombay Telegraph and Courier*, 17 July 1851. [Mehta, p. 150.]

24 *The Bombay Times*, 30 July 1851. [Mehta, p. 150.]

25 [Mehta, p. 150.]

26 [Mehta, p. 151.]

27 [Mrs Deacle was a professional actress who had originally been brought from England to the Sans Souci Theatre in Calcutta by J. H. Stocqueler. Stocqueler was a member of the Committee of Management of the old Bombay Theatre. Mehta, p. 132.]

28 [Mehta, p. 151.]

29 *The Bombay Times and Courier*, 28 August 1855. [Mehta, p. 155.]

30 Foras Salt Batty, Vol. 8, for 1858–68; Vol. 12 for 1868–78. Foras Salt Batty, Vol. 7 for 1878–85. [Mehta, p. 155.]

31 Foras Transfer File, Register No. 103. [Mehta, p. 155.]

32 [Mehta, pp. 117–18.]

33 [Mehta, pp. 120–23.]

34 [Mehta, p. 124.]

35 [These are the rates advertised for a performance of *The Drummers* in 1797. Mehta says they remained constant until 1830. This section thus refers to the Bombay (Amateur) Theatre, not the Grant Road Theatre. Mehta, pp. 21, 43.]

36 [Mehta, p. 45.]

37 *Bombay Theatre Diaries*, No. 602, p. 20. [Mehta, p. 46, Appendix 5.]

38 Ibid., pp. 7–8.

39 [Mehta, p. 46, Appendix 6.]

40 [Mehta, pp. 134–37.]

41 Allardyce Nicoll, *British Drama*, Chapter III.

42 *The British Indian Gentleman's Gazette*, 12 February 1846. [Mehta, p. 139.]

43 [The names of the playwrights have been added.]

CHAPTER 2

The Origins of the Parsi Theatre[1]

The word 'theatre' entered Hindi from English and is used in various senses. A playhouse or auditorium is called a theatre, and drama (*natak*) is also called theatre, as in 'We are going to the theatre', or 'We are going to see theatre.' There is an even broader use of the word, as in 'English theatre' or 'French theatre'. Here, 'theatre' means theatre in the English or French language or the theatre of the English or French people. Included within the meaning of 'theatre' are all its accessories: the auditorium, the play, the playwright, the actors, the stage and its scenery, gestures and mime, the director, and music.

The phrase 'Parsi theatre' signifies the playhouses built and operated by the Parsi community, along with Parsi playwrights, Parsi dramas, Parsi stages, Parsi theatrical companies, Parsi actors, Parsi directors, and so on. Also included are those playwrights and actors who were not Parsis, but who worked on a salaried basis for the Parsi theatrical companies. Further, those companies, owners, and actors are counted who, while not being from the Parsi community and not being residents of Bombay, added the words 'of Bombay' to their theatre companies in order to show their connections to the Parsi theatre. For example, 'The Jubilee Imperial Theatrical Company of Bombay' had its origin in the present Uttar Pradesh (former United Provinces). Its owners added 'of Bombay' to connect it to the Bombay companies. These companies had earned a name in the art of drama, and there was a chance to make a greater profit by using this association.

There were two forms of the Parsi theatre. In the first, the personnel and owners were solely Parsis. They performed dramas in and around Bombay and at times travelled outside of Bombay to other provinces. The second was made up of company owners based in other provinces who toured with their troupes. The present monograph has been written with both in mind.

A brief description of the English theatre in Bombay has been given in the previous chapter. It appears that there was an English-style playhouse on Grant Road variously called the Grant Road Theatre, Shankar Seth's Old Playhouse, and the Royal Theatre. At first English plays were performed here, in accord with the pre-existing traditions of the Bombay Theatre. But after 1846, the English populace took less pleasure in this playhouse because of its distance from their residences and the difficulties in reaching there. Slowly the Grant Road Theatre audience began to change. As the number of Parsis and Hindus increased, performances were required that met the taste of the new spectators. From 1853 onward, performances of plays in Marathi, Gujarati, and Hindustani began to take place in this theatre.

From *The Bombay Telegraph and Courier*, 27 and 31 October 1853, it is learned that one Parsi Dramatic Corps took birth in Bombay and performed a play in the Grant Road Theatre in Gujarati on the theme of Rustam and Sohrab.[2] The plot was taken from Firdausi's *Shahnama*. According to Dr A. A. Nami, this Corps performed two additional dramas on 5 November 1853 and 6 February 1854.[3] The titles of the dramas are not given by Dr Nami. Another advertisement for a performance under the heading 'Parsi Theatre' was published in *The Bombay Times*,[4] announcing the performance of *Shyavaksh ki Paida'ish* (The Birth of Shyavaksh) and a Hindustani farce, *Tikhe Khan*, on 6 May 1854.[5] The same advertisement was published in *The Bombay Gazette* on 5 May 1854. *Shyavaksh ki Paida'ish* was based on the *Shahnama*, whereas the farce satirized the life of the Nawabs. This was the fourth play of the Parsi Dramatic Corps. The fifth drama was advertised in *The Bombay Times* of 18 May 1854, according to which the second part of the Shyavakhsh story was to be performed on 20 May 1854 at the Grant Road Theatre. The farce shown with it was called *Haji Miyan aur Unke Naukar, Fazal aur Tikhe Khan* (Haji Miyan and His Servants, Fazal and Tikhe Khan).[6] The play received a favourable review.[7] Some super-natural elements were included in the performance such as cleaning the teeth with the trunk of a tree and moving the mountain Al-Burz with one hand. *The Bombay Times* of 2 June 1854 published another advertisement for a dramatic performance on 3 June 1854. With this drama the farce of Haji and Tikhe Khan was performed, as well as the plays of a German dramatist for the amusement of the audience.

With this series of six dramas performed in one season, the Parsi theatre was launched. The main plays were in Gujarati, and the farces were written in Hindustani. All of the actors were Parsi youths. The names of the playwrights are not known, and perhaps these plays and farces were never published. All were performed in the Grant Road Theatre.

Advertisements under the headers 'Parsi Dramatic Corps', 'Parsi Theatrical Committee', and 'Parsi Theatre' were published in the Bombay newspapers of the time. A curiosity naturally arises as to whether these names all referred to one organization or whether they belonged to separate companies. Dhanjibhai Patel makes reference to the establishment of the Parsi Natak Mandali (Parsi Theatrical Company) in 1853.[8] The founder of this company was Pestanji Dhanjibhai Master, himself an actor with the company.[9] The other actors were Nanabhai Ranina, Dadabhai Eliot, Manchershah B. Mehrhomji, Bhikhabhai K. Mus, Dr Kavasji H. Bilimoriya, Dr R. H. Hathiram, and Kavasji Nasharvanji Kohidaru who later became famous as Kavasji Gurgin.[10] All these Parsis were famous citizens of their time. Nanabhai Ranina and Kavasji Gurgin remained connected to theatrical activities for most of their lives. The rest got involved in their own occupations. The owner of the company was Framji Gustadji Dalal, who was known as Phalughus. For the overseeing and proper management of the company, a committee was formed made up of Professor Dadabhai Naoroji, Khurshedji N. Kama, Ardeshar Fram Mus, Jahangir Barjorji Vaccha, Dr Bhau Daji Lad, and others.

The Parsi Theatrical Company was the first company established by the Parsis. It performed Parsi dramas, and the ads published in the newspapers all refer to this company under different names. Thus the origin of the Parsi theatre occurred in the form of this same Parsi Theatrical Company. The Parsi community supported it, and it probably developed first as an amateur group and later as a professional company. The enthusiasm of the Parsi youths was not quenched. On 16 September 1854, the company presented *Pathan Safarez aur Kallu* and *Alladin aur Banu Zulekha* at the Grant Road Theatre.[11]

Reference has already been made to the categories of admission for English plays. The entrance fees for the Parsi Theatrical Company were as follows. In the beginning, dress circle tickets were Rs 3, stalls Rs 2, gallery Rs 1.50, pit Re 1. Later in 1854: box Rs 2, stalls Rs 1.50, gallery Re 1.25, pit Re 1. Performances started at 8 p.m.

In the Parsi Gujarati-language newspaper *Rast Goftar* dated 25 February 1855, this notice was published:

PARSI THEATRE

For the benefit of the Patriotic Fund

The Parsi Theatrical Company

wishes to inform the public that its twelfth show

will take place

on February 27th in the Grant Road Theatre

during which the following plays will be performed:

The Tale of Padshah Faredun

and an amusing farce entitled *Uthaugir Surati*.

Ticket prices: Rs 2.50, 1.50, 1.25, pit Re 1.

From this it is learned that the Parsi Theatrical Company continued to perform its Gujarati plays on different occasions. In 1856 it performed *Rustam ane Ekdast*, whose plot was also taken from the *Shahnama*. The name of the playwright is not known. But Bahmanji N. Kabraji and Jahangir Nasharvanji Patel were two well-known playwrights in the Parsi Theatrical Company.[12]

There is no description of how long the Parsi Theatrical Company continued to work in an active way. It is only known that by 1867 when the Victoria Theatrical Company was founded, it had closed down, and its famous actor and originator, Dhanji Master, was appointed director of the Victoria. The end of the Parsi Theatrical Company occurred when all of its stage properties, scenery, curtains, costumes, and so on were bought by J. F. Madan of Calcutta and the company disappeared into deep sleep.

The Parsi theatre definitely began with the Parsi Theatrical Company, but it did not end there. Before 1867, the Hindu theatre had also commenced its activities in Bombay alongside the Parsi theatre. In order to understand the rage for Parsi theatre, one must look at the Hindu theatre as well, because it too provided encouragement to the

Parsi theatre. *The Bombay Times and Journal of Commerce* reported that in 1846 a theatre had started under the name of Khetwaddy (Khetvadi) Theatre.[13] It was announced under the header 'Theatre Committee'.

We have much pleasure in directing attention to an announcement published in another column, by The Theatrical Committee intimating that the Theatre will be opened next Monday evening. It is rather late in the season to make a beginning but on the principle 'better late than never' we must be content with what is now offered to us, and have no doubt that the efforts of the Committee to provide amusement for the public will meet with deserved success.

The reference in the above is to the following:

Our readers are not generally aware than an attempt which has hitherto proved eminently successful, has lately been made to revive the legitimate Hindoo Drama in Bombay. The Theatre in Khetwaddy, where this has been attempted, is as yet without moveable scenes and . . . what is usually reckoned the pit serves the purpose of the stage, benches all round rise tier about tier, and are occupied rightly by hundreds of respectable, well-conducted, and most attentive natives of all classes and creeds. We need not inform the readers of Horace Wilson—to those who are not such, the information may be new—that the Hindoo Drama is of very old date . . . The plays acted at Khetwaddy Theatre have been translated from Sanskrit by a learned Brahmin, who appeared on the stage. A buffoon or chorus first comes in, somewhat after the manner of Greeks and shortly recites the leading particulars of what is about to occur. The actors next appear gorgeously and fantastically dressed and the play proceeds—the buffoon through the whole, even in the gravest scenes, intrudes his impudence or wit.[14]

Thus the Khetwaddy (or Khetvadi) Theatre was active in 1846, and plays translated from Sanskrit were performed there under the name of 'Hindoo Drama'. This theatre was not built in the English style like the Grant Road Theatre, but was possibly an open-air theatre, with the stage constructed after the traditional folk style and folk traditions followed for audience seating, entrance of characters, etc. There is no mention of the language into which the plays were translated, but it can be assumed that perhaps they were in Marathi because the Khetvadi area was a Marathi neighborhood, as it is today, and entertainment must have been geared accordingly. The performance conventions included the entrance of a jester or chorus, followed by narration of the main incidents to be performed. From the beginning to end, the jester was present. All these factors suggest that the dramatic tradition could be called Marathi, although it was not very different from the Nautanki or Svang style either. It seems that the phrase 'Hindoo Drama' was taken from Horace Wilson who had written a book on Sanskrit drama, which he called not Sanskrit theatre but 'the Theatre of the Hindoos'.[15] Perhaps this was why the rubric was used in the column. Whatever the case, it is certain that before the rise of the Parsi theatre in 1853, the Hindu theatre was actively present in Bombay, and in it popular dramas were performed in the local language. This trend must surely have given impetus to the Parsis.

It is surprising that Professor Banhatti in his *History of Marathi Theatre* has not mentioned this theatre and its plays.[16] Kulkarni and other historians of Marathi dramatic literature are also silent on this topic. Thus one wonders whether these dramas were not in Hindustani? Let it be.

Dr Dhanjibhai Patel and Shyavaksha Darashah Sharof have given separate lists of the theatrical companies and clubs that were extant in Bombay by 1861. There are some discrepancies between them. The lists are as follows:

PATEL	SHAROF
Parsi Theatrical Company (Phalughus)	Parsi Stage Players
Amateurs Dramatic Club	Gentlemen Amateurs Club
Elphinstone Dramatic Club (Nazir)	Zoroastrian Dramatic Club
Elphinstone Amateurs (Nazir)	Oriental Dramatic Club
Parsi Stage Players	Persian Club
Gentlemen Amateurs (Phalughus)	Persian Oriental Dramatic Club
Zoroastrian Theatrical Company	Parsi Theatrical Company
Zoroastrian Dramatic Society	Parsi Elphinstone Dramatic Club
Persian Zoroastrian Theatrical Company	Baronet Theatrical Club
Persian Theatrical Company	Anglekar Hindu Company
Oriental Theatrical Company	Original Zoroastrian Club
Baronet Theatrical Company	Parsi Club[18]
Albert Theatrical Company	
Shakespeare Theatrical Company	
The Volunteers Club	
Victoria Theatrical Company	
Original Victoria Club	
Hindi Theatrical Company	
Parsi Victoria Opera Troupe (Nazir)[17]	

Comparing these two lists, some matters are clarified but others obscured. First take Patel's list. According to him, the Victoria Theatrical Company was founded in 1868.[19] The Persian Theatrical Company, also called the Irani Theatrical Company, was founded in 1870.[20] The Persian Zoroastrian Theatrical Company was also founded in 1870–75.[21] The Zoroastrian Theatrical Club was formed in 1866.[22] The Original Victoria was founded by Dadi Patel at the time he separated from his partnership with Nazir in the Victoria Theatrical Company. This incident happened around 1870–71; hence, this company cannot be considered as existing before 1861.[23] In 1879–80 the Zoroastrian Dramatic Society was formed.[24] The Baronet Club was started by Nasharvanji Forbes in 1871, when the Zoroastrian Club performed Edalji Khori's *Khudabakhsh* and Forbes left this club.[25] Thus the Baronet Club's existence before 1871 cannot be confirmed.

These examples prove that Patel's list includes various clubs and companies that came into existence after 1861, and it cannot be considered authoritative. Sharof's list similarly is problematic. Thus the conclusion is that before 1861, there were various Parsi theatrical companies in existence, and they entertained the populace from time to time with plays in the Shankar Seth Playhouse. Most were amateur companies. The club at Elphinstone College only performed English plays, especially Shakespeare, in English with English costumes. The costumes generally were made by the actors themselves. One must also acknowledge that the interest of the Parsi community in dramatic arts kept growing. At first they did not look on it from the standpoint of commerce; rather they attempted to make it attractive from an artistic point of view. Without doubt, the dramas were mostly in Gujarati, but occasionally performances occurred in English and Hindustani. In 1858 the Zoroastrian Theatrical Club performed *Hindi aur Firangi Raj men Muqabla* (Contest between the Indian and Foreign Regimes), which was in Hindustani.[26] Around 1858 a new company called the Indian Theatrical Club was formed. They performed a drama entitled *Nana Sahab*. This was the same Nana Sahab who was considered the hero of the independence struggle of 1857. To show their loyalty to the British government, the Parsis addressed the hero as follows:

Oh tyrant Nana, you've done a foul deed,
Betrayed your salt and insulted our honour.
Sinner, thief, untouchable, who brought death to the
     innocent,
Your example remains, but you'll meet a bad end.[27]

This drama became extremely popular. Some of its songs were sung in Parsi homes.

It is unfortunate that the plays from the early period of the Parsi theatre are nowhere to be found today. It may be that they were not published. Nonetheless, from the descriptions that are found here and there, it seems that the interest of the Parsis went first of all towards the history of Iran. Taking stories from the *Shahnama*, they made the warriors and kings of Persia their heroes. These dramas were performed on stage in the original settings as much as possible. In the beginning, mechanical scenes were not used. The painters of the curtains were not Indian, and the suitability of the costumes was not given much attention. It is surprising that the Parsi actors, although native speakers of Gujarati, spoke Hindustani and had no particular difficulty in pronouncing it on stage.

In brief, the rise of the Parsi theatre dates from 1853. Parsi efforts continued over the years. At first, the plays were in Gujarati, accompanied sometimes after the main drama by one or two farces in Hindustani, which were generally written by Parsis. English dramas were also performed from time to time. The Parsi theatrical companies were both amateur and professional. Plays were performed after adequate rehearsals under the guidance of a director, and there was just one playhouse in use, located on Grant Road and known as the Shankar Seth Playhouse, Grant Road Theatre, or Royal Theatre.

Balwant Gargi's statement, 'In 1870, while Bengal was laying the foundation of its first professional theatrical company, some Parsi business men became interested in the arts and the theatre, and were the founders of the first professional company to use Hindustani as a language for drama,'[28] is entirely false. By 1870–71, the Parsi theatre had already made great strides. Such Parsi playwrights as Kaikhushro Kabraji, Edalji Khori, Nanabhai Rustamji Ranina, Bahmanji Navrojji Kabra, and Nasharvanji Navrojji Parakh had already raised the Parsi stage to a high level through their works.

Gargi's assertion, 'Pestonji Framji launched The Original Theatrical Company and was soon followed in 1877 by Khrushidji [sic] Balivala, who founded the Victoria Theatrical Company in Delhi,'[29] is also incorrect. First, there was no Rustamji Framji [sic], founder of a Parsi theatre company, in the history of the Parsi theatre. Second, the first company was the Parsi Theatrical Company, as has already been described. The word 'original' was required when a company fragmented into more than one part, and it was used for the part that retained most of the original actors. This is demonstrated by the history of the Victoria Theatrical Company. Kunvarji Nazir and Dadabhai Patel were once partners in the Victoria, but in 1870 they could not get along, and the company split in two. Nazir's group was called simply the Victoria Theatrical Company, whereas Dadi Patel named his group the Original Victoria Theatrical Company. The founding of the Victoria Theatrical Company by Balivala in Delhi is also not correct, as will shortly be shown. The Victoria was founded in 1867 by Kaikhushro Navrojji Kabra. Balivala was an actor in it. Later the Victoria went through various ups and downs. Finally it came under the direction of Balivala; he was not its founder.

The development of the Parsi theatre in reality is the history of the Parsi theatrical companies, which will be found in the following sections.

Notes

1 [Gupt's chapter is titled simply 'Parsi Theatre'. The above title corresponds to the chapter's only subheading.]

2 [The advertisement in *The Bombay Telegraph and Courier*, 28 October 1853, names the sponsor as the Parsi Theatrical Committee, not the Parsi Dramatic Corps, and calls the main drama (in English), *Roostum Zabooli and Sohrab*. The language of performance is not mentioned. However, the review of the 29 October performance in the issue of 31 October 1853, in the same paper, styles the drama *Rustom and Sohrab* and refers to performance in Gujarati.]

3 Abdul Alim Nami, 'Urdu drama gadar se pahle', in *Urdu Adab* (Aligarh), March 1955, p. 87.

4 *The Bombay Times*, 2 May 1854.

5 [The Urdu title given in Gupt appears to come from Nami's article in *Urdu Adab*.]

6 [Title probably based on Nami.]

7 *The Bombay Times*, 23 May 1854.

8 Dhanjibhai N. Patel, *Parsi Natak Takhtani Tavarikh* (Bombay: Kaisar-e Hind Press, 1931), p. 2. [Henceforth PNTT]

9 PNTT, p. 393.

10 [PNTT, p. 3.]

11 [Source unknown; no such reference in PNTT or in Gupt's discussion of this company in Chapter 5.]

12 [Gupt apparently confuses this early formation of the Parsi Theatrical Company (referred to in Chapter 5 as 'No. 1') with a later group of the same name. B. N. Kabra and J. N. Patel 'Gulfam' both wrote plays in the 1880s and 90s. Because of this error, the rest of Gupt's paragraph has been deleted.]

13 *The Bombay Times and Journal of Commerce*, February 1846, p. 316

14 Ibid. [It was not possible to compare the passage cited against the original. Obvious typographical errors have been corrected.]

15 [Horace Hayman Wilson, *Select Specimens of the Theatre of the Hindus, Translated from the Original Sanskrit*, 2 vols. 3rd edn, London: Trübner, 1871.]

16 [Shrinivas Narayan Banhatti, *Marathi Rangbhumi cha Itihas*, Pune: Venus Prakashan, 1957.]

17 PNTT, pp. 2–3.

18 Shyavaksha Darashah Sharof, *Purano Parsi Natak Takhto* (Bombay: Kaisar-e Hind Press, 1950), pp. 17–19.

19 PNTT, p. 82.

20 PNTT, pp. 101, 103.

21 PNTT, p. 102.

22 PNTT, p. 192.

23 PNTT, p. 183.

24 PNTT, p. 237.

25 PNTT, pp. 194–95.

26 PNTT, p. 191.

27 PNTT, p. 191.

28 [The original English has been supplied from Balwant Gargi, *Theatre in India* (New York: Theatre Arts Books, 1962), pp. 154–55. Gargi's statement is not as inaccurate as Gupt suggests, since the professional as opposed to the amateur Parsi theatre only got established around 1870.]

29 [Original supplied from Gargi, ibid. p. 155. Gupt mistakes 'Pestonji Framji' in the original for 'Rustamji Framji.']

CHAPTER 3

The Development of the Parsi Theatre

From its beginnings in 1853, the Parsi theatre gradually evolved and developed. It is certain that some theatrical companies emerged but did not survive for long. There were others that were reborn and achieved a certain amount within their lifetimes. But only those companies that had talented performers and serious directors in addition to financial backing were able to compete successfully. Slowly the audiences too became acquainted with dramatic arts and began to show their opposition to shallow plays and farces. A stream of enthusiasm flowed from these theatrical companies through the Parsi community. To whatever extent possible, they attempted to create an atmosphere of entertainment.

The greatest difficulty faced in the early days of the Parsi theatre was the shortage of playhouses. In 1853 only two theatres seem to have existed in Bombay. One was on Grant Road, the Grant Road Theatre, and the other was the Khetvadi Theatre, perhaps an open-air theatre that featured performances in traditional folk styles. The result was that theatrical companies could not present their plays for long runs. The Grant Road Theatre was rented out each week to a given company while the other companies sat idle. In terms of business and revenue, the dearth of playhouses created a formidable situation. Therefore the attention of company owners went first of all to fill this lack. They took two approaches. The companies performed in Bombay as much as they could, but then they took all of their actors, scenery, and props and went on tour, establishing an itinerant theatre so as to perform their plays for as long a duration as possible. These performances took place in different parts of the country during suitable seasons of the year.

The playhouses built in Bombay during the development of the Parsi theatre were extremely important. However, the dates of construction of these theatres and their internal and external dimensions are mostly unknown. Today they have almost all been destroyed or converted into cinemas. Due to the lack of information about the chronology of their construction, the following is presented in alphabetical order.[1]

PLAYHOUSES BUILT BY PARSIS

Edward Theatre: Probably constructed in 1850–60 and still standing on Kalba Devi Road. Like the other theatres, it has been overhauled and is now used for cinema. Gujarati dramas were performed here.[2]

Elphinstone Theatre: Built around 1853 and named for Bombay's popular governor. No other details are available.[3]

Empire Theatre: Constructed in 1908 and owned by the City of Bombay Improvement Trust Limited, whose principal trustees were Mr Nathan of the E. D. Sassoon Company and A. J. Bilimoriya from Tata and Sons. Its seating capacity was one thousand. Dramas were still being performed here in 1930, the year in which the theatre's first talkie, *Vagabond King*, was exhibited. In 1948 Seth Kekhashru Modi had it completely rebuilt and put into operation as a cinema hall.[4]

Eros Theatre: Constructed in 1937 by Shyavaksha Khambata. This elegant theatre was erected opposite Churchgate Station, and lakhs of rupees were spent on it. It still maintains its illustrious character,

Bombay Empire Theatre

FIGURE 4. Printed postcard of the Empire Theatre. Courtesy: Phillips Antiques.

being counted as one of the most famous theatres of Bombay. Today it is used as a cinema hall. Sharof has listed it among the theatres, but he gives no information as to which dramas were performed here or which company played on its stage.[5]

Esplanade Theatre: Built by the Natak Uttejak Company. Located near the present-day Crawford Market, it was constructed of wood. All of the Natak Uttejak Company's dramas were performed here, including Ranchhodbhai Udayram's long-running hit, *Harishchandra*. Kaikhushro Kabra was intimately involved in the construction of this playhouse, just as he was with the founding and operation of the company. The company lasted about thirty-five years; thus the playhouse must have been in use for at least that long.

Gaiety Theatre: Its owner was Dahyabhai Dholsaji, but whether he directed a theatrical company is not known. Earlier, Nazir had built a theatre of the same name on this site, and companies that came from

England would perform here. After Nazir left the Victoria and Elphinstone companies, his main source of livelihood was this theatre. It was here that he acted so successfully in *The Honeymoon*, appearing opposite the English actress, Miss Agnes Birchenough.[6]

Grand Theatre: Another theatre on Grant Road constructed by Balivala. He spent a lot of money on this project and, it is said, fell into a financial crisis as a result. Balivala was a courageous man, and he plied his boat across the troubled waters. But disasters never happen singly. The theatre caught fire and burned to the ground. According to Sharof, the theatre was opened by police commissioner S. M. Edwardes in 1907.

Golpitha Playhouse: Constructed opposite to Golpitha by Pestanji Framji Belati. He had been an actor in the Persian Club and played in the Farsi-language production of *Barjor ane Rustam*. Then he formed the Persian Zoroastrian Club, for which this theatre was built. Here the famous drama *Poladband* was performed using various mechanical scenes.[7]

Hindi Playhouse: Built by Dadabhai Ratanji Thunthi. When Dadi Patel took over the Victoria Theatrical Company, Dadabhai Thunthi left due to disagreements with him. Dadabhai Thunthi founded a new company, the Hindi Theatrical Company, and decided to establish a new theatre. He bought a large house on Grant Road where rehearsals were held and began constructing the playhouse in its compound. He supervised the construction during the day, took his midday meal there, and at seven in the evening started rehearsals. A number of famous Parsi actors were with his company. The first play performed here was *Faredun*, a Gujarati drama written by Kaikhushro Kabra. Then *Bejan ane Manijeh* was performed, and also *Benazir Badremunir*, which was in Urdu. Finally the theatre was turned over to a wealthy creditor whom Dadabhai Thunthi had been unable to repay.

National Theatre: Built by Dvarkadas Lallubhai. Although it was not built by a Parsi, it may be mentioned here. Nothing else is known.[8]

Novelty Theatre: Built on the Maidan in front of the Boribandar Railway Station by Khurshedji Balivala, the famous actor and one-time sole proprietor of the Victoria Theatrical Company. Because it was so popular, the lemon soda and almond-pistachio vendors who sat nearby made good profits. Entrance prices for the orchestra were Re 1.00 or Rs 1.50, and for the pit only one anna. Both seat classes afforded equal pleasure to the spectators. According to *Parsi Prakash*, it was built in 1887. Today the Excelsior Theatre stands in its place.

FIGURE 5. Printed postcard of the Excelsior Theatre. Courtesy: Phillips Antiques.

Original Theatre: Sharof mentions that this theatre existed in 1853. Aside from this, there is no information.[9]

Ripon Theatre: Nothing is known about it.[10]

Royal Opera House: This impressive theatre was built by Jahangirji Fardunji Karaka for seven and a half lakh rupees. Maurice Bandmann of the Bandmann Company provided advice on the construction. The building was completed in 1925, and ten years later it was converted into a cinema hall.

Tivoli Theatre: Constructed by Kunvarji Paghtivala opposite Victoria Terminus (formerly Boribandar Station), where the *Times of India* office is currently located. It was extant in 1886, but the date of construction is uncertain. Built for the Alfred Theatrical Company, it was a rough and ready playhouse. The Alfred's owner in those days was Nanabhai Rustamji Ranina. He had purchased the company from Kavasji Palanji Khatau.

Victoria Theatre: In 1868, when the Victoria Theatrical Company was established, the question arose as to where their plays would be performed. According to Sharof, there were five theatres in existence in 1853, but by the time of the Victoria's emergence, the only one worth mentioning was the Shankar Seth Playhouse on Grant Road. Possibly the other theatres had closed. It was in the Grant Road Theatre itself that the Elphinstone, Zoroastrian, and Victoria companies had to perform. Each company got to use it only a few days a week, limiting their profits. In 1870, when the Victoria Company came into the hands of Dadi Patel, he recommended the construction of a new theatre. The Victoria Theatre was built on a plot of land right on Grant Road, ensuring that this company, the largest of its time, would have no difficulty in performing its plays. No picture of the Victoria Theatre has thus far become available, so it is impossible to give any information about it.[11] However, some people have described it as equivalent to a buffalo stable. Whatever the case, from the standpoint of utility it was an important and well-known theatre.

Wellington Theatre: Constructed by Seth Rustamji Dorabji and inaugurated in 1925 by Bombay Governor Leslie Wilson. It too was converted into a cinema in 1930.

Without a doubt, the main playwrights of the Parsi theatre in its earliest phase were themselves Parsis, and they wrote in Gujarati. The first play, as has already been mentioned, was performed in 1853, but its author is not known, nor is a copy of the play available. Nor are there any authentic details about the author of the dramas subsequently performed by the Parsi Theatrical Company. Another play, *Karan Ghelo*, is mentioned in this period as being performed by Kunvarji Nazir. Karan was Gujarat's last Hindu emperor, and the

FIGURE 6. Kunvarji Sohrabji Nazir, founder of the Elphinstone Dramatic Club (1863). Source: Namra.

drama is based on his story. Because it dealt with Hindu culture, the play contained certain scenes and rituals that required the expertise of Hindus to advise the Parsi actors on their proper performance. After thorough preparation, Nazir had the courage to mount the play. His effort was successful, and the performance proved a source of inspiration to the fledgling Parsi theatre. The play itself is not available, and nothing is known about its author either. Perhaps none of these early plays was even printed. They might have existed as handwritten copies that were destroyed in the course of time. The same situation prevails with the farces and their authors, which were performed along with the first dramas. Although these farces were mainly in Hindustani, their authors were Parsi.

The material available on the Parsi playwrights, with a few exceptions, is negligible. Here and there bits of information are found in various books, but nowhere is the description detailed. Given this situation, as in the case of the playhouses, whatever is available has been collected and recorded here. Kaikhushro Navrojji Kabra can be considered the first Parsi playwright, but in the absence of dates for the other playwrights, the information is presented as follows.[12]

Ranina, Nanabhai Rustamji (1832–1900)

One of the best-known writers of Parsi society, he penned everything from children's books to a trilingual dictionary. As a member of countless *sabhas* and societies, he was also very active in social uplift. He ran his own press and edited a newspaper for a number of years.

Ranina translated one act each of *The Comedy of Errors* and *Othello* into Gujarati for the Shakespeare Theatrical Company; the two plays were published in 1860 by Ashkara Press.[13] The third play Ranina wrote was a translation of *Romeo and Juliet*, published in 1876 by the Fort Printing Press. The translator's name was printed as 'Delta'. It is not known why Nanabhai Ranina did not give his full name.

Dhanjibhai Patel says that the real author was Dosabhai Framji Randeliya, and that Ranina plagiarized him.[14]

The names of Ranina's other plays are: (1) *Karni Tevi Par Utarni* (As You Sow, So Shall You Reap), (2) *Kala Mendha* (Black Sheep), (3) *Homlo Hau* (Cheating Play Never Thrives), (4) *Nazan Shirin*, (5) *Vehmayli Zar* (Suspicious Gaze), (6) *Sati Savitri*.[15] *Karni Tevi Par Utarni* and *Nazan Shirin* illustrate that Ranina was accomplished at writing comedy and satire. *Nazan Shirin* is a comedy that takes up the problem of child marriage. A mother and father are worried about finding a suitable bridegroom. The boy's family takes a loan and tries to impress the girl's parents with their wealth, but in the end the ruse is revealed. Hindi writers also used this episode in their plays and farces. The social problem is roughly the same for all castes and communities. *Sati Savitri* is based on the famous legend, and the playwright provides interesting facts about how and why it was written in his foreword.

Khori, Edalji Jamshedji (1847–1917)

Edalji Khori passed his matriculation in 1865. However, it seems that reading and writing were in his genes. Even in 1865 he translated a book into Gujarati with two of his Parsi friends, dedicating it to the respected Rustamji Jamshedji Jijabhai, who had encouraged the three students.

Edalji Khori was very fond of writing history. He published *France ane Germany Bachche ni Ladai* (The Franco-German War) in 1871 and *Asia ane Turkey Bachche ni Ladai* (The Asia–Turkey War) in 1878. The owner of the newspaper *Mumbai Samachar*, Manakji Barjori Minochehr Homji, commissioned Khori to write the latter history, which was serialized with pictures. His other non-fiction includes *Prani Vidya* (Animal Lore), published in 1880 by Ashkara Press. It covers mammals, birds, reptiles, carnivores, herbivores, and so on.

Khori's dramas were written in Gujarati, and many were later translated by Aram into Hindustani. The rights for Khori's plays were held by a number of different drama companies. Possibly his first drama was *The Lady of Lyons* (1868), based on the eponymous English play by Bulwer Lytton that proved such a hit with the Bombay public. It was written for and performed by the Gentlemen Amateurs Company, headed by Framroz Gustadji Dalal (Phalughus). It is said that during rehearsals for this play, a disagreement developed between Framroz Joshi and Phalughus, resulting in Joshi's departure from the company and its folding thereafter.

His second play was *Rustam ane Sohrab* in five acts, based on Firdausi's *Shahnama*. The Victoria Company owners published it in 1870 at Ashkara Press in Bombay. The author sold the play to the company for 300 rupees. After Kaikhushro Kabra left the Victoria, Dadi Patel became manager and then sole proprietor. Dadi Patel had Aram translate this play into Hindustani and directed it, himself playing the part of Rustam.

Hazambad ane Thagannaz was his third play, published in 1871 by Ashkara Press. This publication too was sponsored by the Victoria Company, and the play was performed by them. At that time, Kunvar Sohrabji Nazir and Dadabhai Patel were joint owners of the Victoria Company. It is said that this play was not a success. Dr Nami calls this play *Hazam Abad aur Thagni Tar*. But the title published in *Parsi Prakash* is the one I consider to be correct.

The fourth play of Khori's was *Khudabakhsh*. This three-act drama was published in 1871 by Jam-e Jamshed Press. It was written for the Zoroastrian Theatrical Company. It was perhaps translated into Hindustani by Aram. The Gujarati version was quite popular. The plot is rather bizarre. A youth named Nadir Shah hears accounts of Pari Banu, the daughter of a wealthy Damascus family, and falls in love with her. He attempts to obtain her and expresses his desire to his friend Zafaruddin. Hearing the full story, Zafaruddin also falls in love with Pari Banu. As a result, the two friends become enemies. They set out on a long journey to find their beloved. On the way, a band of robbers attacks them. Although deprived of their luggage and assistants, both continue on their mission unaided. One of the robbers, Khudabakhsh, finds out that Pari Banu's parents cannot recognize Nadir Shah by sight. He disguises himself as Nadir Shah and arrives in Damascus. By deception and trickery, he is successful in wedding Pari Banu.

Khori's fifth play was *Sunana Mulni Khurshed* (Khurshed for the Price of Gold), published in 1871 by Ashkara Press. It was translated into Hindustani by Behramji Fardunji Marzban. That translation is considered by Urdu scholars to be the first play in the Urdu language. It was performed by the Victoria Theatrical Company under Dadi Patel's direction. The famous Parsi actor Balivala played the role of the heroine Khurshed, and his father Mancherji Balivala played Khurshed's father. The other famous actor in the production was Pestanji Madan. The drama was extremely popular. The amusing thing about it was that the father lays a trap so that his 'daughter', played by his real-life son, Khurshed Balivala, is sold off and forced into married life.

Nurjahan, the sixth play, was translated into Hindustani by Aram. It was performed by the Elphinstone Theatrical Company and published by the Elphinstone partners, Kunvarji Nazir and Dadabhai Patel in 1872 from the Apakhtyar Press. In those days both the Elphinstone and Victoria were owned by Nazir and Dadi Patel in a joint partnership, and thus the top actors of both the companies were involved in the performance of this play. Sir Salar Jang, the prime minister of Hyderabad, was invited to see *Nurjahan*. He was so very pleased by the performance that he invited Patel and his troupe to visit Hyderabad.

Khori's *Jalam Jor* was written for the Zoroastrian Theatrical Company and was originally in Gujarati. Afterwards, Aram translated it into Urdu. It was published in 1876. Altogether Khori wrote about eighteen plays, of which nine were translated into Urdu by Aram.

Kabraji, Kaikhushro Navrojji (1842–1904)

A major contributor to dramatic literature and the development of the stage, Kaikhushro Kabraji was an extraordinary individual. He was not only the proprietor and editor of the leading Parsi newspaper, *Rast Goftar*, but also a playwright of high calibre.

Kabraji alone should be credited with establishing the Victoria Theatrical Company. He wrote his first play, *Bejan ane Manijeh*, in Gujarati for this very troupe in 1869, based on a story from Firdausi's *Shahnama*. It is said that in performance it was not as successful as had been anticipated. Jamshed Daji played the part of Manijeh, and the public gave him the title of Jamsu Manijeh. Kabra presented a benefit night for Jamsu and played the part of Manijeh himself in it.

Kabra's second play was *Jamshed*, composed in 1870 again for the Victoria Theatrical Company. Although it too was based on the *Shahnama*, it departs from the original significantly. In his preface to the play, Kabraji clarifies:

> Still there is some difference between these two stories. If the story of Bejan was full of *shringar ras*, then Jamshed's story is full of *karuna ras*. In the first was amusement and in the second advice; in the first primarily story and in the second more of history; and due to this, although the famous Goldsmith thinks that the task of writing plays is very easy for the writer familiar with theatre, nevertheless to transform the story of Jamshed into an interesting or amusing play is even more laborious than to transform the story of Bejan. Incidents and situations suitable for a play can be found quite easily in the

FIGURE 7. Kaikhushro Navrojji Kabra, social reformer, journalist and playwright. Source: Delphine Menant, *The Parsis* (1917).

story of Bejan . . . but Jamshed's story is . . . history without the interesting incidents suitable for a story. If the matter of Jamshed's entrapment in the noose of love had not been placed in the background, then Jamshed's story would be considered the driest in the memorable *Shahnama*.

King Jamshed's mind was swollen with his own power. Due to arrogance he made a claim of divinity, on account of which there was rebellion in his kingdom. After being defeated and crushed, he died in a state of penury. In just these words can Firdausi's colourful story be entirely summarized. However fine a description Firdausi has eloquently given of

Jamshed's magnificence and great deeds, still this account is of little use in arranging the structure of a play, because in a play explanations are more necessary than incidents. Which events happened in Jamshed's glorious reign so that the mind of this emperor, appointed by the exalted God, became swollen like this? As he became puffed up with arrogance, what happened to cause the population to rebel and finally deprive him of his kingdom? All these matters this 'Homer of the East' has left to the imagination of his readers. Their absence can be excused in a book like the King of Poets' *Shahnama*, but in a play one cannot avoid bringing these events before the spectators.

That is why in this play all the events pertaining to Jamshed's reign have had to be invented. Whatever sorrowful finale Firdausi described for Jamshed's kingship, even more sorrowful reasons have had to be inserted in this play from the imagination. What is the meaning of Jamshed's losing his kingdom through arrogance, and how did it happen? Great care has been taken to show these things in this play, and I now explain my plan in brief. First, due to the prosperity derived from the king's grandeur and control, his authority and pomp, he considered himself the greatest, on account of which he became proud and arrogant. His arrogance slowly increased, and the flame of his pride was fanned by the breeze of flattery. The Padshah, trapped by flattery, made the claim of divinity, which several innocents with a true heart accepted. Certain cheats with their own interests in their hearts gradually fed the Padshah's arrogance, and I have attempted to show how it steadily increased.

In this manner, herein the king has been placed among ignorant and self-interested people, whereas far-sighted and wise people have been shown as disheartened at his misfortune. And importantly, the efforts of his wise advisors and councillors to break his arrogance have been depicted . . . Finally his arrogance takes the form of tyranny, he attempts to enforce his claim of divinity, and confident of his learning and power, he distances himself from the wise courtiers who are like his hands and feet, because of their opposing advice. In the time of need without advice and help, he finds himself in an incurable and helpless condition. His arrogance slowly becomes insufficient, and finally the time for repentance comes, but then it is too late. Losing his kingdom, he is in the condition of a wandering beggar: this example of a natural result is shown in this play.[16]

Regarding this three-act play, its plot, dramatic art, and the author's skill, little further needs to be said. If the evidence for a play's excellence be its success on the stage and popularity with the audience, then *Jamshed* must be counted among the top class of dramas.

After *Jamshed*, Kabra wrote *Faredun*, also based on the *Shahnama*. Like *Jamshed*, this too is a historical drama, but it treats a dynastic period somewhat later than Jamshed's. Kabra presents his self-justification, as he did in *Jamshed*, in the preface to *Faredun*:

Among all kinds of plays, those pertaining to history are the most difficult to write. There is a kind of enmity between the peculiarities and topsy-turvy incidents needed for success in the composition of the play and the truth required in history. Just as a poet is unsuccessful in giving a true history—that we have seen with the great poet Firdausi—similarly, if a playwright seeks to stick to true history, then he is forgoing his duty to theatre. If history is shown on the stage just as it is, it will be unsuccessful as theatre. The playwright must use a little imagination, but then in true matters he may not use his imagination . . . Luckily like Jamshed, the history of Faredun is also small and simple, without many incidents. The whole history of Jamshed is that he became a majestic king, ranking with the prophets, but when he made a claim of divinity his vainglory broke him, trampled him under foot, and caused him to be murdered at the hands of Zohak.[17]

According to Kabraji, Firdausi did not need to explain how everything happened with Jamshed. But the playwright, in order to do justice to his hero, must use his imagination or else the character will be incomplete. The author divides *Faredun* into two parts. The first contains two acts, the first of which has four scenes and the second five. The second part similarly has two acts with five scenes each. The first part of the drama is largely invented whereas the second is more historically based.

The playwright acknowledges that although he tried to depict the entire life of Jamshed, from a dramatic standpoint this is not appropriate because it is a fault to try to pack too much into a two- or three-hour play. But in *Faredun* he did not commit this mistake. The playwright says the following about the intention behind his composition:

My main objective is only now, when Parsis have begun to forget their land, their power, their glory, and their feelings towards their people, to freshen the memory of previous glory by presenting before them a picture of that previous rule mingled with amusement and knowledge. And if my feeble efforts are of any help in increasing an enthusiasm for these matters among Parsis, I will consider myself amply repaid.[18]

From this it is clear that the author wanted to remind the Parsis of their past and fill them with a new enthusiasm, and undoubtedly he was successful in this.

Kaikhushro Kabraji was a reformer who led the movement for the betterment of Parsi society. He wrote essays, wrote plays, and even promoted music education by forming the Gayan Uttejak Company. For the social advancement of Parsi women, he brought out the magazine *Stribodh*.

Kaikhushro not only propagated Parsi history and culture, he wrote plays like *Harishchandra*,[19] *Sitaharan*, *Lavkush* and *Nand Batrisi* and thereby encouraged reformist Hinduism. Although *Harishchandra* and *Sitaharan* were originally plays by Ranchhodbhai Udayram and Narmada Shankar respectively, Kaikhushro helped to endow them with performability and became known as their author. *Nand Batrisi* was his original composition.

The plot of *Ninda Khanun* (Scandal House) was taken from the English poet and dramatist Sheridan's famous play, *The School for Scandal*, but the author adapted it to fit contemporary Parsi society. *Bholi Jan's* plot was based on *The Colleen Bawn*,[20] but it was a highly instructional play. In it, the famous actress Mary Fenton played the part of the heroine Gul very effectively. The piece *Sudi Vache Sopari* (Betelnut between the Scissorblades) was based on *Wives as They Were and Maids as They Are*,[21] according to Dhanjibhai Patel. The play was written in 1884 and published in the same year by Ranina's Union Press. However, in his foreword the playwright claims that it was based on *The Wonder* by the famous English writer, Mrs Centlivre. It too depicts the condition of Parsi society. On pages 7 and 19 a *dhrupad* and a *ghazal* are included in Hindustani.

Parsi Vachho Kaka Pahlan is another of Kabraji's plays, also known as *Shehriyani Safai, Virudh Gamdiyan Sadai* (The Cleanliness of the

Citydwellers vs the Simplicity of the Villagers). The second title sheds greater light on its subject. The scenes take place in Malesar and Navsari. *The Hut of the Red Mountain*[22] formed the basis for *Vinash Kale Viprit Buddhi* (Contrary Logic in a Time of Destruction).

Without a doubt, Kaikhushro Kabraji was a successful dramatist and actor. Each character emerges fully developed in his writing. Ordinarily a playwright depicts his characters in conflict with other characters, in both the personal and collective aspects; otherwise his characterization is not attractive. This art is also visible in Kabraji's characterization. His characters are of all types—murderous, savage, crazed, immoral. His specialty is that the sinner is shown as a sinner, the hypocrite as a hypocrite, the truthsayer as a truthsayer. King and pauper, hero and coward, sinner and ascetic, high and low, lover and beloved are all drawn in their own way. Jamshed's call, Arjasp's intelligence, Jamasp's heroism, Sapanjan dissolving in love, Arnavaz burning to ashes, crazy Shehrnavaz, Manijeh ensnared in love's net, Sita in separation from Rama, Tara lamenting for her husband and son, Harishchandra ready to give up his life for truth: all in their own places represent human virtues and characteristics. What can be greater proof of the artistic achievement of an accomplished author?

All told, Kaikhushro N. Kabraji's contribution to the Parsi theatre was very unique and important. He deserves credit for giving stability to dramatic literature and performance. Thus it is entirely appropriate that he is known as 'Father of the Native Stage'.

Apakhtyar, Nasharvanji Dorabji (1835–1878)

Apakhtyar was a famous Parsi scholar and family man. He was very interested in music, being a singer as well as a dramatist, writer, and journalist. He was the proprietor of *Parsi Panch*. Although this paper was started in 1854 by Dadabhai Shoheri, Apakhtyar took over in 1878 and ran it until his death.

Apakhtyar was born in 1835. At first he was known as Kikadavar, but in 1854, when he started the paper *Apakhtyar*, this name became attached to him. Apakhtyar and Kaikhushro Kabraji were sworn enemies. On one side the Victoria Theatrical Company was performing Kabraji's *Bejan ane Manijeh* and Khori's *Rustam ane Sohrab*, while on the other Apakhtyar determined to mount a musical production of *Sohrab Rustam*. Apakhtyar took on the task of giving *Sohrab Rustam* a musical structure. Luckily, he got Manakji Barbhaya who had a sweet and attractive voice to play the role of Sohrab. Apakhtyar performed the role of Rustam himself, and Jamsu Kandevala played Tahmina. *Sohrab Rustam* was the first opera in Gujarati and was very popular with the spectators.

Apakhtyar produced a number of 'sketches' that included music. The most popular was *Kajora no Skech* (The Unfit Match), in which a twelve-year old girl is married to an old man. Apakhtyar's Parsi Stage Players performed these sketches. The impact of Apakhtyar's music was such that Kaikhushro Kabraji began to include songs in his prose dramas, and Edalji Khori had Ranchhodbhai Udayram compose songs for his dramas. The tradition was thus established. In this sense, the contribution of Apakhtyar to Parsi drama is quite important.

Aram, Nasharvanji Mehrvanji Khansahab

Several dramas of Aram's are famous, but not all were originally written by him. Most were translations into Urdu of Khori's Gujarati plays, e.g. *Sone ke Mul ki Khurshed* (1871), *Nurjahan* (1872), *Jahangir* (1872), *Mazhab-e Ishq, urf Bakavali Tajulmaluk* (1872), *Hatim* (1872), *Qamar uz-Zaman* (1874), *Jalam Jor* (1876). Aram also wrote original dramas, such as *Jahangir Shah Gauhar* (1874), *Benazir Badremunir, Gulva Sanovar Cha Kurd, Chhail Batau Mohana Rani, Padmavat, Shakuntala, Lal-o-Gauhar, Farrukh Sabha, Chandravali*.

Aram stands in the front line of Parsi writers in Urdu, both from the standpoint of quantity and literary quality. His language however was very difficult. The ordinary Urdu speaker could not readily understand it. This was because, in his words, 'My native language is neither Urdu nor Braj.'[23] *Benazir Badremunir* was Aram's first musical play. The second musical was *Jahangir Shah aur Gauhar*. Its language was relatively simple, being a good example of contemporary Hindustani. The Urdu of *Gulva Sanovar Cha Kurd* is, on the other hand, relatively difficult. Some people consider *Sone ke Mul ki Khurshed* to be the first Urdu drama.

Dhabhar, Dorabji Rustamji, aka Dolu

Around 1875, there was a slow period in the dramatic profession. The Zoroastrian Company began to retreat, but Irani plays continued. The Alfred Theatrical Company was also inactive during this time. In 1876 the company had Edalji Khori write *Jalam Jor*, an adaption of *Pizarro*. Then Dhabhar, a singer of Turra and Khyal, mixed some of his songs and others into the existing Urdu plays and began to perform them. A new company, the Shah-e Alam Theatrical Company, was established, and it performed *Jan-e Alam Anjuman Ara*. Behramji Katrak played the role of Anjuman Ara. Dhabhar wrote a play and gave it a strange, long name: *Jabuli Selam ane Aflatun Jin; Gullala Pari ne Pakdaman Shirin*. The names of several dramas are included in this name, from which one concludes that Dhabhar wanted to bring the excellent qualities of several plays into one. His play was only performed thrice, and then it settled into deep sleep.

Dhabhar himself was a good actor and director. One day a Parsi actor started drinking alcohol on the stage. Dhabhar saw this and immediately marched him to the green room, where he seized the bottle and threw it away. He later said, 'If you are going to drink, then don't come back to my club.' As an actor, Dhabhar played the *hijra's* part in *Anjuman Ara* with great success. It is said that his gestures were very natural and attractive.[24]

Mistri, Edalji Dadabhai (Edu Kalejar)

On the basis of one of Kaikhushro Kabraji's novels, he wrote *Dukhiyari Bachu* (The Unfortunate Bachu), and based on another, *Paisa Paisa* (Money, Money). An amusing story is attached to the composition of the first. Edu Kalejar often attended the rehearsals of the Parsi Theatrical Company out of friendship with its members. Three friends of Dhanjibhai Patel's had established this company: Framji Dadabhai Apu's brother Dinshah Dadabhai Apu, Bapuji Jamshedji Mistri, and Dadi Ba. Edalji Mistri wrote a musical play, *Gul-o-Bulbul* (The Rose and the Nightingale), and gave it to Dinshah Apu, but it was not very successful. Then Edu Kalejar advised him to stage a play in Parsi dress. Apu replied, 'Oh, go away! How will people like it if Parsis come on stage wearing their long cloaks and saris? They'll look like peeled sugarcane!' To this, Edu Kalejar answered that the Zoroastrians performed their comedies in Parsi dress.

After this incident, Edu Kalejar dramatized Kabra's *Dukhiyari Bachu* and presented it to Apu. Framji Apu played the part of Bachu's husband and Edu played the loafer. The play was a big hit. This was the first attempt at performing a social drama on the Parsi stage. Inspired by his own success, Edu then wrote *Paisa Paisa*. This too was a dramatic adaptation of a Kabra story. Ardeshar Mamo played a much-acclaimed part in it.[25]

Kabra, Bahmanji Navrojji (1860–1925)

A famous Gujarati writer, his plays number over one dozen, including *Jebanejar ane Shirin* (based on Shakespeare's *Othello*), *Sipah Bachani Sajni, Jebanejar, Bholi Gul, Gamreni Gori, Kal Jug, Dorangi Duniya, Bagh-e Bahest, Bapna Shrap, Faramarz* (based on *Hamlet*), *Vafa par Jafa, Diljang Diler, Khushro ane Parichehar, Bahera Bahela Kaka, Jugar, Bhulo Padelo Bhimbhai, Nur-e Neki*, etc.[26] Bahmanji holds a high place among Parsi writers. In addition to plays, he wrote stories and novels, and he was also involved in journalism. From the above list, it is apparent that he was fond of writing comedies. Manners and morals were the main themes of his dramatic works.

Gamreni Gori (The Village Belle) was written for the Alfred Company of Kavasji Khatau. Later it was performed hundreds of times by Balivala's Victoria Company. The actresses Mary Fenton and Munni Bai played the leading role. The play's subject is a comparison between the pure life of the village and the arrogant lifestyle of the city. *Bholi Gul* (Innocent Flower) was based on Mrs Henry Wood's novel *East Lynne*. Bahmanji Kabra was the brother of the famous Parsi writer and reformer, Kaikhushro Navrojji Kabra.

Balivala, Khurshedji Mehrvanji

He was mainly an actor, director, and company owner, but he was also proficient in writing comedies. His Gujarati comedies include *Matlab Beharo*, *Khudabakhsh*, *Gustad Dhamar*, and *Kavlani Kachumbar*.

Bandekhuda, Dadabhai Edalji Ponchkhanevala

This Parsi writer is famous for three plays: *Yazad-e Zard*, *Barjor ane Mehrsimin Ozar*, and *Khushru Shirin*. The second of these, published in 1871, was a four-act play written for the Persian Zoroastrian Theatrical Company. There are a large number of characters, including Iranis, Turanis, Jabulis, Negroes and giants. Pestan Framji Belati played the hero Barjor's part, and Ardeshar Jahangirji Chinai played the female role of Mehrsimin. The playwright tries to show that true love illuminates the darkness of men's souls, and whoever is immersed in love always enjoys blessings and good fortune. The play is in both prose and poetry.

Batlivala, Firoz

Only two of his plays are famous. *Nekbakht Tehmina* was a three-act play written for Balivala's Victoria Theatrical Company. In it the author sheds light on Irani history and customs, and also clarifies the difference between Irani and Turani culture. The drama is named after the heroine, and it is written in verse. His other play was *Kharid Lo Khavind* (Buy a Husband). It was performed by the Parsi Theatrical Company. Batlivala also published two works entitled *Sarod-e Avasta* and *Firozi Gayan.*

Bharucha, Framji Sohrabji

He wrote *Alauddin ane Jadui Fanas* (Aladdin and the Magic Lamp), which was performed by the Elphinstone Theatrical Company.

Bhedvar, Shahpur N.

He is known to have written only one drama, entitled *Haq Insaf.* In regard to the performance of this drama, Dhanjibhai Patel says that various girls acted in it. Each one wore a sari of a different colour. The owner of the company was not interested in buying so many saris, but the playwright was also the director, and he insisted that the company owners bite the bullet and lay out the money.[27]

Dhondi, Edalji Framji

He wrote *Sitam-e Hasrat.*

Framroz, Khurshedji Bahmanji (1847–1920)

He wrote *Pakdaman Gulnar* for the old Elphinstone Company. At first it was thought that this drama's creator was Nanabhai Ranina, but Ranina's son said that the actual author was Framroz himself. Ranina only made a few improvements in the play.[28] Two other plays by Framroz were also successful on the Gujarati stage, *Jahanbakhsh ane Gulrukhsar* and *Shahzada Shyabakhsh.*

Khambata, Hirji

Ab-e Iblis was his most famous play. Generally speaking, Hirji was a successful actor and director. After the performance of this play, he left the Parsi theatre and spent the rest of his life in a government job.

Khambata, Jahangir (1856–1916)

The nephew of Hirji Khambata, he had a great interest in the art of drama. He wrote an Urdu drama called *Khudadad*. His other plays were written in Gujarati. Famous among his works are *Juddin Jhagro, Kohiyar Confusion, Mad House, Mako Bhil,* and *Dharti Kamp*.[29] Jahangir was most interested in writing social dramas based on Parsi mores. Because he himself was a good actor and a company owner, his plays were very successful.

Nazir, Kunvarji Sohrabji

Kadak Kanyane Phisela Paranya was the only play he wrote, although he wrote a great deal in English.

Parakh, Dr Nasharvanji Navrojji

He was an actor as well as a playwright. *Sulemani Shamshir* (The Sword of Solomon) was published in 1873.[30] Kunvarji Nazir helped to inspire it. After the *Indar Sabha* had achieved such success, Kunvarji Nazir had Dr Parakh rewrite it. It was a big hit, starring the author and Jamshedji Framji Madan in the main roles. A very popular farce, *Asman Challi*, was also performed on the same bill. The heroine's part was played by Jamshedji Framji Madan, and it contained a number of miraculous scenes. Parakh's second play was *Phalkasur Salim*, which was published one year after the first one.

Patel, Ardeshar Behramji

He primarily wrote farces. First, he wrote *Nanivai Viruddh Junivai* for the Alfred Company, but it was not successful. Then he wrote *Taqdirni*

Taksir. It too met with little success. *Aslaji* suddenly brought him into the front ranks. After that his comedies brought him considerable fame. *Sudhareni Shirin Thikane Avi* and *Kaka Mama Kahaivana* proved to be quite successful.

Patel, Dhanjibhai N. (1857–1937)[31]

Dhanjibhai Patel was a doctor by profession, but he enjoyed writing and performing in plays. Six plays are attributed to him. These are *Khaslat-e Shaitan, Feraun, Tufan, Laila, Rustam Sohrab* (a musical), and *Habil* (based on Milton's *Paradise Lost*).

Sanjana, Seth Pestanji Kavasji

He wrote *Barjor ane Mehrsimin* for the Baronet Club. His second play was *Shahzada Erich*. The plot was based on ancient Parsi history. Sanjana was the director of the Baronet Club. *Shahzada Erich* was written for the Bombay Amateurs.[32]

Tarapurvala, Darashah Sohrabji

This writer was a respectable householder who always liked to write. 'A Young Parsi' was the pseudonym under which he composed fiction. In 1867 he wrote the story *Velayti Gori Golamadi* and sold it just a few days after its publication. In 1868 he wrote *Zanankhanani Bibio* and it too became very famous. He was also interested in drama, and therefore he joined the Victoria Theatrical Company. For this company, he wrote *Kaikaus ane Safed Dev* (Kaikaus and The White Devil). The playwright himself played the white devil, and Kaikaus was played by Phalughus, Rustam by Kakaval, and Gurgin by Kavasjiba, which contributed to its success. After a time, Darasha Tarapurvala quit the Victoria and formed his own company, the Khoja Dramatic Club. For them he wrote the play *Kaikaus ane Saudaba.* Kavasji Khatau played the part of Saudaba in it. The third play he wrote was *Dukhiyari Bhul* (A Poor Girl's Error), in which Tarapurvala himself played a part.

Then he left the world of drama. Aside from Gujarati, he had a good knowledge of Italian. This enabled him to become the manager of the Italian shipping company, Rubetino. He left Bombay for Singapore, and it was there that he died.[33]

Wadia, Mehrvanji Nasharvanji

He was a creator of social and moralizing dramas. His play *Satano Nigahvan Khuda* was very popular.[34] His second play was *The Honeymoon*.

Notes

1 [The list has been rearranged in Roman alphabetical order.]

2 Sharof, *Purano Parsi Natak Takhto*, pp. 22–23. [Note Gupt's error: the Edward Theatre is not listed by Sharof.]

3 Sharof, p. 22.

4 Sharof, pp. 22–23.

5 Sharof, p. 23.

6 Sharof, p. 23.

7 *Kaisar-e-Hind*, 2 December 1928.

8 Ibid.

9 Sharof, p. 22.

10 [The former Ripon Theatre is now the Alfred Talkies on Grant Road.]

11 [A photograph of the Victoria Theatre was published in C. J. Sisson, *Shakespeare in India* (1926). It does not match the pejorative description given here.]

12 [The names of the eight most significant playwrights have been rearranged in approximate chronological order, according to their dates of birth, when known, and dates of their publications. The minor playwrights have been listed alphabetically after the major playwrights. For dating of playwrights, various sources have been consulted, principally Pilam Bhikhaji Makati, *Parsi Sahitya no Itihas* (Navsari: Makati, 1949).]

13 *Parsi Prakash*, vol. 2, p. 172.

14 Ibid., Vol. 1, p. 572.

15 [The English titles of three of Ranina's plays are derived from J. F. Blumhardt, *Catalogue of Marathi and Gujarati Printed Books in the Library of the British Museum* (London: 1892).]

16 [Preface, *Jamshed* (Mumbai: Ashkara Press, 1870). Translated by Samira Sheikh and Kathryn Hansen.]

17 [Preface, *Faredun* (Mumbai: Ashkara Press, 1874). Translated by Samira Sheikh and Kathryn Hansen.]

18 [Ibid.]

19 'The drama *Harishchandra* was written in Gujarati based on the original by R. R. Ranchhodbhai Udayram. Modified with permission for the Natak Uttejak Company, in four acts, published in Bombay at the Ashkara Press of Behramji Fardunji [Marzban] Company.' *Parsi Prakash*, Vol. 2, p. 562.

20 [By Dion Boucicault.]

21 [By Elizabeth Inchbald.]

22 [By Henry M. Milner.]

23 Aram, Preface to *Jahangir Shah aur Gauhar* (Cooper Company, 1874).

24 *Kaisar-e Hind*, 3 March 1929.

25 *Kaisar-e Hind*, 17 March 1929.

26 [Titles corrected against the Gujarati-language lists in Appendix 2 of Gopal Shastri, *Parsi Rangbhumi* (Vadodara: Sadhana Shastri, 1995) and the list on the cover page of B. N. Kabra's novel, *Banva Kal*.]

27 *Kaisar-e Hind*, 7 April 1929.

28 PNTT, p. 14.

29 *Kaiser-e Hind*, 21 April 1929, and PNTT, p. 370. [Titles corrected against Shastri's Appendix 2.]

30 *Parsi Prakash*, Vol. 2, p. 459.

31 [Dhanjibhai Patel was also the author of *Parsi Natak Takhtani Tavarikh*, a history of the Parsi stage, one of Somnath Gupt's principal sources.]

32 *Kaisar-e Hind*, 28 April 1929.

33 *Kaisar-e Hind*, 10 March 1929.

34 PNTT, p. 368.

CHAPTER 4

Urdu Dramatists of the Parsi Stage[1]

Raunaq, Mahmud Miyan Banarasi (1825–1886)

Dr Nami states that Raunaq's full name was Mahmud Ahmad. Sheikh Mahmud was his own name and Sheikh Ahmad his father's name. In the southern system he was known as Mahmud Ahmad after his father, although the Parsis called him Mamud Miyan.[2] Mahmud Miyan's pseudonym was 'Raunaq'; it is not known how he began to be called 'Banarasi'.

Raunaq came and settled in Bombay, where he died on 25 April 1886, at the age of 61. He began his livelihood as a worker in a textile mill and ended it as a playwright, having served as an employee of the Victoria Theatrical Company until his death.

Raunaq's plays reveal that he was a good scholar of Farsi and Urdu. The number of his plays is very large. The list given by Dr Nami is as follows:

Benazir Badremunir
Laila Majnun
Anjam-e Ulfat, urf Humayun Nasir
Puran Bhagat
Saif us-Suleman, urf Masum Masuma
Sitam-e Haman, urf Fareb Israel
Ashiq-e Sadiq, urf Hir Ranjha[3]

Hatim Bin Tai, urf Afsar Sakhavat

Tilasm Zohra, urf Ranj ka Badla Ganj

Fasana-e Ajayab, urf Jan Alam Anjuman Ara

Insaf-e Mahmud Shah Ghaznavi, urf Is Hath De Us Hath Le

Insaf-e Mahmud Shah, urf Zulm Umran

Ashiq ka Khun, urf Daman par Dhabba

Ajayab Paristan, urf Baharistan-e Ishq

Zulm-e Azlam, urf Jaisa Bona Vaisa Pana

Khvabgah-e Ishq, urf Bedad Vahshat

Khvab-e Muhabbat, urf Nadan ki Dosti Ji ka Janjal

Gharur Rud Shah, urf Chanda Hur va Khurshed Nur

Sangin Bakavali

Naqsh Suleman, urf Shadadi Vahisht

Fareb Fitna, urf Chahat Zar

Kalka Bhog, urf Ghari ki Ghariyal

Nuruddin aur Husn Afroz

Chameli Gulab

Miyan Pissu aur Bibi Khatmal

The description of these plays follows:

Benazir Badremunir (Benazir and Badremunir): In 1872 when Dadi Patel was the manager of the Victoria Theatrical Company, he got the idea of having an opera written and performed in Urdu. He asked Nasharvanji Khansahab (Aram) to write such an opera, and accordingly he composed *Benazir Badremunir*. Dadi Patel's production of it was very successful, and he gained great popularity from it.

This original play is not available anywhere today. Raunaq composed his opera based on Aram's 1872 drama of the same title. Possibly it was written in 1879, but I have only seen evidence of a copy published in 1880 by the Victoria Company in the Gujarati script. Until both Khansahab's and Raunaq's texts have been compared, it is difficult to say what similarities and differences may exist between the compositions. Dr Nami states that according to Dadabhai Ratanji Thunthi, Raunaq rewrote the dramas of his company and other companies and published them under his own name. If Raunaq's plays had been published under his name by other publishers, Thunthi's statement could be considered true. But *Benazir Badremunir* was published by the Victoria Company itself, and Raunaq's name is printed in the author's position. If this were an emendation of Khansahab's play, then it would have stated, 'Munshi Raunaq has written this play on the basis of a play of the same name by Khansahab.' It was the practice at the time to print such statements. Thus we will have to accept that the play is Raunaq's own.

In the first act, the fairy Mahrukh declares her love for Benazir, the Prince of the East, but he rejects her. In order to conciliate him, Mahrukh gives him her flying cot. When Benazir's parents find out that their son has disappeared, they set out for the jungle as ascetics. In the second act, the princess of Sarandip, Badremunir, appears, walking in her garden. At that very moment, Benazir passes by seated on his flying cot, and seeing Badremunir, he falls in love with her. Badremunir sees Benazir and falls in love with him too. Mahrukh hears of this via a *dev*, and she imprisons Benazir. Badremunir laments at the separation from her beloved and sends her best friend Najmunnisa to search for him. Najmunnisa, in the disguise of a *jogin*, sets out to find Benazir. In the third act, Badremunir meets up with Benazir's parents. They all proceed together to look for Benazir. In the jungle, Najmunissa encounters Firoz Shah, king of the *jinns*. With his help, Benazir escapes from prison. Firoz Shah sends for Benazir's parents, and in the end he reunites parents and son. Mahrukh is forgiven and a warning is issued that in future, no one should fall in love.

From the standpoint of characterization, consider the infatuation of Mahrukh:

Each moment I'll strive to please you, my love,
Each wish of yours will be my command.
Stay with me all night and wander by day,
But give your heart to none, if you value your life.

BENAZIR

Your love is touching, fairest flower of all,
How could I ever leave you and seek another?
As a favour lend me your flying horse
And I'll tour the skies filling my heart's desire.

In this opera, Raunaq has Badremunir and Benazir each sing a *ghazal* in Farsi, written respectively by Maulana Jami and Faughani. Probably Raunaq did not know Farsi himself or could not compose poetry in it. In those days there was a fashion for Farsi *ghazals*. Farsi *ghazals* were sung in Urdu plays to attract the Parsi spectators, or possibly a touch of Farsi was added to raise the calibre of the Urdu.

After Raunaq, a number of playwrights made this story the basis of their compositions. From this it is evident that the story was very popular. Because of its magical scenes, the drama became the object of audience appreciation. Hafiz Mohammad Abdullah and Faqir Mohammad Tegh reworked the story in their own dramatic versions.

Jafa-e Sitamgar, urf Ghari ya Ghariyal (The Bloodthirsty Tyrant, or Clock or Deathknell): Dr Nami calls this play *Kalka Bhog, urf Ghari ya Ghariyal*. He does not say who its printer and publisher were, and therefore it is impossible to prove whether the edition is authentic or not. On the copy of the edition in my possession, it is written: 'Drama in three acts; written for the Victoria Theatrical Company by the late Munshi Mahmud Miyan Raunaq and published for the third time for the benefit of the public by order of the owners of the Victoria Theatrical Company, by Lakhmi Das's company, in the Urdu language and Gujarati script.' The authenticity of this edition is proved by the statement that it was published by the order of the owners of the Victoria Theatrical Company. Thus its title ought to be more authoritative than the edition cited by Dr Nami. Nevertheless, from the standpoint of content, the title *Kalka Bhog* is more fitting, because the incident described in the play is based on the notion of tasks being completed or not completed on time. The incident is as follows.

A poor soldier named Sitamgar becomes the king of Roshanabad by means of magic. As a worshipper of the goddess Kalka, he sacrifices a human being once a year on a full-moon night to propitiate her. The goddess has given him a boon, ensuring that his reign will continue as long as he performs the sacrifice. Should he fail to perform the ritual correctly however, he himself will be sacrificed by the goddess. Midnight is the time that is specified for the completion of the sacrificial act.

Sitamgar captures Nekbakht, the son of the previous king, and plans to sacrifice him to the goddess. He also wants to eliminate a certain official in his kingdom. But Nekbakht escapes from captivity and goes to Nur Alam, a village girl, who loves him more than her life and promises to protect him. Sitamgar wants to make Nur Alam his wife. One day Sitamgar chances to find Nekbakht at Nur Alam's house, and he captures and imprisons him in his palace once more. Nur Alam, after searching and searching, arrives there just as Nekbakht is about to be sacrificed. Nur Alam protects Nekbakht, and Sitamgar agrees to substitute her for him in the sacrifice. While they are fighting, Nekbakht escapes and the clock strikes midnight. Sitamgar fails to perform the sacrifice on time. The goddess becomes angry, makes herself manifest, and devours Sitamgar. In this manner, the clock becomes for Sitamgar the deathknell, and Sitamgar's cruelty makes him the offering for Kalka's feast. The play ends with the marriage of Nur Alam and Khush Chehr. The play is an opera.

Ashiq ka Khun (The Murder of the Lover): Dr Nami has given only the first name of this drama in his list. Unlike other dramas, he has not described it, which suggests that the text was not examined by him. Nami mentions a play entitled *Ashiq ka Khun* in his list of Talib's plays, wherein he notes, 'This is a drama of Raunaq's to which Talib made very minor changes. The title page reads, "From the drama written by the late Munshi Mahmud Miyan Raunaq, in a new setting by Munshi Vinayak Prasad Talib." In addition, there is a couplet: "With the sword of cruelty the lover is slain. It takes precious metal to kill the silver-bodied." At the end of the book, Talib's name is mentioned.'[4]

The copy of the drama in my possession was published in 1903. It is the fourth edition and it reads, 'Published by Khurshedji Mehrvanji Balivala, company owner, Victoria Theatrical Company.' Thus this is an authentic edition published in the Gujarati script. It also contains the same couplet cited by Dr Nami from his copy. No doubt remains that its original author was Raunaq.

It is an opera in two acts. The incidents take place in Kiniyan, an imaginary location. The story is about Mastenaz, a girl whose father has died. She has three lovers named Ashiq, Shuja, and Ibnemir. At first Mastenaz is in love with Ashiq, and she writes letters promising to marry him. Next she toys with Shuja. Then she starts lusting for wealth and inclines towards Ibnemir. She begs Ashiq to free her from her promise. Ashiq's cousin-sister Dilnavaz warns Ashiq about Mastenaz's craftiness and infidelity, but blinded by love he ignores her. As a result, Mastenaz plots to kill Ashiq, hiring an assassin from the coffeehouse for two thousand rupees. Before carrying out the murder, the assassin tries to dissuade her, complaining of the hard hearts of women in love.

> The stain of a lover's murder can never be removed
> Though you may wash it from your skirts till doomsday.
> You've never been known to pity your lover.

Is that iron or a heart that you hold in your bosom?
Fleeing from infidels and the guilty aplenty,
You would still cut off the heads of the innocent.

Nevertheless, Ashiq is eventually murdered. When she hears the news, Dilnavaz becomes very sad, but Mastenaz reasons that the thorn that revealed her unfaithfulness has been removed. Just as Mastenaz prepares to wed Ibnemir, the entire conspiracy is revealed. Raunaq avails of the marvellous and the supernatural in the revelation of the secret. Miraculous effects are exhibited to surprise the spectator and elicit applause. Finally Mastenaz admits to the crime of having Ashiq killed, stabs herself with a dagger, and dies. The lover who is still alive marries Dilnavaz. Ibnemir escapes from the clutches of an unfaithful wife, and the assassin is sent to the gallows. The play ends. Although the drama is in verse on account of its being an opera, the beauty of Raunaq's poetry is visible in several places.

Zulm-e Azlam, urf Jaisa Bo Vaisa Lo (The Tyranny of Azlam, or As You Sow, So Shall You Reap)[5]: This opera is the story of a beautiful young woman named Nurunnisa and the defence of her chastity. Nurunnisa and Shamsru are the offspring of a Turkish noble on the island of Tuman. Azlam, a Negro tyrant, takes a fancy to Nurunnisa and wishes to marry her, but she does not agree. The brother and sister are compelled to flee, escaping Azlam's oppression to protect her honour. Azlam pursues them. Shamsru's ship is destroyed in a storm and the two are separated. A noble of Basra, seeing Nurunnisa floating in the water, tells his cart driver to rescue her. The driver succeeds, and the noble brings Nurunnisa to his home. There he shelters her with humility and respect, but both master and servant (the cart driver) fall in love with her. After many attempts, neither is able to win her heart. Then they try to disgrace Nurunnisa. By coincidence, Azlam's ship has also sunk, and he escapes and shows up at the same noble's home. The noble offers him shelter too. Nurunnisa is despondent, thinking of her brother. Azlam, calling her his sister, also starts becoming despondent. He befriends the cart driver, who takes Azlam in disguise to Nurunnisa. Azlam again starts to torment Nurunnisa. Finally the noble, thinking that Nurunnisa and Azlam are having an incestuous relationship, orders that they both be publicly shamed and sold in the marketplace. Shamsru, who by chance has survived, suddenly turns up in the market and sees what is happening. He recognizes his sister and purchases both her and Azlam. He begins to wonder whether his sister has lost her chastity. For this reason, he becomes bent on killing her. All these incidents take place in a country called Sham. The Prince of Sham, Munavvar Ins, sees Nurunnisa and falls in love with her. He asks his father for permission to marry her. When the father hears the gossip about Nurunnisa and all her suitors—Azlam, the noble, and his cart driver—he tries to dissuade his son, but the prince stands firm. Eventually the whole story is revealed. Azlam, the noble, and the cart driver confirm Nurunnisa's chastity; Shamsru too is satisfied; and in the end Munavvar Ins and Nurunnisa are wed. Each receives his just deserts, and Nurunnisa forgives the sins of all.

Raunaq does not respect the dramatic unities in this play, manipulating the plot however he likes. With the audience in mind, several spectacular scenes have been introduced, such as a flowing river, and boats colliding and capsizing when a storm comes up; the noble's eye popping out when Nurunnisa gives him a slap; a holy man producing a magic bottle, and so on. Various *ghazals* included in the play contain Raunaq's name. The romantic dialogues are good, although by the standards of poetry, the drama cannot be counted as of a high calibre.

Hatim Bin Tai, urf Afsar-e Sakhavat (Hatim Tai, or The Beneficent Officer): Dr Nami calls it *Hatim Bin Te*, but in the version published by the Victoria Company, the word *Tai* is used. This is a play in two acts. It is an assortment of incidents assembled by the playwright to exhibit the generous and helpful nature of Hatim. The main incident concerns a beautiful woman, Husn Bano, and her marriage with Munir Shami. Husn Bano has set seven questions to be answered successfully by the one who would win her as wife. Many men come and go, failing the test. Husn Bano's nurse pleads with her to break her vow, but she is not willing to do so. However, she falls in love with Munir Shami. He comes with answers to three of her questions and is very restless. Then he meets Hatim who promises to help him. Through divine powers, Hatim meets certain ascetics from whom he receives the answers, and on behalf of Munir Shami, replies to Husn Bano. After a fashion, Husn Bano's vow is fulfilled, and Hatim facilitates her marriage to Munir Shami.

But this is not the entire play. The author has added some other characters and pokes fun at the hero and heroine. With this innovation a layer of humour has been added. The play ends with the celebration of the marriages of Hatim and Zarrin Posh, and of Munir Shami and Husn Bano. The weaving together of the incidents does not display a high level of artistry. Whenever necessary, some supernatural element or other is used to manipulate the plot. Character development is minimal, and the play is not an example of high dramatic art. Aram and Abdullah also wrote plays using the same episode. However, their plays are not available and thus cannot be compared with Raunaq's.

One more composition of Raunaq is in my possession. It is titled *Bhole Miyan*, but it is incomplete. It is a farce. Until the entire copy is available, we cannot say what the author wanted to show in it. The farce is divided into scenes, not acts. My copy has six full scenes and a seventh incomplete one. Dr Nami has not mentioned this play in his list. It was published in 1882.

There is no doubt that Raunaq and Zarif are the oldest non-Parsi writers of the Parsi theatre. Zarif generally took earlier dramas and gave them new form. Raunaq too reworked dramas that had previously been written by Parsis, in addition to composing original dramas. His plays exhibit two main elements. First, they end on a note of idealism and morality. His dramatic sense of justice makes the character reap what he has sown. Secondly, because his dramas are operas, there is a great deal of versification in them. One does not find a high level of poetry. Even the *ghazals* that are full of romantic sentiments do not reach a superior level. Raunaq should be considered a poet of middling ability.

Finally it is worth noting that some plays of Raunaq's were altered by other writers and are available now in this form. As an example, Raunaq's drama *Sangin Bakavali* was revised by Munshi Talib. Hafiz Mohammad Abdullah and Ghulam Husain Zarif also reworked it. The case of *Khandan-e Haman* is similar.[6] *Puran Bhagat* was rewritten by Abdullah, Zarif, and Maulvi Bakhsh Ilahi. Zarif and Tegh gave a new form to *Anjam-e Ulfat*. *Saif us-Suleman* was published by Zarif and Abdullah under their names. In this manner, a number of Raunaq's dramas fell into other hands and came before the public in altered forms. However, because of the unavailability of both the original and the later versions, it is difficult to say how much credit should be given to each author.

Zarif, Husaini Miyan

Not much is available about Zarif, as is the case with his contemporary playwrights. He lived in Bombay and worked for Jamnadas Mehta Booksellers and Printers for three rupees a month. Later he began to write poetry, developing an interest in composing dramas. There is no evidence that Zarif wrote any original plays, but he certainly transformed a number of them. His pseudonym 'Zarif' is found frequently. As an example, *Gul Sanovar* is listed among the plays of Zarif. Aram first wrote it with the title *Gulva Sanovar Cha Kurd* (What Gul Said to Sanovar). Its plot was based on an old story. Whatever changes Zarif introduced can only be known when the two texts are compared. However, most of Zarif's plays cannot be found. *Chhail Batau, Lal-o-Gauhar, Farrukh Sabha, Hatim Tai, Tamasha-e Allaudin urf Chiragh-e Ajib, Havai Majlis, Laila Majnun,* and *Gul Bakavali* were all originally written by Aram. It remains to be seen what changes were made by Zarif.

Zarif made adaptations of other authors' plays as well. Aside from the above, the following plays of Zarif are well known: *Natija-e Asmat, Khudadost, Chand Bibi, Tohfa-e Dilkusha, Bulbul-e Bimar, Tohfa-e Dilpazir, Shirin Farhad, Ali Baba, Chitra Bakavali, Badremunir, Naqsh Sulemani, Aksir-e Azam, Ishrat Sabha, Husn Afroz, Nairang-e Ishq, Sitam-e Haman, Fareb Fitna, Nasir-o-Humayun, Matam-e Zafar, Bazm-e Suleman,* and *Khudadad*.[7] From this list, the plays *Benazir Badremunir, Nasir-o-Humayun, Sitam-e Haman, Naqsh Sulemani,* and *Fareb Fitna* were also written by Raunaq. Perhaps Zarif adapted them, because Raunaq's period predates Zarif's.

Dr Nami has given some information about other plays of Zarif, which is worth examining.[8]

Zarif's biggest contribution was that he took popular old plays and turned them into new operas. It is not known whether his plays were performed, or whether they were simply read and the publisher Jamnadas Mehta made a good deal of money because of the similarity between the old and new names of the plays.

Talib, Munshi Vinayak Prasad (d. 1922?)

Talib was born in Banaras, a Kayasth by caste. From the beginning, he was addicted to poetry. He came to Bombay and stayed there until the end of his life. He died in 1922.[9]

Dr Nami provides the following list of Talib's plays:

Lail-o-Nihar, urf Khubi-e Taqdir
Nal Damayanti
Fasana-e Ajayab

Chaman-e Ishq

Nigah-e Ghaflat

Diler Dilsher

Khazana-e Ghaib

Karishma-e Qudrat

Tilasmat-e Gul

Gopichand

Harishchandra

Sangin Bakavali

Aladdin

Vikram Vilas

In addition to the above tally, I have seen copies of *Ramlila* and *Ali Baba aur Chalis Chor, urf Nasib ka Zor.*

Sangin Bakavali (Bakavali of Stone): It is said that Raunaq wrote it originally, but Talib made some changes and revised it. In the edition brought out by J. Sant Singh, Talib's name appears in the first scene in the invocation. At the end of this scene, a song also contains Talib's name. Talib's name is used in the punishment Indar gives Bakavali: *asl ho hal tera, vasl ho talib ka, hai teri yah saza.* At the beginning of the second scene when Tajulmaluk enters, Raunaq's name appears: *shama ki tarah se jal jal ke hun bas main bhi tamam / raunaq-e bazm-e raqib aj vo mera yar hua.* The same text appears in the edition edited by M. S. Jauhar and published by Bhai Daya Singh and Sons. Thus it would appear that Raunaq first wrote *Sangin Bakavali* and then Talib revised it. This is confirmed by the edition published by the Victoria Company. The form of the change and estimate of its extent can be determined by looking at both editions; however, at this time Raunaq's *Sangin Bakavali* is not available. A copy of the play published by Khurshedji Balivala is in my possession, dated 1891.

As is apparent from the title, the plot of *Sangin Bakavali* concerns the love of Bakavali and Tajulmaluk. Bakavali is a fairy in the court of

Raja Indar who falls in love with Tajulmaluk, a mortal, and incurs Indar's wrath. Cursed by Indar, the lower half of Bakavali turns to stone; thus the adjective *sangin* (made of stone). Later, the king forgives her and both are joined in marriage. A second plot also runs through the play, relating to the loves of Chatravat and Chaturbudh, and Nirmal and Sais. Both stories move simultaneously, although they are not connected. It is not known why the author gave the drama this form.

Sangin Bakavali was a very popular play, and several companies aside from the Victoria Theatrical Company performed it. However, from a literary standpoint, it lacks the quality of Talib's other plays. Possibly this is because Talib did not completely rework Raunaq's play. Under orders from his employers he may simply have made a few changes in it, so that when performed, the drama would not seem old and uninteresting.[10]

Ali Baba aur Chalis Chor, urf Nasib ka Zor (Ali Baba and the Forty Thieves, or The Power of Destiny)[11]: This is a three-act play based on the famous story, written for the Victoria Theatrical Company. Ali Baba was a poor woodcutter in the land of Paras. His wife's name was Zarina and he had a son, Ghanim. The family managed to survive by doing odd jobs and taking out loans. Finally when they had nothing left even to pawn, their sorry situation attracted the attention of Muzaiyyan, who was staying with them as a maid-servant, and she gave them her savings to spend. Not only that, she told Ali Baba to sell her off, repay some of his loans, and start a business. But Ali Baba rejected her proposal. Helplessly Ali Baba grovelled at the feet of Qasim, his elder brother, but with no result. Qasim's servant Sattar also wished to give Ali Baba his earnings, but Ali Baba refused. Disappointed on all counts, Ali Baba left for the forest. After cutting a pile of wood and heaping it up, he sat down to contemplate the condition of the world. At that moment he was interrupted by the arrival of his son, Ghanim. Just then a group of thieves were heard singing in the distance. Father and son went into hiding and watched their exploits. They learned where the thieves kept their treasure and how the gate to the storehouse opened and closed to the words 'Open sesame' and 'Close sesame'. Having found the key to becoming rich, they waited for the thieves to leave and then raided their store. After they returned home, Zarina went to fetch the scales to weigh the goods, but her clever sister-in-law put glue on the base of the scales and the entire secret was revealed. Qasim himself went to the thieves' den when he discovered its location, but before he could escape with more goods, the thieves arrived and murdered him.

Ali Baba, motivated by his nephew's weeping and wailing, went to fetch the dead body of Qasim and had a tailor sew a shroud for him. The tailor was blindfolded so that he would not learn the way to the house. The thieves were eager know who had robbed them and went on the alert. Mustafa, the tailor, found out the way to Ali Baba's house. The thieves tried various stratagems to kill Ali Baba but could not succeed. In the end, their thievery was punished and Ali Baba spent the rest of his life in splendour. Ghanim and Muzaiyyan were married and lived happily ever after.

The play is primarily written in poetry. The language is Hindi mixed with Urdu. Little literary beauty is apparent. It is likely that the music facilitated the drama's success. From the standpoint of character, the drama contains villains as well as valiant heroes. In a small canvas, the author tells a full story.

The play also contains spectacular scenes. The thieves' storehouse and its door that opens and closes at the sound of 'sesame' was itself a wondrous sight. The scene in which Muzaiyyan kills the thieves and their leader was not short on the marvellous. Seeing such scenes, the public would be highly pleased. The drama's movement was fluid, and the plot was very attractive to the spectators.

Vikram Vilas (Vikram's Joy):[12] Also called *Sat Andhe* (Seven Blindmen). Vikram, the king of Ujjain, bestows the title of Vikram Vilas on his son Rajratan; this gives the play its name. There are seven principal male characters: Vikram the king, prince Rajratan, the army officers Hiralal, Maniklal, and Motilal, and two clowns at Vikram's court, Dangal and Mangal. These seven fall for various women and, making a mockery of their intelligence, indulge in activities that otherwise would not occur.

The plot is very peculiar. Vikram once married Madanmanjari, the daughter of a lord in Karnatak, then left her and returned to Ujjain. Rajratan is their son. Mother and son somehow get along until one day the son, now grown up, opens his mother's pendant with the aid of a servant. There he finds a letter informing him that his father is the king, Vikram. Together with his mother, Rajratan immediately sets out for Ujjain. When he arrives, he sends the king a letter through the gardener Sevati and her son Chaman, which says:

You who sit on your lofty throne
I am your pride and joy.
The whole world will kiss your feet,
But I am the one whose feet you should kiss.
Where is my rule, where is my wealth?
Where is your vow, where your promise?
Abandon the throne, I've come to claim it!
I am a robber, but you are the robber's father.
I've roamed the country, the kingdom is mine.
Whoever catches me wins the crown.

The king is startled, hearing the word 'promise', and declares that he does not remember and asks for proof. He orders that the thief be arrested, and the entire play rests on this command. Dangal and Mangal undertake to make the arrest, but they fall victim to the wiles of Rajratan and Chaman, disguised as women. Dangal and

Mangal are enchanted by them, lose their wits, and are taken captive themselves.

One day the king enters a temple, and Rajratan and Chaman capture him too. They lock the temple from outside and refuse to open it. In the same scene, Vikram meets Rajratan and Madanmanjari. The king recognizes his former sweetheart and recalls that he performed a Gandharva marriage with her. Then he remembers the curse pronounced by her father, that her beloved would forget her and she would suffer until she came before him and reminded him of the past. Actually the play should have ended at this point, but the author did not choose to do so.

In the second act, Manorama, the daughter of Lekhraj Thakur, is married to Rajratan. Manorama insists that women are superior to men by nature, thereby inciting the wrath of Vikram and landing herself in jail. The king had been praised in this couplet: 'Few in all the world can boast the character of Vikram, who is the most noble of all.' Manorama had rewritten the lines as, 'Who is Vikram and what is his character? The noblest nature is that of women.' The author has made women's nature his subject, showing how Manorama's girl-friend Chapala releases her from prison and proves that the seven men mentioned above are blind fools. This is the key to the second name of the drama.

The drama is in Hindi. Different aspects of womanly wisdom have been shown in various contexts. One man is blinded by love, another by delusion. King Vikram is a good man; Madanmanjari vanishes from the stage after their first visit. The couplet composed by Manorama proves to be true. Everyone owns up to their individual weaknesses.

A number of miraculous scenes have been incorporated. When King Vikram ascends the throne, climbing up a flight of stairs, a hand-maiden poses a riddle:

O Raja Vikram Bali, tell me at length—
The throne belongs to you, but what are the four stairs?

The king answers:

Justice, truth, and liberality are the first three stairs.
The fourth stair is mercy, now you know all four.

The king climbs the four stairs, and then a second handmaiden asks:

Who lives on these and on the next four?
Describe them as well, O Dharma incarnate.

The king says:

Observance, devotion, humility, and respect,
These are the next four steps, know them as such.

Vikram climbs another four steps. Then the third handmaiden asks:

And what are the third set of four stairs?
You must remember them, O my lord.

Vikram answers:

Patience, contentment, and bravery, my beauty;
The fourth is persistence, the means of happiness.

Then the king proceeds to the throne. The three handmaidens hide behind three columns. As the king climbs, each column falls one by one, and the handmaidens appear from behind.

In the sixth scene of the first act, a Shiva temple is shown beside a river. Rajratan and Chaman are seen washing their clothes, beating them against a stone along the riverbank. The sight of flowing water on the stage is achieved by special effects.

The author's craft is comparable to other dramas of the time, although the plot is very loose and there is a great deal of mediocre humour. The jokes are lacking in civility and tend towards the obscene. The play cannot be counted among the superior works of Talib.

Nigah-e Ghaflat, urf Bhul men Bhul, Kanton men Phul (The Careless Gaze, or Error upon Error, Rose among Thorns): Talib composed this four-act play for the Victoria Theatrical Company. The title page contains the couplet

> He who calls the world mad is prone to acts of rashness.
> How wise the person who said, 'A rash man is a crazed man.'

These words underscore the entire plot. Nazim, a peasant, is duped by the villain Shatir into believing that his wife Nargis is disloyal and in love with another man. Although he loves her very much, Nazim in his rashness makes various accusations against Nargis and eventually abandons her and their young son Kazim. Nargis and Kazim manage to survive thanks to Salim, Nazim's uncle, and his wife Jinat. The story begins with Nargis taking in mending and eking out a living. From a distance, Shatir points out to Nazim a woman expressing her love for a man. In actuality, the woman is Nargis's stepsister Sambul and the man is her husband Masrur, an evil character. Sambul's appearance resembles Nargis's and because Nazim only sees her back, he believes Shatir and falls into his trap. Shatir and Aurang manage to collect a lot of money through their trickery, but in the end they are caught. The bundles of notes indicate that Faiyaz distributed all the money to his two daughters. Therefore they receive the money. Meanwhile Masrur has abandoned Sambul and taken up with another woman. The rejected Sambul comes to drown herself in the same river where Nazim is preparing to commit suicide because of separation from Nargis. Nazim rescues his sister-in-law Sambul, and when she regains consciousness the whole matter comes out. Sister meets sister and husband is reunited with wife. Sher Khan, the police constable, and Uncle Salim facilitate matters, and Shatir and Aurang are arrested and meet with due punishment. In this fashion, careless gazing or *nigah-e ghaflat* creates a strange situation in which two individuals give up their lives in order to find release from hardship, but in the end whatever is God's will prevails.

Talib's plot is based on everyday incidents from daily life, and his imagination makes them appear fantastic. The play is definitely a satire on the inferior character of women and the lustful behaviour of men. The language of the drama is Hindustani, and most of the lines are in verse. The poetic standard is not high. The dramatist has not created characters who would require the lofty expression of sentiments. His plot is of the middling, serviceable sort that would please an eight-anna ticket holder. Consider this dialogue:

SHATIR

What do you say? Are you incapable of speech, sir?
It's amazing! Am I awake or do I dream?
For six months I've been wondering about this,
And today it is plain before my eyes.
How should I tell you what Nargis has done?
She has wronged the one who was good to her.

NAZIM

A friend is a person who acts like a mirror,
Who is clear as water and clean in his bosom.
Loyal and concerned for his friend's welfare,
He removes any malice before it settles in the heart.
You suspected this for six months, and yet,
What kind of friend are you, that you did not warn me?

SHATIR

A man is one who thinks before he acts,
Who weighs each matter and ponders it first.
How could he shame a friend in any way?
He would not do this, or lose face in God's sight.
Until I saw vice with my own eyes,
How could I tell you of my surprise?

(*Act II, Scene 2*)

The setting of the play is Egypt.

Lail-o-Nihar, urf Taqdir ka Khel (Night and Morning, or Fate's Game): The edition I have of this play was published by Khurshedji Balivala, Victoria Company, 1904. There is no mention of the edition. Dr Nami calls this play *Lal-o-Nihar, urf Khubi-e Taqdir*, which indicates that the edition he consulted is a private publication. It should not be considered to be as authentic as the one published officially by Balivala.

The main plot of the play is based on Bulwer Lytton's famous novel, *Night and Morning*, which has been expanded and modified in the new work. The couplet on the cover states:

When even angels fail to get free of sin's net,
How can men born in sin hope to gain goodness?

The dramatist makes this his main theme. Deceitful and wicked characters are punished and the truth is revealed. Firoz and Dil Afroz, and Ashraf and Nastaran, are joined in love's bonds. After the removal of all difficulties, they eventually find peace.

Ramlila:[13] Talib wrote this for the Victoria Theatrical Company. In his own words, 'This drama was written in the Hindi language because of its Hindu story.' It is in four acts and in mixed poetry and prose. The author's purpose is indicated in the couplet on the cover page:

What does the arrogant man gain from his imagination?
His egoism would argue that he attains to God.

This drama is based on the famous *Ramcharit*. It begins in Mithilapuri with Sita's *svayamvar* and ends with Ravan's death, the reunion of Ram and Sita, and the return to Ayodhya. Most of the important episodes that occur in between are depicted in this drama.

All of the well-known characters are included, but Manthara's husband Bhushan is an invention of the dramatist. He apparently has been added to bring the necessary comic touches to the play and create a link between the exiled Ramchandra and Bharat. Bhushan tells Ram about Bharat and Bharat about Ram. The characters have all been depicted in accordance with their temperaments. However, when Ram and Sita speak their Urdu dialogues it is extremely discordant. Rather than appearing as the *sadhvi* speaking to her husband Ram, Sita seems like some *begam* addressing her lord. Note the following from Act I, Scene 3:

SITA

Diklao apna chehra-e taban kabhi kabhi
Zarre ko kar do mehr-e darakhshan kabhi kabhi.

RAM

Pahlu men jab raho tum ai bilqis ru mere
Ho jaun main bhi rashk-e suleman kabhi kabhi.

SITA

Ji jate hain ham apne masiha ko dekh ke
Mushkil hamari hoti hai asan kabhi kabhi.

RAM

Ulfat ne vo kamal dikhaya zaval men
Rahta hun khvab men bhi tumhare khyal men.

SITA

Tum mil gaye jo mujhko to goya khuda mila
Zahir hai uska nur tumhare jamal men.

RAM

Bad az fana bhi talib jana rahenge ham
A jae su-e gor-e ghariban kabhi kabhi.

SITA

Show your shining face sometimes to me,
Make of these parts a radiant sun for me.

RAM

With you at my side, oh Queen of Sheba,
The wealth of King Solomon pales before me.

SITA

Seeing you, my Messiah, I gain new life:
Difficulties grow easy sometimes for me.

RAM

The wonder of desire is that even in pain
I live in a dream, while fixed only on you.

SITA

When I found you, 'twas as if I'd found God,
It's his light that shines in your glow upon me.

RAM

Even after death we continue our quest, oh Talib.
Let the cold grave be our lot for some time.

Because of the instructional nature of the play and its being replete with wondrous scenes, it was a great hit with the spectators.

Diler Dilsher (Dashing Dilsher): This drama is named for its valiant hero, a robber, thug, murderer, and conspirator who through his deceptions has a terrific time of it. When he is finally captured by the police, he cleverly pulls out a vial of poison and ends his life. The niece of a trader named Musharraf is in love with him. Even though she knows of his wicked deeds, she falls into his clutches out of passion. When Dilsher is caught, she dies of shock. Both end their lives at the same time and place.

The drama is an odd tragedy. It abounds in scenes in which thieves and bandits murder travellers and wealthy people, and Bahram, a thug, is murdered by his own wife. The entire drama is constrained by the net of deceit and trickery. It is mainly in verse, indicating that Talib wrote it when opera was in vogue on the Parsi stage.[14]

Karishma-e Qudrat, urf Apni ya Parai (The Wonder of Fate, or One's Own or Another's): The copy of the play in my possession has a torn title page, thus the name of the publisher and date are unknown. Nevertheless this too appears to be a drama published by Balivala. Dr Nami has listed it as *Karishma-e Muhabbat*. This name is proof of the fact that different publishers made slight changes and republished the famous dramas.

The events take place in Rome under the cruel king Titus. There are three nationalities present among the characters: Roman, Jewish, and Turkish. Titus's son Marcus is first attracted to his cousin-sister Dessia and the two decide to get married. But shortly thereafter he falls for Rahil, the adopted daughter of a Jewish trader. The trader saved her from a burning fire and brought her up as his daughter. Rahil's real name is Paulina, and she is the daughter of the religious leader of Ardiya, the pontiff Brutus. Thus she is not a Jewess but a Roman.

Marcus sees Rahil and falls head over heels in love with her. He seeks ways to elope with her, and the Turk Nasir Beg becomes his accomplice. Rahil's adoptive father doesn't want her to speak to Marcus, but love's arrows are too strong. Marcus consequently declares to his beloved Dessia:

Don't sacrifice yourself, my dear, for my sake.
How can I explain the secrets of my heart?
Don't give your heart away, for my sake.

Because:

Now my heart is incapable of loving anyone.
The heart I took pride in once is no longer a heart.

The entire play is full of this sort of foolishness.

Finally Marcus and Rahil get married. Dessia gives up her rights, and the reality of Rahil's background is revealed. The play is in both poetry and prose.

It is not known why Talib took this un-Indian story and made it the subject of his play. Perhaps it is based on some English drama or novel.[15]

Harishchandra: The tale of *Satya Harishchandra* was already prevalent. The Victoria Company had Talib take up the theme in order to attract the Hindu spectatorship. Earlier, the Gujarati version by Udayram Ranchhodbhai had attained great popularity in the production by the Uttejak Theatrical Company.

My copy of the play has the monogram of the Parsi Amateur Dramatic Society imprinted on it. 'For private use' is also written on it, and 'rehearsal copy', that is, not for sale. It was printed by Jam-e Jamshed Press where most of the Victoria Company's dramas were published. Thus this appears to be an authentic copy.

There is no novelty in the drama's plot. Following an argument between Vashishth and Vishvamitra in the court of Indra, it is decided to test Harishchandra's truthfulness. Talib includes all of the trials and difficulties imposed on Harishchandra and his family in the various legends. Vishvamitra's chief accomplice in this scheme is his disciple Nakshatra, a comic character. There is also a *vidushak* named Pandit Mangal Mishra who is brave in speech and timid in action.

This drama is unique for its language, Hindi. Talib mainly wrote in Urdu, but here he shows that a Banarasi Kayasth is as capable of writing smoothly in Hindi as in Urdu. Several Hindi plays were written based on the legend of Harishchandra. Bharatendu's *Satya Harishchandra* is well known. From the standpoint of arousing religious sentiments, this play was very appealing, and Talib earned much success from this work.

Gopichand: Three editions of this play are in my possession. The oldest was published in 1893 and the other two in 1901 and 1904, by the owner of the Victoria Company. Talib took the play from Nasharvanji

Mehrvanji Khansahab Aram's drama, which he 'rewrote in a new style.' The story tells of Gopichand, king of Bengal, who became a yogi and achieved an immortal body. This deed was accomplished with the aid of two yogis, Jalandharnath and Kanif. Gopichand's mother Mainavati was also an important figure.

The plot is based on a well-known folk tale. Various remarkable scenes and supernatural events have been incorporated into the drama. These demonstrate the extraordinary powers of yogis and yoginis on the one hand, and quench the thirst of the audience to view spectacular effects on the other.

The dramatist attempted to satisfy the need for humour through the character Lotan. In one scene, a Jogin beats him with a whip and makes him dance. Once when Balivala himself was playing the part of Lotan, his foot caught on a nail while dancing, but he continued his dance and didn't even let out a sound. Afterwards, his foot was in agony for days. Mary Fenton played the part of the Jogin, and it is well known that a new costume was made up especially that enhanced her beauty.

The language of the drama, the reverence of the populace (especially the Hindu populace) for yogis, the use of attractive actors, and other elements made *Gopichand* a very successful drama. Talib's poetic powers are best observed in the dramas *Harishchandra* and *Gopichand*.

Betab, Narayan Prasad (1872–1945)

Betab was born in 1872 in Aurangabad in Bulandshahr district, Uttar Pradesh. His father's name was Dhulla Ray, and he was a Brahmabhatt by caste. The family was very poor. At first Betab worked in a sweet-shop, and then he became a compositor in a printing press in Delhi. One day Jamadar Saheb's drama company came to Delhi and made preparations to perform in the Rama Theatre near the police station.

Someone from the company came to the press to place an advertisement for the performance. It was there that Betab met the company owner and received an invitation to see a drama for free. Thus was Betab bitten by the drama bug. Somewhat later, the New Alfred Company arrived in Delhi, and the contract for printing the notices for Murad's drama *Khurshid-e Zarnigar* was given to the press where Betab worked. Bctab revised one line of the couplet in the advertisement, which led to an argument with the dramatist. Finally the dramatist agreed that he had made a mistake. Betab's prestige was on the rise. A little knowledge of music, a certain love for poetry—it was enough to make Betab shine.

Betab's first play was *Husn-e Farang* (Foreign Beauty). Next he wrote *Qatl-e Nazir* (Nazir's Murder). Nazir was a prostitute who had been murdered around that time. It was a hot topic, and the company profited financially. The play was especially successful in Lahore. Jamadar's company began to take off. Betab's third play was *Krishna Janm* (The Birth of Krishna) and the fourth *Mayurdhvaj*; both were unsuccessful.

Next Betab joined the Parsi Theatrical Company of Bombay, a partnership company owned by Framji Apu, Ratanji Apu, Edalji Dadabhai Mistri, and Bajan. The director was Amritlal Keshavlal Nayak. Here Betab wrote *Kasauti* (Touchstone), *Mitha Zahar* (Sweet Poison) and *Zahri Sanp* (Poisonous Snake). In memory of Amritlal Nayak, he also wrote *Amrit* (Ambrosia). Then he took leave of the Parsi Theatrical Company.

In 1909 Betab went to Calcutta with Kavasji Khatau's Alfred Company. From Calcutta, he went to Quetta and wrote *Gorakhdhandha* (Labyrinth) based on Shakespeare's *The Comedy of Errors*.

On 29 January 1913, Betab's *Mahabharat* was performed in Delhi. The company made a huge profit from it. The greatest impact of this drama was that it put an end to the dominance of Urdu on the Parsi

FIGURE 8. Narayan Prasad Betab, playwright in Urdu and Hindi. Courtesy: Natya Shodh Sansthan.

stage. Company owners perceived the pulse of the audience and began to have plays written and performed in Hindi. Three years later, on 16 August 1916, Betab's *Ramayan* was performed in Lahore. Soon after, Kavasji Khatau died and Betab left the company and returned home. After some time, the Alfred Company owner, Jahangir Khatau, again called Betab and employed him at a salary of 500 rupees per month. In the meanwhile, Betab wrote *Patni Pratap* (The Splendour of the Wife). After this play, Betab went to work for the Madan Theatres in Calcutta at a salary of 750 rupees per month. Under

FIGURE 9. Scene from *Zahri Sanp*, a drama by Betab, with actor Keravala. Source: Namra.

FIGURE 10. Gold medal awarded to Betab for his drama *Mahabharat* (1913). Source: Namra.

contract to them, he wrote *Ganesh Janm* (The Birth of Ganesh). In 1931, Betab met Chandulal J. Shah and Dayaram J. Shah, owners of the Ranjit Film Company. He wrote the screenplay *Devi Devayani* for them and entered the film industry. Betab died in 1945.

Betab's claim that his *Mahabharat* was the first Hindi play is incorrect. Before him, Talib had written *Harishchandra* and *Gopichand* in Hindi and *Ramlila* in Hindi-Urdu. Betab's daughter Mrs Vidyavati Lakshmanrao Namra wrote her PhD dissertation on Betab and submitted it to Bombay University.[16] Therefore there is little need to reiterate what she has already written about him.

Hashr, Agha Mohammad Shah Kashmiri (1879–1935)

Hashr was born in 1879 in Banaras. He was a Kashmiri whose maternal uncle had come with his shawl business and settled the family in Banaras. Hashr's first drama, *Aftab-e Muhabbat* (The Sunshine of Love), was published in 1897. After that, he went to Bombay and gained employment in the Alfred Company of Kavasji Palanji Khatau. He wrote *Murid-e Shak* (Disciple of Doubt), *Mar-e Astin* (The Enemy Within), and *Asir-e Hirs* (Captive of Desire) for this company.

Dr Nami says that he had half completed *Hamlet* when he quit his job, and that Ahsan finished it, titling it *Khun-e Nahaq*. But this is dubious because neither Ahsan nor anyone else has shed light on the matter. *Khun-e Nahaq* is an independent and whole drama, not an incomplete one. It is certainly true that some people began to write the name of *Khun-e Nahaq* as *Mar-e Astin*. In 1901, Kavasji Khatau published a synopsis of *Mar-e Astin* together with its songs. This shows that *Mar-e Astin* was a drama written by Hashr. The synopsis shows no similarity to the plot of *Hamlet*. The story seems to be completely independent. Thus that part of *Hamlet* that Hashr is said to have created must be available somewhere else, or perhaps it does not exist at all and this rumour circulated simply as hearsay.

FIGURE 11. Agha Hashr Kashmiri, Urdu playwright. Courtesy: Natya Shodh Sansthan.

After leaving the Alfred Company, Hashr was attached to a small company. Here he wrote *Mithi Chhuri, ya Dorangi Duniya* (Sweet Knife, or Two-faced World) and *Dam-e Husn* (Beauty's Snare). But he did not stay on and soon was back with Khatau's company. This time he wrote *Shahid-e Naz* (Martyr to Coquetry) and *Achhuta Daman* (The Inviolable Robe). Then he left and joined Sohrabji Ogra's New Alfred Company. Here he composed *Khvab-e Hasti* (Life Is a Dream) and *Khubsurat Bala* (Beautiful Affliction).

Next Hashr had the idea of forming his own company, and thus the Indian Shakespeare Theatrical Company came into being. In

Calcutta this company performed a number of dramas, and after arriving in Allahabad it folded. Hashr then took up employment with the Madan Theatres. Here his famous plays *Madhur Murali* (Sweet Murali), *Bhagirath Ganga*, *Hindustan*, *Turki Hur* (The Turkish Vixen), and *Ankh ka Nasha* (Eye's Delight) were written.

A characteristic of Agha Hashr was his equal command over both the Hindi and Urdu languages. Reading his plays, it is not easy to discover any infelicity. His understanding of Hindu legends was as acute as his knowledge of Muslim tales. He wrote both social and religious dramas successfully, and all of them became popular. Truth be told, very few writers have achieved his level. Among the superior playwrights for the Parsi stage, Talib, Ahsan, Betab, and Hashr can readily be listed. Pandit Radheshyam also wrote a number of plays, but aside from *Abhimanyu*, they were inferior as works of dramatic art.

Agha Hashr died in Lahore in 1935. Hashr's drama has been treated in a PhD dissertation written by a lady for Bombay University. There is thus no need to discuss and analyse it here. Hashr and Radheshyam are also treated in Pavan Kumar Mishra's thesis, *Parsi Rangmanch*. A few critical studies of Hashr have also been published in Pakistan, which will supply some further information about him.

Ahsan, Mehdi Hasan

Ahsan was from Lucknow; his father served in the army. His maternal grandfather had achieved renown as a *vaidya* and a poet.[17] He began his education with Persian and Arabic. It is said he also had some practice in English. Being fond of music, his inclination towards poetry was natural.

Near Ahsan's home was a large building in which theatrical companies from outside the city often performed. Ahsan began to frequent these performances. When Dorab Shah's troupe performed *Ghazala Mahru* and *Jashn Kunvar Sen* there, Ahsan was a spectator and became fired with the desire to write dramas.

He is considered to have written ten dramas altogether:

Zahar-e Ishq, urf Dastavez Muhabbat

Chandravali Nekniyat, urf Gulistan Asmat

Khun-e Nahaq, urf Mar-e Astin (Hamlet)

> (*Mar-e Astin* was also the name of a separate play, which was performed by the Alfred Theatrical Company. I have examined its songs, which are distinct from those of *Khun-e Nahaq*. Therefore it can be concluded that *Mar-e Astin* was a different play from *Khun-e Nahaq*. Who knows why Dr Nami considered the two to be one and the same?)

Bazm-e Fani, urf Gulnar Firoz

Dilfarosh

Bhul Bhulaiyan

Chalta Purza

Sharif Badmash

Kanak Tara

Othello

Bhul Bhulaiyan (Labyrinth): Dr Nami says, 'Ahsan composed this drama on the plot of Shakespeare's *The Comedy of Errors* as told to him by Sohrabji Ogra in 1901.' But the statement is incorrect. That play of Shakespeare's hinges on the identical appearance of two brothers, whereas in *Bhul Bhulaiyan* it is a brother and sister who are said to be identical. The error that occurs is on account of the brother-sister similarity, not that of two brothers. Thus Ahsan's play is not based on *The Comedy of Errors* but upon *Twelfth Night*, in which the similarity of a brother and sister is the source of the entire deception.

Although Ahsan wrote this drama on the basis of a work by Shakespeare, his play is quite different from the original. First, Ahsan has given all the characters Muslim names. He has attempted to cast the play in a Muslim light. The events are said to take place in the Tatar country, again departing from Shakespeare. In the original, Malvolio, Sir Andrew Aguecheek, and Maria form a very interesting subplot in which Shakespeare has satirized the decadent lifestyle of the contemporary feudal elites. But Ahsan in his play has added an insipid subplot featuring Abdul Karim, Fazita, and Vafadar, to please the lower order of spectators through an emphasis on women's waywardness and amorous nature. To clarify the picture, the author has had to invent an incident involving thieves.

As far as the main story is concerned, it resembles Shakespeare's. In both, brother and sister are separated because of an accident of fate. Shakespeare has their boat capsize in an oceanic storm, whereas in Ahsan they are in a train that is struck by lightning while crossing a river. In both, the heroine dons male dress and appears to the king's beloved bearing a love letter. The beloved rejects the letter but falls in love with the messenger. When the brother and sister suddenly meet, the king's beloved (Olivia in Shakespeare, Jamila in Ahsan's version) marries the brother (Sebastian/Jafar), and the king marries Viola (Dilara).

Shakespeare has a subplot with Sir Toby, Andrew Aguecheek, and Maria, but Ahsan has created the trickery of arranging a marriage between Abdul Karim disguised as Rafiquddin with Ayyara disguised as Hasina, Jamila's sister. Although this subplot is roughly similar to Shakespeare's, in style and culture it is very different. The endings in both versions are the same.

Shakespeare's duke is a music lover who pines with love sickness and is shown in this condition at the opening of the drama. However, Ahsan begins his play with Jamila[18] and Jafar taking refuge in the forest because of an assault by their enemy. Ahsan's strategy exemplifies the tradition of the then Parsi stage to appeal to spectators through sensational scenes. In this manner, both versions contain similarities and differences. Shakespeare is a fatalist. Ahsan's poetic competence is exemplified in several places, especially in the dialogues between the Nawab and Jamila.

Dilfarosh (Merchant of Hearts): This play by Ahsan is based on Shakespeare's *The Merchant of Venice*. Among the English characters, all of the suitors of Portia (Shirin in Ahsan) have been omitted except for one, Mahmud, the brother of Qasim (Bassanio). However, he is unsuccessful in his suit and returns home dejected. Qasim's brother is in fact a product of Ahsan's imagination, created to show that Qasim's entire fortune and wealth is usurped by his brother, forcing him to spend his life as a pauper. Shylock has been kept by Ahsan as is, and Zar (Antonio in the original) is shown as taking a loan of six thousand rupees from him for Qasim. The conditions of the loan are in accordance with the original. Mohsin (Shakespeare's Lorenzo) elopes with Shylock's daughter Talha (Jessica). The casket scene is not shown as in the original but merely in a flash. The rest of the story follows the original. Portia/Shirin pleads for justice in the judge's court, but Shakespeare's persuasive language is lacking in Ahsan's Shirin. The outcome in both is that Shylock's wealth is turned over to Talha and Mohsin. Finally Qasim and Shirin, Talha and Mohsin, and Masud and Sulha—all three couples are joined in marriage and celebrate.

Although the language of *Dilfarosh* is somewhat simpler than *Bhul Bhulaiyan*, wherever the opportunity arises the author has not stinted to make it more difficult. Some examples of Ahsan's poetry are also visible in this play. All of the various incidents that Shakespeare has combined in the creation of his play are there in Ahsan's work, but the way in which they are woven together is much looser than in the original.

Chalta Purza (Shrewd Operator): The play begins with a debate between two angels. One is named the Angel of Thought and the other the Angel of Action. The question concerns the manner in which man, living on earth, performs his part on the world stage. The Angel of Action says that man has suppressed the secret of his origin and merely fills hell's stomach by adopting the features of wild animals. In the rest of the drama, a picture is drawn of mankind's decline and demonic character. A bandit named Sikandar Khan disguises himself as a respectable man and lays a trap. In the end he is caught, but he escapes from police custody. Sikandar is the shrewd operator (*chalta purza*), the one who murders, goes to jail, imitates a respectable person, and in the end is exposed.

Ahsan wrote this drama full of disguised characters for the New Alfred Company. The director Sohrab Ogra was very fond of this play, and he himself played the part of Sikandar. The female impersonators Amritlal Nayak and Narmada Shankar were very popular in it. The company spent a lot on the set for this play and made quite a large profit. The dialogues are very tight, and characterization is quite natural.

Khun-e Nahaq (Unjust Murder): This play is based on Shakespeare's *Hamlet*. As in his other plays, Ahsan has made various changes in his adaptation from the original. Ahsan's characters are Muslims, and the events are centred in the city of Damascus. Ahsan has compressed the entire story into three acts, whereas in the original there are five. This makes it clear how the plot has been reduced. The number of characters has also been altered. The number of Hamlet/Jahangir's friends has been reduced and the number of companions of Ophelia/Mehrbanu increased.

The original drama opens with a guard at the castle of Elsinore. This is because of Shakespeare's interest in the supernatural. Also, it creates the proper atmosphere for the introduction of the ghost, who bears the responsibility of encouraging Hamlet to take revenge. Ahsan did not consider this appropriate. In Act I, scene V, the dramatist has

Jahangir (Hamlet) speak a soliloquy in which he himself relays the news of the appearance of his father's dead spirit to him. Later he summons the ghost, saying:

I had no knowledge of my desire's logical end.
Why did you abandon me in this helpless state?

To this, the ghost suddenly appears and replies:

I died but found no peace in the tomb.
I am ashamed to speak the name to you now.

In this way, both engage in a dialogue. Finally Jahangir addresses his uncle, saying:

You black snake! You hissed and killed him.
May ruin befall me if I let you live.

The first act ends here and Jahangir's future plans are laid out. This act also illustrates that the queen, Jahangir's mother, wants her minister Humayun (Polonius) to usurp the throne of Farrukh (Claudius), but Humayun does not agree. The mutual attraction between Jahangir and Mehrbanu is also depicted in this act. The words of Mehrbanu are those of a true lover, but Hamlet's reply is scattered and obtuse. He thinks of women only as deceivers and tricksters, and Mehrbanu finds no response to her expression of love. The love banter between Rihana (Mehrbanu's friend) and Salman (Jahangir's servant) has been given a humorous slant in the play which seems inappropriate. Shakespeare never had Hamlet say directly that his mother should see the picture of her former husand. But Ahsan has Jahangir show his mother his father's picture and tell her that his uncle murdered his father. Finally Jahangir fires his pistol at Farrukh and dies himself. This is the ending of *Khun-e Nahaq*.

Khun-e Nahaq was a very popular drama. Various companies played it over and over again. Actors such as Joseph David and Sohrab

Modi played the part of Hamlet and were very successful. A Muslim actor from Jaipur also is said to have been famous in this role. This play was adapted for the screen too, but it was not as popular in the film world as on the stage.

Chandravali: Ahsan attempted to weave a Hindu tale into this drama. Murad Barelvi had written a drama named *Chitra Bakavali* which became very popular. Pleased at its success, Dadabhai Ardeshar Thunthi asked Ahsan to write a play just like it, and *Chandravali* came about. It was first performed in Lucknow, and the fortunate Ahsan attained fame in his own birthplace. Later it was performed with great fanfare by the Alfred and New Alfred companies.

The focal point of the drama is the defence of the marital fidelity of women. The king Raj Mohan and his minister have an argument over whether women are able to maintain their purity. The king's guru, who plays his part under the name of Mahatma, claims that he will be able to undermine Chandravali's chastity, but he is not successful. In the end Chandravali proves her womanly virtue, and the Mahatma is very embarrassed.

Two subplots are intertwined in *Chitra Bakavali*, which reduce the naturalness of life in the drama, but in *Chandravali* the plot follows only one thread. Thus the dialogues are linked smoothly and the plot is unified. But Ahsan did not forget to bring a Muslim atmosphere to this play. The inclusion of Gungi, a bawd, is evidence of this.[19]

Bazm-e Fani (The Transitory Assembly): This play of Ahsan's is based on Shakespeare's *Romeo and Juliet*. As always, the main characters' names have been changed to Muslim ones. In consequence this play is also known as *Gulnar Firoz*. Ahsan has developed the plot in his own fashion. He shows that Ghafur ud-Daula and Zahur ud-Daula are both respectable citizens of Firozabad. Firoz (Romeo) is Ghafur's son, thus according to the original he belongs to the Montague clan, whereas

Gulnar (Juliet) is Zahur's daughter and is a Capulet. The most significant characters retained by Ahsan include the king, his minister, Zarif (the king's jester), Masud and Anjam (Firoz's companions), Mirza (Zahur's nephew) and Musharraf (Gulnar's fiance). Among the female characters, aside from Gulnar there are the wives of Zahur ud-Daula and Ghafur ud-Daula.

Musharraf and Firoz quarrel, and Musharraf is killed. Gulnar marries Firoz. Ahsan has changed the tragedy of Romeo and Juliet to a happy ending, completely turning the original upside down. The picture that Shakespeare draws of his times, in which two high-ranking families because of their mutual enmity lose their children and then are reconciled, is not present in Ahsan's drama. The dilemmas of life that Shakespeare depicts are not even hinted at in *Bazm-e Fani*. A sting is inflicted but it produces no pain.

Othello: This is also an adaption of a Shakespeare play, but it could not be viewed. *Kanak Tara*, *Zahar-e Ishq*, and *Sharif Badmash* are all unobtainable.

After Talib, Ahsan is one of the playwrights who maintained the impact of the Parsi stage through his forceful writing. His language is difficult Urdu, his poetry is full of feeling, and his dialogues are strong and touching. If there is a lack in him it is simply that he does not represent any of life's depth in his plots. His gaze is focused on the superficial aspects of society. Possibly this was the hollow demand of his age. The audience enjoyed a low order of humour and could not imagine high romance. Ahsan did not write about any problem of society. His patrons were also focused upon making money. As a result Ahsan could not give us plays that would have a lasting place in the dramatic literature.

Abbas, Abbas Ali (1889–1932)

His name was Mir Ghulam Abbas, but he was better known as Abbas Ali. He was born in Lahore in 1889 and died in Bombay in 1932. Little is known about his life. It appears that he came to Bombay from Lahore and settled there. His interest in theatre was sparked by the theatrical companies that used to tour Lahore. He also became rather fond of poetry. As a result, he began to frequent the theatre and also to write for it.

Abbas's first play was perhaps *Nairang-e Sitamgar* (Tricks of the Oppressor), which was written in 1906 for the Star Theatrical Company, originally of Lahore. Because of internal disagreements the company folded, and the play never appeared on the boards. However, Abbas achieved a certain amount of fame through it, and he was able to take advantage of this when Balivala's Victoria Theatrical Company came to Lahore soon after. Abbas read a few scenes of his play to Balivala. As a trial, Balivala had him compose some additional scenes, and finally, being satisfied with Abbas's work, he offered him the position of *munshi* in his company. With that, Abbas came to Bombay and began living there.

Balivala related the plot of a drama by Beaumont and Fletcher to Abbas and asked him to compose a play based upon it. This was the beginning of *Zanjir-e Gauhar* (The Chains of Gauhar). Rehearsals of the play began in Lucknow in 1907, and after the company returned to Bombay it was performed in Balivala's own Grand Theatre. The play was directed by the famous actor Harmuz Tantro. Among the cast were the director himself, the Peshavari Brothers, Bijli, Fatima, and Khurshed. Balivala invited the dramatists Talib, Hashr, Murad Ali, and Betab to see the play, and they praised him on its success. This play was published by Balivala during his lifetime and after his death by his daughter and company manager Mehrbai.[20]

In *Zanjir-e Gauhar* Nauroz kills his uncle and occupies his throne. He causes great torment to his nephew, Prince Mazhar, because Mazhar is opposed to his sister Gauhar's love for Nauroz. Gauhar however wants to make Nauroz her life partner. Mazhar tries to get his sister murdered, but at the critical moment Nauroz shoots the murderer with his pistol and saves Gauhar. Next, the sister (Gauhar) arrests the brother (Mazhar), but then Nauroz rescues Mazhar, and in the end Nauroz and Gauhar are married. According to Muslim culture, these murders were not considered immoral.[21] Such tragic-seeming incidents therefore lacked the gravity that could transform the drama into a genuine tragedy. This kind of plot structure was a typical feature of Parsi plays. Abbas's imagination was unexceptionable.

Dr Nami enumerates thirty-one dramas of Abbas.[22] They were written for a number of different companies. Several were written for the Victoria Theatrical Company, such as *Zanjir-e Gauhar, Nairang Naz,* and *Nurjahan, urf Nur-o-Nar.* The plays written for other companies include *Nairang-e Sitamgar* for the Star Theatrical Company of Lahore, and *Dukhiya Dulhan* (The Miserable Bride) for Framji Apu's company, which was rewritten under the name of *Jahanara* for Vatlam Kesho Nayak's Shakespeare Theatrical Company in 1911. *Shamshir Islam* (The Sword of Islam) was performed by the New Jodhpur Bikaner Theatrical Company in the Coronation Theatre, Bombay. After this, Abbas wrote *Khazana-e Din* (Storehouse of Faith) in 1916, *Nai Zindagi* (New Life) in 1917, and *Kiski Bhul* (Whose Fault) in 1918. These plays were performed in Akola and Amravati.

Abbas Ali was also employed by the Natyakala Pravartak Company. It is said that he wrote *Panjab Mail* for this company in 1919. However, the *Panjab Mail* published by J. S. Sant Singh lists Dilavar Shah as its author, and in 1924 he dedicated this play to his guru. Dr Nami says it was written in 1919, and Sant Singh's edition indicates it was dedicated by Dilavar Shah in 1924. This raises doubts about the date of composition. It may be that the original date of composition was 1919, but there is much confusion about the author's identity. Further investigation is needed into this matter. Another discrepancy is that Sant Singh's edition says *Panjab Mail* was written for the Alexandria Mandali, and Dr Nami says it was written for the Moralizing Theatrical Company of Rahyubai.[23]

Among Abbas Ali's other dramas, *Shrimati Manjari* (Mrs Manjari) and *Mohini B.A.* are very well known. *Shrimati Manjari* became especially popular. *Farz-o-Vafa* (Duty and Loyalty) and *Kal Kya Hoga* (What Will Tomorrow Bring?) were written after it, both for the Natyakala Pravartak Company. When this company was sold to the Maharaja of Bhandara, Ganpatrao Pandey, he changed its name to the Rising Moon Star Theatrical Company. *Lady Lajvanti*, considered the sequel to *Shrimati Manjari*, was also written by Abbas Ali and performed by Seth Chandulal's company.

In 1928 Abbas Ali again was employed by the Natya Pravartak Company, and he composed eight plays for it: *Sevak Dharm* (A Servant's Duty), *Ek Hi Paisa* (Just One Penny), *Sone ki Chidiya* (The Golden Bird), *Post Master*, *Mumtaz*, *Indar Vijay* (Indar's Victory), *Shadi ki Pahli Rat* (The Wedding Night), and *Puranmal* in two parts. In 1930 he wrote *Nek Khatun* (Noble Lady) for the Madan Theatres. In the same year he composed *Shan-e Rahmat* (The Glory of Mercy) and *Shahi Farman* (Royal Command) for Seth Motilal's George Theatrical Company of Bombay, both of which were performed in Hyderabad. Abbas Ali's last play was *Sakhi Sundari* (Sundari, the Companion), which he was unable to complete.

In sum, Abbas Ali wrote approximately thirty plays for various theatrical companies. The language of these plays was Urdu, Hindustani, and Hindi. The poetry was not of a high standard, but it was characteristic of what was popular on the stage at that time. Some of the plays were set in an Islamic milieu, and some were written under the influence of the nationalist movement to strengthen Hindu-Muslim unity. It is probable that the degree of contact Abbas Ali had with various drama companies was unequalled by any other play-wright. Almost all of his plays were published by J. S. Sant Singh and Sons, Lahore, but the entire body of work is unobtainable.

Mahshar, Muhammad Ibrahim Ambalavi

His full name was Muhammad Ibrahim and pseudonym 'Mahshar'. 'Mahshar' means Day of Judgment. From this it appears that he was very energetic and of a fiery temperament, at least in his way of thinking. Being a resident of Ambala, he wrote 'Ambalavi' after his name.

Dr Nami considers the following plays to be his:

Dushman-e Iman
Josh-e Tauhid, urf Religion of Yunan
Dozakhi Hur
Khuni Sherni, urf Chamakti Bijli
Khun-e Jigar, urf Sham Javani
Sunhari Khanjar, urf Intaqam Ruh
Atashi Nag, urf Bap ka Qatil
Gunahgar Bap
Shakuntala, urf Gumshuda Anguthi
Mirabai, urf Krishnadev ki Bhakti
Satyagrah
Rasila Jogi, urf Yogshakti
Gharib Hindustan, urf Inqalab yane Svadeshi Tahrik
Hashr Mahshar
Khud Parast, urf Daulat ka Ghulam
Jang-e Jarman, urf Lalchi Qaisar
Nigah-e Naz
Hamara Khuda

Krishna Avtar (In the play published by J. S. Sant Singh and Sons, the title appears as *Raja Sakhi va Krishna Avtar*, which seems more correct.)

Dushman-e Iman (Enemy of the Faith): This is a kind of tragedy. In the beginning, Beauty and Love have a quarrel. The devil settles the dispute. A king named Avid is tormenting the daughter of the king of Portugal, who had been exiled and sought refuge with Avid. One day he tries to rape her and gets killed. In this manner, women's righteousness is preserved.

Josh-e Tauhid (Zeal for the One God): This is a kind of religious drama in which the characters are depicted as converting to Islam.

Dozakhi Hur (Hellcat): A play written to show the harshness and destructive nature of women. Both of these plays were written for the Orpheus Theatrical Company, whose owner was Mr Jacob.

Khuni Sherni (The Bloodthirsty Lioness): Also based on a story about a harsh woman, it is full of incidents of murder and distrust caused by women. The happenings take place in Greece and Rumania. There is no attention paid to the dramatic unities.

Khun-e Jigar (Heart's Blood): Here too, Princess Naubahar displays the might of her bullets. The drama is full of murders and conspiracies.

Sunhari Khanjar (The Golden Dagger): This play is completely concerned with the loves of princesses and their conspiracies. There are countless murders. The events occur in Rumania and Bulgaria.

Atashi Nag (Fiery Serpent): Its subject is fighting and murder for the sake of the throne. The ending is shown to be happy.

Gunahgar Bap (Father's Faults): This is an accomplished play about a Hindu family. Two princes, Chandar Singh and Bal Singh, are the sons of King Vikram and Queen Nirmala. They all are living together happily until Vikram meets the courtesan Madankala and marries her. Discord ensues between Nirmala and Madankala. Vikram's friend Sajjan Singh visits him with a proposal of marriage between his daughter Rupvati and Vikram's son, Chandar Singh. Rupvati accompanies her father and meets both Nirmala and Madankala. However, Madankala tells Rupvati that Chandar Singh has many faults, and as a result Rupvati rejects the prince. Madankala had been a court singer for King Samar Singh. He sends a message to King Vikram to return his singer, but Vikram does not comply. Samar Singh's army attacks Vikram. Vikram escapes with Madankala. Nirmala and Chandar Singh are also forced to flee. They are all separated from each other. Hearing news of the *svayamvar* of Maharaja Sopat Singh's daughter Surajbai, Chandar Singh arrives there, and he gets married to her. Bal Singh, with the help of allies, assumes his father's throne. When he hears that Chandar Singh has become king, he goes to meet him. Vikram and Madankala endure many difficulties in the jungle. In the end, Madankala elopes with Mauj Singh. Vikram comes to Chandar Singh to decide what to do. Madankala dies of snakebite. Nirmala, after much wandering, also arrives at the same palace. Mother, father, and sons are all reunited.

There is a great difference between this play and plays about Muslim culture. After writing this play, Mahshar appears to have turned towards Hindu history, because he later wrote *Shakuntala*, based on the famous legend.

Mirabai: This was written on the basis of the popular story.

Satyagraha, urf Sukanya Savitri: Based on the story of Savitri and Satyavan. The author has given ample evidence of his imagination as well.

Rasila Jogi, urf Yogashakti (The Amorous Yogi): The plot of this drama is very strange. When Raja Salamat Singh falls ill, Lal Singh tries to bribe the royal doctor and have him fed poison, but the doctor refuses. Raja Salamat Singh dies anyway, and his daughter Mahlavati secretly invites Lal Singh to the palace and promises to marry him. However, the prime minister Bisaldev and commander of the army Karan Singh find out, and they have Lal Singh assassinated. Mahlavati becomes enraged and removes the men from their posts. In their place she appoints women. She also rejects a marriage proposal from one Kesari Singh, causing him to attack the kingdom. In this circumstance, Mahlavati marries Guru Machhandarnath and through his yogic powers she defeats the enemy. After twelve years, Machhandarnath's disciple Gorakhnath joins him and takes him away. Kesari Singh takes advantage of the situation and makes another attack, but this time is defeated by Machhandarnath's son who has the assistance of both Machhandarnath and Gorakhnath. Finally Gorakh puts the crown on his head and blesses his ascent to the throne.

The plot illustrates that Mahshar was completely ignorant of the Hindu *sant* tradition. The marriage of Mahlavati with Machhandarnath is a misconception, and the idea of the yogi's son becoming king is even more bizarre. This sort of business is nothing other than the defective imagination of a Muslim playwright. The spectacle of the supernatural has been created through these nonsensical, made-up incidents, but in all other respects the drama is lacking in artistic value.

Gharib Hindustan, urf Svadeshi Tahrik (Indigent India, or The Indigenous Products Movement): The principal subject is the Swadeshi campaign, as expressed in these lines:

He who desires life should buy goods of his own place.
Instil a sense of honour in the ignorant and ill-mannered ones
    at home.
Read out the teaching to your wives and daughters.

The plot that has been constructed to illustrate this theme is very odd. Suraj Singh returns to India after completing a law course in England. His elderly father goes to meet him at the station, and his son calls him a fool. Hari Pandey, Shiv Pandey, and Maulana Bashiruddin debate the issue of untouchability. On Id, Wahid and Aziz want to sacrifice a cow. Maulana, putting his son in the place of the cow, tells the two to halt the sacrifice. Thakur Hari Singh throws his son Suraj Singh out of the house. Suraj Singh comes to his senses and begs forgiveness from his father for his bad behaviour. The Thakur embraces him with satisfaction. The education received abroad is proven to be incomplete and worthless. Swadeshi values are proclaimed. This is the strange plot of this play. It is the result of the poverty of Hindustan.

Hashr Mahshar (The Tumult of Doomsday): This is the story of how an illegitimate claimant murders a ruler and embezzles his money.

The plays of Mahshar are mainly filled with incidents of murder and deception. Some of them have also been written concerning the contemporary problems of the country, but within the old mould in which the illegitimate remove the legitimate and establish their power. One sin becomes the seed of another sin, and after much destruction and gore, the story returns to the straight path.

Joseph David

All that is known is that he was attached to several theatrical companies. He played Hamlet with great success in the Arya Subodh Theatrical Company production of *Khun-e Nahaq* in Poona. The famous actor Sohrab Modi considered him his guru.

He successfully directed several plays for the New Parsi Theatrical Company, among which are *Dhup Chhaon*, *Har Jit*, *Kali Nagin*, and *Dukhtar Farosh*. Almost all of these plays were adaptations from Shakespeare. For the Alexandria Theatrical Company, he directed

Intaqam, Ah Mazlum, Sunhari Khanjar, Hasin Qatil and *Khuni Sherni*. For the Imperial Theatrical Company he directed *Naqli Shahzada, Andaz Vafa, Bhola Shikar, Tir-e Havis, Hur-e Ab, Khaki Putla, Matlabi Duniya, Ghafil Musafir, Eshiyai Sitara, Nur-e Vatan, Sansar Nauka, Bagh-e Iran, Karm Prabhav, Sher-e Kabul, Qaumi Diler,* and *Nur men Nar*. For the National Theatrical Company he directed *Aftab-e Dakin*.

Sometimes he was also a partner in these drama companies. It is said that he composed the following plays: *Dara Sikandar, Josh-e Vatan, Duniya Jitnevala, Khurshed-e Iran, Dariya-e Nur, Tasvir-e Sharafat, Purana Gunah, Sharif Shahzada, His Highness, Zulm-e Narvan, Husn Parast, Tegh-e Sitam* and *Hitler Married*.

Joseph David did not live a long life. He died at the age of thirty. The Parsi stage has never forgotten the services of Joseph David nor can it ever forget him.

Pandit Radheshyam Kathavachak

Pandit Radheshyam was a resident of Bareli. He started out as a professional reciter in the *katha* tradition. He attained considerable fame in this art and acquired wealth as well. His performances of the *Ramayan* became extremely popular and still are.

He wrote a number of plays. Pavan Kumar Mishra has described them at length in his dissertation, therefore it is unnecessary to write much more here. Radheshyam enjoyed a special relationship with the New Alfred Theatrical Company. He also wrote several plays which were performed by the Surya Vijay Theatrical Company.

In his book *My Time in the Theatre* he has discussed his own plays in detail.[24]

OTHER URDU PLAYWRIGHTS

The number of playwrights in Urdu is quite large. Only the most popular and accomplished ones have been described above. Some additional playwrights worth mentioning are Saiyad Anvar Husain Lakhnavi 'Arzu', Mohammad Abdul Aziz 'Zayak', Abdul Latif 'Shad', Ghulam Muhiuddin Dehlavi 'Nazan', Saiyad Qazim Husain Rizvi Lakhnavi 'Nashtar', Pandit Tulsidas 'Shaida', and others.

Muhiuddin Nazan's Contribution

Although like other *munshis* Nazan situated most of his dramas outside of India, nonetheless there is variety in the content of his plays, unlike the run-of-the-mill Muslim plots. Take *Sher-e Dil* (Lionheart) as an example. Its storyline is basically historical, connected to the period after the attacks on India by Nadir Shah and one side of the political situation in the country. After Nadir Shah's departure, Murshid Kuli Khan became the ruler of Bengal. He had no son, and thus his son-in-law Shuja Khan (1725–39) became his heir, then Shuja's son Sarfaraz Khan (1739–40), and after that his uncle Alivardi Khan (1740–46). Alivardi Khan had no sons, only three daughters who were married to three sons of his nephew Haji Mohammad. The oldest among them, Falak Jah, also known as Shahamat Jang, is the hero of this play. The middle son Sirajuddaula was the ruler of Dacca, and the youngest son, Zainuddin Ahmad, was the ruler of Cuttack. Falak Jah was the governor of Patna. His contemporary was Surendra Singh, king of Munger.

Falak Jah attacked Surendra Singh. For assistance Surendra Singh called on his commander Safshikan Khan, whose father had given him the title 'Lion of Kabul'. Safshikan Khan defeated Falak Shah and had him agree to the following treaty conditions:

(1) Four lakh rupees for military expenses would be paid as punishment.

(2) The Kohinoor diamond possessed by his wife would be given to Surendra Singh.

(3) In future, Falak Jah would commit no further hostilities.

Upon agreeing to the conditions, the Lion of Kabul told his lieutenant Kadir Beg to respectfully deliver the Nawab to the border and to turn the four lakhs of rupees and the Kohinoor diamond over to the treasurer Asad Yar Khan. After Safshikan, Falak Jah lured Kadir Beg, saying that if he killed Safshikan and retrieved the Kohinoor, he would make him his minister. The disloyal Kadir Beg agreed.

On his way back from battle, Safshikan's son Shahzor went to meet his future wife, Munirunnisa, the daughter of Asad Yar Khan. Munirunnisa's mother Chandni Begam also came to the spot, and she insisted that if Shahzor went to his father and asked for the Kohinoor as his family's possession, she would agree to her daughter's marriage with him. But Safshikan said the diamond belonged to the king and refused. The marriage was not consummated.

King Surendra was conversing with his queen Radharani when Kadir Beg entered and gave news of the victory, saying that Safshikan had taken the Kohinoor as a bribe to free Falak Jah. The king was taken in but the queen said it was impossible. Kadir Beg did not deposit the Kohinoor in the treasury but sent it to Safshikan. This was his craftiness. Kadir Beg told the king about Chandni Begam's condition. At this the king became enraged and told Kadir Beg to arrest Safshikan. Asad Yar Khan found out that the Kohinoor diamond was not in the treasury. Meanwhile Kadir Beg arrested Safshikan. The king, thinking that Safshikan was guilty, had him condemned to death.

Bedad Khan, taking the order of Safshikan's execution from Kadir Beg, reached Falak Jah. Seeing the work half completed, he became pleased. The manacled Safshikan went to meet his guru, Khaki Shah. The guru advised him to do nothing against the king and Safshikan returned. Hearing the order for his father's death, Shahzor became bent on rebellion, but his father told him to cease hostilities. The son vowed to abide by his father's wishes. Kadir Beg tempted Chandni Begam with the Kohinoor and promised to marry her daughter himself. Shahzor and Munirunnisa met secretly. At that moment, Chandni Begam arrived with Kadir Beg and began to speak about the proposed marriage. Munir refused. Kadir Beg resolved to destroy Shahzor.

Shahzor left home for guard duty and met Kadir Beg in the forest. Kadir Beg incited Shahzor to put on royal clothing and finish him off. Shahzor refused. Kadir Beg then threatened to kill Shahzor. Meanwhile Shahzor's mother arrived there. While they were both quarrelling, Kadir Beg escaped and ran off. Munir told her father what her mother had said, and Asad Yar Khan, seating his slave Nasiban in a palanquin, sent her to Munir's place where the Nikah was being read. King Surendra Singh was told the secrets of Kadir Beg's treachery, Safshikan's innocence, and Chandni Begam's lust for the Kohinoor diamond by Nihar Singh. Both set out to determine the truth. Kadir Begam and Munir, seeing Nasiban get out of the palanquin at the time of the secret marriage, took the Kohinoor and figured how to go to Falak Jah. This news reached Shahzor and Nihar Singh. Shahzor set out to capture Kadir Beg.

At the time Nihar Singh was taking Safshikan to the execution ground to be killed, an invisible voice was heard, and Nihar Singh, hiding Safshikan, disguised him in Arab dress. Adversity befell King Surendra. Living in the forest, Safshikan learned that Kadir Beg had met Falak Jah at the border and was planning to attack. Safshikan went in search of Falak Jah. Both met by accident and Safshikan imprisoned him. In the same forest, Raja Surendra separated from his companions and emerged alone. Kadir Beg surrounded him and took him captive. At the same time, Shahzor too arrived there. Nihar Singh and Safshikan in Arab dress also turned up. The king was freed and Kadir Beg was killed at the hands of Shahzor. The king called them to court and expressed his gratitude. Safshikan was shown justice. Falak Jah too recognized his innocence. The king performed penance. The drama ended happily. There is also a farce within this drama, in which women's wiles are displayed. Altogether the drama contains nineteen songs.

In the same way, Nazan's other plays too hold their own importance. Nazan's plays were directed by Joseph David, a famous and successful director of the Parsi theatre. In *Nur-e Vatan*, in the context of war between the Moors and the Israelites, there is a very affecting description of a father's vow. This was a very popular drama in its time.

Notes

1 [Gupt lists the dramatists somewhat randomly. They have been rearranged in chronological order based on life span and period of activity in the theatre. At the end of the chapter, the entry on the Urdu dramatist Nazan, originally included in Chapter 5, has been inserted.]

2 [Evidence indicates that Raunaq was probably from 'the Deccan', signifiying Gujarat, Maharashtra, or points further to the south. See Imtiaz Ali Taj, ed., *Urdu ke Klasiki Adab [Drame]*, Vol. 5 (1969), pp. 3–8.]

3 [Corrected against Taj, Vol. 5, pp. 16 ff.]

4 Abdul Alim Nami, *Urdu Thetar* (Karachi: Anjuman-e Taraqqi-e Urdu Pakistan, 1962), Vol. 2, pp. 117–18.

5 Published June 1883.

6 [Possibly Gupt means *Sitam-e Haman*.]

7 Rambabu Saksena, *A History of Urdu Literature* (Allahabad: Ram Narain Lal, 1940), p. 354.

8 Nami, pp. 118–34.

9 [According to Saksena, Talib died in 1914. *A History of Urdu Literature*, p. 354.]

10 Based on the 1900 edition published by Khurshedji Balivala.

11 Published by Khurshedji Mehrvanji Balivala, Jam-e Jamshed Steam Press, Bombay, 1900.

12 Published by Balivala, The Jamshedji Nasharvanji Petit Parsi Orphanage, Captain Printing Works, 1908.

13 Published by Khurshedji Balivala, The J. N. Petit Parsi Orphanage, Captain Printing Press, Mumbai.

14 Based on the edition published by Balivala, Jam-e Jamshed Press, 1901.

15 [The same plot is taken up by Agha Hashr Kashmiri in *Yahudi ki Larki*.]

16 [Vidyavati Lakshmanrao Namra, *Hindi Rangmanch aur Pandit Narayanprasad Betab* (Varanasi: Vishvavidyalaya Prakashan, 1972).]

17 [According to Saksena, *A History of Urdu Literature*, p. 355, Ahsan's grandfather was Hakim Navab Mirza Shauq of Lucknow, author of the masnavis *Zahr Ishq* and *Bahar Ishq*.]

18 [Should be Dilara, instead of Jamila.]

19 [Contrary to his usual balance, here Gupt indulges in the stereotype of Muslim culture as licentious. The bawd or *kutni* was a stock character in Sanskrit drama and continued into medieval literature.]

20 I have a copy published in 1908.

21 [Gupt here and later in the chapter strays into communal stereotypes. He characterizes 'Muslim culture' and dramas set in a Muslim environment as full of violence and deception, which he claims are accepted as routine and not viewed with approbation.]

22 Nami, pp. 290–91.

23 Nami, p. 296.

24 Radheshyam Kathavachak, *Mera Natak Kal*, Bareli: 1957.

CHAPTER 5

The Parsi Theatrical Companies

Zoroastrian Theatrical Club (Old)

It was in 1866, about two years before the Victoria Theatrical Company came into existence, that the Zoroastrian Theatrical Club was founded.[1] The newspaper *Rast Goftar* was used to notify those who were aficionados of drama. The principals who thought of establishing this company were of the opinion that it should perform new plays. The Shankar Seth Theatre was already available for performance. The actors were eager and the playwrights, Bandekhuda and Rustam Jabuli, were ready to assist the founders. Some stage props had also been collected. Finally, the following gentlemen decided that dramas should be put on. They resolved to dedicate their minds, bodies, and resources to running the company. The pillars of the club were Nasharvanji Behramji Forbes, Dhanjibhai Rana, Dosabhai Biliya, Pestanji Dadabhai Pavari, Rustam Jabuli (playwright), Dhanjibhai Bimadalal, Dadabhai Pastakiya, Framji Kavasji Mehta, Dadabhai Ponchkhanevala (Bandekhuda), and Anand Rao (a Marathi painter).

In addition to these ten, the names of Seth Manchershah Bejanji Mehrhomji and Seth Mancherji Hoshangji Jagosh are also listed. The life of the club was Nasharvanji Forbes. He was the one who stressed that the playwright Edalji Khori be brought on board. He thought that if Khori could be enrolled, he would not give his works to other companies, and only the Zoroastrian Club would prevail on Grant Road. It should be recalled that two companies named Gentlemen Amateurs and Musical Sketches were already operating. It was primarily Khori who wrote for them. But he was an independent spirit and could not be entrapped. However, he promised to give the option on his new work first to the Zoroastrian Club and then only to other companies. When the Victoria Theatrical Club rejected *Khudabakhsh*, which had been written for them, Khori offered it to the Zoroastrian Club, according to his word. They performed this play in 1871 in the Shankar Seth Theatre. This increased the fame of the company, and the Victoria Company greatly regretted their mistake.

Before *Khudabakhsh*, the Zoroastrian Club had performed Bandekhuda's *Khushru Shirin* and earned quite a name. Forbes played the role of Khushru Parvez's companion, Shahpur, very attractively. Dhanjibhai Patel believes that Nasharvanji Forbes perhaps left the Zoroastrian after *Khushru Shirin*, because he was not seen in any other play performed by the club. His absence riled the spectators, to the point that they complained about his failure to appear.

The Zoroastrian had certain unique traits that distinguished it from the companies of the day. Before the drama began, three actors would collectively chant a prayer. After the prayer, one actor would step in front of the drop scene and deliver a prologue. At the end of the drama, an actor expressed the company's thanks to the audience and sang a benediction or salaam. As long as Nasharvanji was with the club, he sang the salaam accompanied by the band. The salaam from *Khushru Shirin* was as follows:

> *kariye salam, kariye salam,*
> *khab khoi aya, tamo kharchine dam.*

> Perform the salutation, perform the salutation.
> You awoke from your dream, having spent your money.

FIGURE 12. Scene from *Khushru Shirin*, a drama by Bandekhuda, first performed by the Zoroastrian Theatrical Club. Source: Namra.

After Nasharvanji's departure, the company declined but kept performing at a lesser pace.

Some others in the company were also known for their artistry. One was the Hindu partner, Anand Rao, who lived in Poona and painted the curtains. Dadabhai Mancherji Pastakiya was a fine comic actor, and people respected him for his amiable nature. Framji Kavasji Mehta was an expert dancer although he danced in English style. Among his friends he was known as 'Phalu Photographer'. Rustamji Kavasji Jabuli also helped the company as a writer. Dhanjibhai Bimadalal was a well-known comic actor of the Zoroastrian Company.

The Zoroastrian performed a number of dramas, but their most famous was *Khushru Shirin*. The Persian plot and costumes were like sweet-smelling gold. Two or three things in this play enchanted the audience. While travelling through a deserted forest towards the city of Madayan, Shirin loosens her hair and submerges herself in a fountain to wash the dust from it. This scene was very captivating and worth viewing. Some spectators came only to see this one scene. Sitting naked but modest, washing her hair in the spring water, Shirin scattered her beauty and won everyone's hearts. Another scene showed the large Kiyani army raised by Behram to fight against Khushru Parvez, each person's heart inflamed with martial passion. The third scene was Khushru Parvez's *dakhmu*; *dakhmu* in Gujarati means a fort that is constructed for concealment.[2] It was built on the top of a mountain, with stairs on the outside that led to a door. As soon as the door opened, the scene inside was shown. The entire fort presented an atmosphere of sombre silence. While climbing the stairs, Shirin sees her Khushru, bows to him, comes out and stabs herself, and falls off the mountain. This heart-rending scene full of pathos gave new life to an episode from ancient times in Persian history. Shirin's part was played by Khurshedji Behramji Hathiram.

The Zoroastrian Company also performed farces of a topical nature. One such was *Pateti ni Fajeti*. Like other farces, this one contained a moral lesson as well as various jokes. All the main actors of the company took part in this farce, including the partners Dhanjibhai Rana, Dosabhai Biliya, Dadabhai Pastakiya, and others. The fame of the company grew accordingly. Other smaller companies became envious and wanted to bring the Zoroastrian down. One time someone from the gallery threw an old chappal that landed near the footlights. Dosabhai Biliya became enraged, and he immediately came out from behind the curtain and sternly condemned the perpetrator. The spectators also supported him. Nonetheless, from that day on the company's fortunes began to decline. Khushru Hathiram, because of illness, and another actor named Hormasji Hathiram left the company. The company was weakened, but this was not its end. Dosabhai Biliya again joined forces and performed Khori's *Jalam Jor* in the Shankar Seth Theatre, based on Sheridan's *Pizarro*.

The Old Zoroastrian Club proudly maintained its reputation. Some of its actors' names are given above. Others worth mentioning are Framji Kanga Dosabhai who played the lead in *Jalam Jor*, and Mehrvanji Pestanji Mehta and Hormasji Behramji Hathiram who were female impersonators. This company performed Kavasji Dinshahji Keash's three-act play *Behramgor ane Banu Hoshang* in 1873.[3]

The Zoroastrian Theatrical Club was also called the Old Zoroastrian Theatrical Company, because in 1877–78 a new company, the Zoroastrian Dramatic Society, was founded. Moreover, the Persian Zoroastrian Club, a different group from the original or 'old' Zoroastrian Theatrical Club, was founded in 1870. It was also called the Irani Theatrical Company. It performed *Rustam ane Barjor* in the Grant Road Theatre in the Farsi language.[4]

FIGURE 13. The Helen Theatrical Company from Hyderabad. Courtesy: Indira Gandhi National Centre for the Arts.

Persian Zoroastrian Club [5]

This club was born in 1870. Pestanji Framji Belati left the Irani Theatrical Company and founded it. Its actors were mostly Irani, not Parsi, although Dadi Patel was among its chief supporters.

The Persian Zoroastrian Club performed Bandekhuda's *Barjor ane Mehrsimin Ozar*. Various mechanical scenes were used in this drama. A giant named Poladband and a witch, Morjan, especially drew the spectators' interest. Pestanji Belati himself was a good actor. At one place in this drama, the witch Morjan flies through the air seated on her throne. At that moment, Pestanji sees her and says, 'Ge-i, ge-i, ge-i ge-i,' with such an attitude and pronunciation that the audience found it very endearing and started calling him 'Gei Gei'. This drama was performed in 1871 in the Shankar Seth Theatre. But after that, without considering the matter from the standpoint of profit, the club started performing Hindustani dramas instead of Gujarati ones.

This club faced the same difficulty that confronted all the companies: where to get boys to play the female roles? Finally Pestanji trained his own brother, Kavasji Framji Belati. The club was unable to survive for long. Kavasji Framji Belati continued to perform in various theatrical companies, in both Hindi and Gujarati plays. Finally because of ill health he left the stage. Pestanji Framji Belati became depressed at his lack of success in the theatre and turned to academic studies.

Zoroastrian Dramatic Society [6]

In 1877–78 when the Shakespeare Theatrical Company disbanded, several of its main actors thought about forming a new company, and three family men decided to join together as partners. They were Pestanji Dinshah Kanga, a good cricketer, Behram Collector, a successful comic actor, and Behram Katrak, who was in the textile industry. The company was called the Zoroastrian Dramatic Society. Kanga also took in some new actors who were his cricket companions. The club was based outside the Fort area, in the school of Dinshah Master located in a lane near the Alahi Gardens.

On the founding night, Dhanjibhai Patel was invited to tell the club members what to do and which plays to stage. It was decided to perform the opera *Rustam ane Sohrab*. After that other partners joined the company. Now there were five: Behramji Pestanji Collector, Behramji N. Katrak, Pestanji Dinshah Kanga, Framji Hormasji Lalkaka, Rustamji Hormasji Bamji. The author of *Rustam ane Sohrab* was Dhanjibhai Patel, but it was based on a play written by Edalji Khori. The drama was full of versification and a high level of singing. The reason for this was that previously Dadabhai Thunthi had introduced good songs in the Urdu opera *Aladdin* when it was performed by the Victoria Theatrical Company. He himself had played the part of the magician Abanezar. Anything less than this standard would have met only with failure.

In the above drama, Behramji Collector played the role of Gurgin very successfully. Behramji Katrak was the bodyguard (*pahalvan*) Hajir, Pestanji Kanga the king Kaikaus, and Rustamji Bamji the prime minister Afrasiyab's bodyguard, Homan. Rustamji Bamji deceived Sohrab in such a way that when Homan entered the stage the audience shouted out, '*Dhurt*, shame, shame!' Rustam Bamji's praiseworthy feature was that he could perform comic roles as well as serious ones with equal ease.

The society also performed a farce called *Ratai Madam*, written by Pesu Petrij. Rustam Bamji played the part of a *mobed* (priest). Because of this, the elders of Bazaar Gate Street in the Fort became very angry at Bamji and the company.

In 1879–80 there was much disturbance because of the dearth of theatres. The Victoria Company was performing in the Shankar Seth Theatre and the Elphinstone in the Victoria Theatre. The Natak

Uttejak Company's Esplanade Theatre, a rough wooden structure built in front of Crawford Market, was the only venue available to the Zoroastrian Dramatic Society. The Society performed their plays in it for a rental fee of Rs 30 per night. These performances occurred every night except Saturday and Thursday, because those were the days reserved by the Natak Uttejak Company for their Gujarati dramas. For some time this arrangement worked satisfactorily, but then one night there was a ruckus. Rustamji Bamji was playing the part of the *mobed* in the farce *Ratai Madam*. It is said that a Parsi named Dinshah Harvar became very agitated at this. He came in the afternoon with several companions and told the manager, 'If Rustam Bamji performs this farce as he did before, I'm going to rush the stage and cut down the curtain. What right does this wretch have to perform this kind of farce?' When he heard this, Pestanji Kanga, an athletic youth who was a company partner, laughed and told Bamji not to worry.

Another incident occurred in which Framji Kavasji Mehta had a booklet of the songs of *Rustam ane Sohrab* published at his own expense and gave a thousand copies to the playwright Dhanjibhai Patel. Mehta also sent a copy to each of the newspapers for review. In those days, Behramji Malabari's newspaper *Indian Spectator* was published at Framji Mehta's Kaisar-e Hind Press. Behramji Malabari published a positive review of the drama in his paper, and Kaikhushro Kabra read it and came to see the play. For a figure such as Kabraji to attend a play was in itself an important event. The managing partner of the Natak Uttejak Company, Framji Gustadji Dalal, who was sitting next to Kabra said, 'Why should you encourage them so much?' Kabra replied, 'Why shouldn't we encourage those who deserve it? I like the songs very much.' Kabra found the songs to be entertaining, and what better proof could there be of the drama's success? After this conversation, Kabra published a review of *Rustam ane Sohrab* in his paper *Rast Goftar*. Framji Gustad became so jealous that he told the Zoroastrian

Society that they could no longer use his theatre. This was because the Saturday shows of the Natak Uttejak Company were losing income due to the Friday performances of the Zoroastrian Society.

Because they could not get the Esplanade Theatre, the Zoroastrian's doors closed. There was no possibility of doing Persian plays on Grant Road. They were not popular there and because of that, Urdu plays had begun to be performed. The effect of this news on the actors was very negative. They had performed *Rustam ane Sohrab* about eleven times and had just begun rehearsing *Bejan ane Manijeh*. The result was that the company began to break up.

Victoria Theatrical Company

'The name of this company was known not only in Bombay but throughout Hindustan. Without a history of this famous theatre company, no history of the Parsi theatre can be considered complete.'—Dhanjibhai Patel

The English proverb 'a cat has nine lives' conveys something of the history of the Victoria Theatrical Company. The company was founded in 1868.[7] There were four owners at the time: Dadabhai Ratanji Thunthi (Dadi Christ), Framji Gustadji Dalal (Phalughus), Kavasji Nasharvanji Kohidaru (Kavasji Gurgin), and Hormasji Dhanjibhai Modi (Kakaval). In point of fact, the company was the brainchild of the famous Parsi scholar and reformer Kaikhushro N. Kabraji. He was the committee secretary of a Parsi gymnasium. Looking at the poor financial condition of the gym, he got the idea of organizing the existing drama companies into one combined company and putting on a play. The income from the performance would be used to enhance the gym's finances. To implement this idea, he called a meeting of all the company managers, and they agreed to the plan. At that time, it should be noted, both the Parsi Theatrical Company and the Gentlemen Amateurs had shut down. A play was

FIGURE 14 (TOP LEFT). Dadabhai Sohrabji Patel, actor-manager of the Victoria Theatrical Company. Source: Namra.

FIGURE 15 (TOP RIGHT). Dadabhai Thunthi, director of the Hindi Theatrical Company. Source: Namra.

FIGURE 16 (BOTTOM LEFT). Khurshedji Mehrvanji Balivala, famous actor-manager of the Victoria Theatrical Company. Source: Darukhanawala.

FIGURE 17 (BOTTOM RIGHT). Kavasji Palanji Khatau, actor with the Alfred and Empress Victoria Theatrical Companies. Source: Namra.

performed, and the gym was improved with the profits. After collecting the money for the gym, the question arose, what would become of the assembled actors? Phalughus had no work just then and his company, the Gentlemen Amateurs, had stopped performing. He wanted to start a new, larger company to prevent the actors from dispersing. Kabraji agreed to this. When Apakhtyar, the owner of Musical Sketches, heard about this he became very angry. He tried his level best to thwart the plan but failed to do so.

Thus the Victoria Theatrical Company was born. It was also called the Parsi Victoria Natak Club, but the former name became the most famous. Kabraji performed another service by making the four actors listed above into owners of the company. Certain actors were given regular salaries, and rules and regulations were established for their service. A managing committee was formed to supervise everything and carry out the company's work in a satisfactory manner. The members of the committee were upstanding, respected citizens, namely: Vinayak Jagannath Shankar Seth (chairman), Dr Bhau Daji Lad, Sohrabji Shapurji Bangali, Khurshedji Rustamji Kama, Ardeshar Framji Mus, Jahangirji Mehrvanji Pleader, Mehrvanji Manakji Shethna, K. N. Kabra (secretary), Pestanji Dhanjibhai Master (director), Khurshedji Nasharvanji Kama.

As soon as the company was founded, it began to rehearse for its first performance, which was Kabraji's production of *Bejan ane Manijeh*. After full preparations, for which the owners had to expend a lot of money, but which they had to accept on account of Kabra's direction, this play was performed on 20 March 1869. About twenty actors, all Parsis, took part. It is said that the drama played for fifty nights, more or less. From this, the level of interest and satisfaction of the Parsis is apparent. Some of the actors were so good that the public added their dramatic roles to their names, calling them Dhanju Bejan, Jamkhu Manijeh, Dosu Godrej, Khushru Kobad, Kavasji Gurgin,

Darashah Afrasiyab, and so on. *Bejan ane Manijeh* was connected to Persian history and hence the costumes were all Persian.

Bejan ane Manijeh earned the owners a good income, but nevertheless they were not very satisfied with the play. Seeing this, Kabraji composed another drama, *Jamshed*. This was more popular than the first drama, and the company owners also filled their pockets nicely. The third play, *Faredun*, was performed next, and this too was written by Kabra. By then the Victoria Company was well established and had begun to mount plays with a lot of fanfare. The other companies fell behind. Because all the performances took place in the old playhouse, the Shankar Seth Theatre on Grant Road, only one or two days a week were available to the company to perform. The owners thought that this was decreasing the company's revenue. If they could acquire their own theatre, they would be able to show plays more often and increase their income. After this decision, Dadabhai Thunthi and three other partners searched for a suitable plot of land on Grant Road. With effort they found a place for Rs 60 per month, and on this spot they had a playhouse built called the Victoria Theatre. When it was completed in 1870, the Victoria Company moved all their paraphernalia from the old theatre into the new one. Now the company's plays were performed only there.

But it seems that the company was not running smoothly. There were disagreements sometimes between the managing committee and the owners. In 1869 Kabraji resigned as secretary of the committee. It was natural that this should have an effect on the company. However, the company kept going and did not collapse. Everyone began to look for a new secretary. Finally Dadabhai Sohrabji Patel, better known as Dadi Patel, MA, was chosen as the new secretary of the managing committee. He was from a wealthy family and had been an amateur actor as well as an influential personality. Ignoring the other members, he began to run the company according to his own ideas. As a result the committee was obstructed, and finally it stopped functioning. Dadi Patel now ran the company by himself, but the owners were not pleased.

In 1870 after getting their own theatre built, the Victoria Company again mounted *Bejan ane Manijeh* and *Jamshed*. After this they performed Edalji Khori's *Rustam ane Sohrab*. Later *Hazambad ane Thagannaz* was performed. This too was written by Khori. Dadi Patel continued to exert influence over the Victoria. In 1871 he insisted that Khori write an Urdu drama, but Khori didn't know Urdu, so he wrote a play in Gujarati called *Sunana Mulni Khurshed*. Seth Behramji Fardunji Marzban translated it into Hindustani, and it was then performed in the Victoria Theatre by the company. Seeing this, Patel's rival, Kunvarji Sohrabji Nazir, had Khori write *Nurjahan* for his Elphinstone Company. Nasharvanji Mehrvanji Khansahab translated it into Urdu, and the Elphinstonians performed it in the Shankar Seth Theatre.

Dadi Patel was the first one to think of producing a play in Hindustani or Urdu, and he implemented his idea at once. Next he devised the notion of getting an Urdu opera written and performed. He had Khansahab write *Benazir Badremunir*, and it too was performed by the Victoria. This opera was extremely successful, due mainly to two actors, Khurshedji Balivala and Pestanji Framji Madan. Later Balivala became the sole manager of the Victoria Company.

The question arises as to what Dadi Patel's relation to the Victoria was in 1870–71. Was he merely the secretary of the disbanded managing committee or was he also a partner in the company? Dhanjibhai Patel and other historians shed no light on this. But it seems certain that in addition to being secretary, Dadi Patel must have had another connection to the company.

Another of Dadi Patel's accomplishments was to divide the company into amateur and professional sections. The amateur group or 'night club' was made up of those actors who held jobs elsewhere during the day and performed only at night, and the 'day club' consisted of those who became full-time employees and worked for the company during the day. Among the day club or professional workers, the chief were Khushru Kobad (Khurshedji M. Balivala), Pesu Avan, and Khushru Kobad's father, Mancherji Balivala. The Balivalas, father and son, both left their jobs as compositors with the Byculla Education Society Press and joined the Victoria Company full-time.

Meanwhile Sir Salar Jang of Hyderabad arrived in Bombay, and Dadi Patel invited him to his theatre. Sir Salar Jang saw a couple of the Victoria's plays and, impressed with what he saw, invited the company to Hyderabad. They began preparations to leave in 1872. Finally, after encountering various difficulties, the company reached Hyderabad. This was the first trip of the day club; night club members could not go because of their other jobs. The company was very successful in Hyderabad. The nobles treated them with great hospitality, and the Nizam himself was very pleased. Some plays were performed in the women's quarters as well.

After the Hyderabad tour, the company returned and once more took Bombay by storm. In this interval, Dadi Patel enhanced the company's reputation even further. He produced several more dramas by Khori, including *Hatim Bin Tai* in which he appeared to great effect as Hatim, and the highly successful *Alamgir*.

Here it should be noted that Dadi Patel was also a partner with Kunvarji Sohrabji Nazir in the Elphinstone Theatrical Company. For some time the two had not got along. In 1873 Dadi Patel turned the Victoria Company over to Nazir and left it. For two years Nazir was the owner. In 1874 there was a government function in Delhi. Nazir thought that the Victoria should go to Delhi and perform an Urdu drama to test its mettle. The obstacle was that Dadi Patel upon leaving the Victoria had started a new company, the Original Victoria Theatrical Club, and taken several key actors with him. Among these the most important was the female impersonator Pesu Avan. Due to his absence the Victoria suffered a great setback. Nazir was worried as to how he could succeed without a female impersonator who could sing well. Finally he launched a search for new boys and with great difficulty located two: Edalji Dadabhai (Edu Kalejar) and Ardeshar (Ado).

The Victoria Company arrived in Delhi and earned great fame as well as profit. The actors and others who went on this tour were K. S. Nazir (owner), Khurshedji Mehrvanji Balivala (Khushru Kobad), Framji Dadabhai Apu (Fram Apu), Dosabhai Fardunji Mangol (Dosu Ekdast), Dhanjibhai Khurshedji Ghariyali (Dhanju Ghariyali), Mehrvanji Mancherji Balivala (Khushru Kobad's father), Kavasji Manakji Contractor (Bahuji), Pestanji R. Lali (Pesu Lali), Nasharvanji Lali (Nasvan Lali), Edalji Dadabhai (Edu Kalejar), Ardeshar (Ado), Sohrabji Badshah (journalist), Pestanji Madan (painter), Kraus (German painter), Ardeshar Chinai (Ardeshar Mamo), Vamanji Garda, and a Parsi cook.

It is not known how many days the Victoria stayed in Delhi, how many and which dramas they performed, or how much money they made. During the sojourn in Delhi, an accident occurred during the performance of *Gopichand*. Khurshedji Balivala was playing the part of Lotan, and Kavasji Contractor (Bahuji) was on stage performing the Jogin's part. Lotan was dancing while being beaten with a whip by the Jogin. Unfortunately there were some nails protruding from the stage. They pierced Balivala's feet and he felt great agony, but he remained intent on his duty and didn't stop dancing. Successful acting often comes at great cost.

Another incident occurred during *Sone ke Mul ki Khurshed*. The scene was a sword-fight between the police constable Jafar Khan and Jahanbakhsh, scion of a royal family. Kunvarji Nazir was sitting in the front row watching with some European friends of his. Dosabhai

(Jahanbakhsh) struck Jafar Khan's sword with such vigour that it broke in two, and one piece flew off and hit Nazir. Nazir was beside himself and started berating Dosabhai. Dosabhai remained silent, but when the play was over he returned the insults to Nazir. Dhanjibhai Ghariyali and Pesu Lali mediated the quarrel.

The season ended in Delhi, and the company travelled to Lucknow. Dhanjibhai Patel has mentioned nothing about the Lucknow sojourn. From Lucknow the troupe arrived in Calcutta, where they stayed in a Parsi family mansion. Prior to 1874, no Parsi theatrical company had visited Calcutta. Nazir rented out the Lewis Theatre on Chowringhee Road, later known as the Royal Theatre. The Bengalis are extremely fond of music, and they had been awaiting the Parsi singers with utmost eagerness. Several eminent Bengali singers invited the Parsis to their homes to discuss various musical matters. At that time in Bengal the Western organ was in vogue, whereas in Bombay the tabla and sarangi were favoured, with only occasional use of the Western fiddle. The effect of these discussions was that the Parsi musicians were deemed deficient in their knowledge of classical music and its *ragas* and *raginis*, leaving a bad impression on the Bengalis. Balivala mentioned this weakness to Nazir, who became quite disheartened and perplexed. But he took the bull by the horns and began to rehearse the opera *Indar Sabha*. He sent telegrams to Delhi summoning Dadabhai Ratanji Thunthi, Dr Nasharvanji Navrojji Parakh, and Dosabhai Dubash. These three had particular expertise in the *Indar Sabha* and could enact it anywhere, under any conditions. In the end, the *Indar Sabha* was a hit in Calcutta. The part of Raja Indar was played by Dadi Thunthi, Gulfam by Dr Parakh, and Lal Dev by Dubash. Thunthi's singing, acting, and attractive appearance impressed the audience tremendously. But jealousies cropped up among the actors. Dosabhai Mangol and Khurshed Balivala, who ordinarily played the roles of Indar and Gulfam, were upset that they did not get a chance to perform.

No mention is made of what other dramas were performed in Calcutta. After staying in Calcutta for some time, Nazir made a plan to return to Bombay. He thought that it would be good to perform a couple of plays in Banaras on the way. Thus the company went from Calcutta to Banaras. There is no news of any play performed in Banaras. Here it is worth nothing that Bharatendu Harishchandra in his essay *Natak*, composed in 1883, makes reference to a play *Shakuntala* performed by a Parsi company. Could this have been the opera *Shakuntala* composed by Nasharvanji Khansahab and performed by the Victoria Theatrical Company? If the drama were obtainable today, this mystery could be solved.

From Banaras the Victoria returned to Bombay. Next, seeing that it was the season in Poona, they proceeded there. Upon returning from Poona, Nazir must have been able to assess the financial condition of the company. There is no list or description of the plays performed during the tour to Delhi, Lucknow, Calcutta, Banaras, and Poona. Meanwhile, the state of affairs in Bombay was that while the Victoria Company was on tour, Dadabhai Thunthi was the director of the Elphinstone. Nazir, the owner of the Elphinstone Company, had turned everything over to Thunthi before setting out on tour. Thus the Victoria left Bombay on two tours, first with Dadi Patel to Hyderabad in 1872, and then with Nazir in 1874.

Upon returning from Poona the Victoria continued to perform, with Nazir running both the Elphinstone and Victoria. But one day he decided to extricate himself from the Victoria. He called all the important employees, those who earned between Rs 30 and 60 a month, to his home for a meeting. He explained clearly that he was incapable of sustaining the financial risk and suggested that the lead actors buy the company and run it on a commercial basis. Hearing Nazir's proposal, all were astounded, but eventually four actors agreed to take the company into their own hands. These were Khurshedji

Balivala, Dosabhai Mangol, Dhanjibhai Ghariyali, and Framji Apu. The fifth, Kavasji Contractor, refused to assume the risk of running the club, but he agreed to serve as an actor whenever necessary. Thus in 1876 began the fourth life, as it were, of the Victoria Company. The first was when it was established by Kabraji, the second when Dadi Patel took over, the third under Nazir, and fourth, ownership by a group of actors.

Freed from the clutches of the capitalists, the company now came under the actors' management. The new owners, however, were faced with the problem of how to run the company. They were experts in performance art but had no experience of management. If they kept quiet, they would wind up paying the rent on the theatre and the actors' salaries out of their own pockets. Balivala suggested that they turn to Dadabhai Thunthi, and they all agreed. Thunthi was then a director and actor in the Elphinstone at Rs 100 per month. Nonetheless they approached him, pleading, 'You are the company's father.' He was asked to become a partner and accept the directorship, with the other partners staying on as joint owners. All of Dadi Thunthi's conditions were accepted, and thus the company acquired five, not four, new owners. The company's cart moved forward in a new fashion.

Taking the reins into his hands, Thunthi's first task was to improve the costumes and touch up the old curtains. He did not allow any but the earlier plays to be performed in the old costumes. He started the practice of beginning each drama with a *jalsa*, in which each singer would sing a song and all would then join in a chorus. Thunthi himself participated, and thus no actor had the courage to refuse. The admiration of the music lovers increased with this new item, and the number of spectators grew. Other Urdu dramatic companies imitated this practice later on.

As before, the Victoria undertook a tour, and this time they performed in Calcutta, Banaras, Delhi, Lahore, and Jaipur. In 1877, there was a further change when Framji Apu and Dadabhai Thunthi resigned. The remaining three partners took the company on another tour in 1878. This time they crossed the sea to Rangoon, Singapore, and elsewhere to display the banner of their artistic expertise.

When Thunthi quit, Khurshedji Balivala became the company's director, using his experience to run the company. In 1881 King Theebaw of Mandalay invited the company to perform, and they settled on a fee of Rs 43,000 for the performance of thirty-five plays. In those days Mandalay was not under British rule, and to go there was a very risky business. Nonetheless Balivala proceeded with great courage. The Victoria reached Mandalay in 1881. Twenty-seven members of the company went to Burma, where the company was received with great hospitality. To understand the Burmese language Balivala retained a Rangoon resident, a Parsi named Kavasji Gandhi, as interpreter.

One day a servant of the king presented the guests with baskets full of small oranges. They considered this an ordinary present and kept the baskets in a corner. When a few people peeled the oranges to eat them, they found that diamonds and gems had been hidden inside. The oranges were not meant for eating, they were the means of welcoming and rewarding the guests. When this news spread, the company members jumped on the oranges to get as many as possible. On another occasion, the king had a small pit dug and filled with rupee coins. Then he asked each actor to fill his hands and take away as many coins as he could hold. The actors were extremely pleased and almost everyone got a goodly sum, but Dorab Bajan because of his fat fists could only get 125 rupees. In addition to these valuable gifts from the king, the company members received many individual presents from the Burmese people. It is said that each earned on average Rs 400–500 plus several diamonds and gems. After subtracting all the expenses, the company returned with a profit of Rs 50,000.

The Victoria then girded its loins for a new adventure. In 1885, a Colonial Exhibition was held in London.[8] Balivala took the company there, but they did not meet with success. In fact, because of their ignorance of certain regulations, they were charged with a heavy fine. The amount was so large that the entire property of the company had to be put up for sale. Not even the tariff to return home was left. Somehow or another they got back. The earnings from Burma were thus squandered in London.

After returning, Dhanjibhai Ghariyali left the company in 1886, perhaps because of the loss in London. Now there were only two owners left. In 1889 when the company toured north India, Dosabhai Mangol caught a fever in Delhi and died. Now Balivala was the sole owner.

The reader must not forget that in 1876 the company had belonged to the actors. From then until 1889, thirteen years with their ups and downs have been described in this abbreviated account. Meanwhile, another chapter of the company's history was unfolding, connected with their travels to the princely states. In 1880 the Victoria Company went to Jaipur. At that time the reigning Maharaja was Ram Singh, who was very fond of drama. To fulfill his passion, he had a theatre built in Jaipur, now called the Ramprakash Cinema. To educate Jaipur's *gunijan*[9] in theatrical art, the Maharaja retained Dadabhai Thunthi as a salaried director for the princely state. Some Parsi youths also joined Thunthi in the service of the court. Similarly the Maharaja of Patiala in 1891 constructed a theatre in his city for the Parsi companies. The Victoria Company presented many benefit perform-ances in these native states. Some of their charitable contributions were as follows:

| 1882 | For a Well in Mandalay | Rs 400 |
| 1884 | For the Dar-e Mehr Fund in Rangoon | Rs 1200 |

1885	Lord Ripon Memorial Fund	Rs 658
	In Remembrance of Professor Fast	Rs 673
1888	Lady Reay's Medical Women's Fund	Rs 863
	Zarthosti Ona Rahethanon Fund	Rs 761
1889	Panjab Mechanic Institute	Rs 200
1892	Parsi Poona Gymkhana	Rs 300
1893	Ambabai Bhavnagari Home for Nursing	Rs 572[10]

When debates were circulating about whether actresses should be admitted to the drama companies, the Victoria also considered the question. In the end, Balivala decided that some actresses would be enrolled to sing and dance. As a result Miss Gauhar, Miss Malika, and Miss Fatima joined the Victoria.

The long story of the Victoria Theatrical Company has been narrated here in brief. But before concluding one other journey must be described. This was to Ceylon. Neither Dhanjibhai Patel nor Jahangir Khambata has referred to this trip. The Victoria went to Ceylon for the first time in 1889 and staged *Aladdin* and *Tilasm Zohra*. *Indar Sabha, Humayun Nasir, Insaf-e Mahmud Shah, Laila Majnun, Sangin Bakavali urf Indra Shrap, Saif us-Suleman*, and *Havai Majlis* were also put on in Ceylon. In the same year the company had two dramas translated into the Sinhala language and performed them. The company again toured Ceylon from December 1916 to March 1917. In this span they performed *Aladdin, Ashiq ka Khun, Ali Baba, Indar Sabha, Karishma-e Qudrat, Khurshid-e Alam, Khubsurat Bala, Hir Ranjha, Tilasmat-e Gul, Diler Dilsher, Nurjahan, Nairang-e Naz, Nazan, Fasana-e Ajayab, Fareb-e Fitna, Pakzad Parin, Mahabharat, Maru, Ramlila* or *Ramayan, Lail-o-Nihar, Vikram Vilas, Sangin Bakavali, Saif us-Suleman, Zanjir Gauhar, Savitri, Zulm-e Azlam, Sitamgar, Sati Anusuya, Harishchandra*, and *Havai Majlis*. The director of the company during this trip was Hormasji Tantra.

The record shows what a brave individual Balivala clearly was. He also had a special theatre built in Bombay for his company, called the Grand Theatre. It was constructed on Grant Road. Unfortunately, in September 1923 Balivala suffered a stroke and left this world at the age of 61. The company struggled for some time afterward, but in the end it was bought by the Madan Theatres of Calcutta. The company had been formed with great enthusiasm and now was slowly extinguished.

'At the end of the beloved's soirée we tried to rise and leave,
Stiff and aching we got up, then we lurched and fell, like tears.'

Empress Victoria Theatrical Company

The founder of this company was Jahangir Pestanji Khambata. It was established in Delhi in 1876 as a limited joint stock company with several shareholders. The owner of the largest number of shares was Lala Lalsingh Dulahsingh. Jahangir Khambata was a member of its board of directors.

According to Sharof, the Victoria Theatrical Company was to perform in the private salon of one Batumal. Dadi Poladband was one of the men who were distributing advertisements for the show. Lalaji mentioned his desire to start a large theatrical company to Poladband, promising to give him a big bonus. Poladband encouraged Khambata to implement this idea. Khambata could not commit himself because he lacked the funds to buy the number of shares needed to become a director. Lalaji made up the deficiency and Khambata joined the company's board of directors.[11]

After becoming managing director, Khambata's first effort was to invite the Victoria Company's famous painter, Pesu Madan, to join the company. Some other performers also changed allegiance and joined Khambata, including actors like Kavasji Khatau and Edu Sailani, melodious singers such as Naslu Sarkari, and all-rounders like Dorabji Sachinvala.

Khambata began to rehearse the *Indar Sabha* along with Khatau. He entrusted the writing of the script to a Bohra *munshi*. In the *Indar Sabha*, Khatau played Gulfam and Nasharvanji Sarkari (Naslu Sarkari) the Sabz Pari. Dorab Sachin was the Pukhraj Pari, and the Lal Dev's role was filled by Kau Kalingar. Raja Indar was played by Kavasji Handa. The play was extremely successful, and the company's fame increased. The ordinary public rushed to see the plays presented by Jahangir Khambata. After the *Indar Sabha, Chhail Batau Mohana Rani* was performed. Kavasji Khatau was Chhail Batau and Naslu Sarkari played Mohana Rani. In *Laila Majnun* also, Laila's part was played by Naslu Sarkari and Majnun by Khatau. In *Gul Bakavali*, Khatau was Tajulmuluk and Bakavali the same Naslu Sarkari.

Even kings from the native states came to see Khambata's plays. In accord with the desire of one of them, a new drama called *Khudabakhsh* was performed, written by Edalji Khori. In it Khatau played the part of Nadir. The drama was very successful, and the king liked it too. After that, *Ali Baba aur Chalis Chor* was prepared in musical style. All the songs were written by Khatau. The leader of the thieves was played by Khambata himself. Khatau became Ali Baba, and Marjina was played by Naslu Sarkari. The drama was very effective on stage, and the fame of the company reached a pinnacle.

There is no description of what play was performed in Delhi after *Khudabakhsh*. But one incident from Delhi is worth remembering. One afternoon after rehearsals were over, a peon approached Khatau saying, 'A memsaheb has come to meet you.' Hearing this, Jahangir Khambata went to meet her. He was astounded by what he saw: breathtaking appearance, delicate figure, a face like the moon. Khambata began to wonder who this doll carved from marble could be. Who was this houri from heaven who had come to meet an ordinary Indian man? He soon learned that the girl was Mary Fenton. Her father was a military pensioner, and she exhibited magic lantern shows together with her father. She had come to book the theatre where Khambata's company was performing on a day when it was not in use. Khambata agreed to rent out his hall for Sunday. The Irish girl left, promising to check with her father and then return. Khambata gave her an entry pass to the evening's performance. Once Mary Fenton had seen the *Indar Sabha*, her desire for watching plays was whetted. Because she lived in India, she spoke good Hindi and Urdu. She was especially attracted to the actor Khatau, and their friendship deepened. When the company left Delhi for Meerut, Mary Fenton went along with Khatau. But her father followed and brought her back. Khatau returned to Delhi and took Mary back to Meerut with him. What transpired after that will be dealt with later.

Another incident had to do with Khambata's quarrel with the police. The problem was that he refused to issue them a free pass. Once when Khambata was in his carriage handing out playbills, the carriage hit a boy. He was taken to hospital and died there. Seeing this chance, the police began to harrass Khambata. A court case ensued. In the end, Khambata was released, but the experience had been very bitter. The company stayed five or six months in Meerut.

From Meerut the company went to Lahore and set up their stage in Hira Mandi. The actors stayed in a Parsi residence called Gulab Bagh, with Khatau and Mary Fenton in a bungalow nearby. The play *Khudadad* was performed in 1878. The tickets were sold out by the afternoon, but the crowd kept pressing in. At eight o'clock the drama began. Because of the large number of people, the benches of the lowest class of seats collapsed. There was a huge uproar, but fortunately no one was injured. The company stayed in Lahore about five months. They performed *Ali Baba* in Chinese costumes with Chinese-style sets. In those days Jamshed Framji Madan's Elphinstone Company was performing plays in Amritsar. Dr Nasharvanji Navrojji Parakh of Rangoon was one of the company partners. One day, some people from the Elphinstone Company came to Lahore for sight-seeing. After seeing Khambata's play, Parakh was very pleased, and he congratulated him on his success.

The Empress was about to complete one year of activity. The actors gave notice that their salaries should be doubled, otherwise they would resign. They had only agreed to perform in the company for a year. Jahangir became enraged; he thought it must be a trick of some sort. Then he learned that a Parsi gentleman wanted to lure the actors away and start his own company. Khambata tried to explain to the actors that their salaries would be embezzled, but they didn't understand. Khambata wrote a farce on this incident entitled *Bhangar Sabha*. It showed how a greedy person starts a new company and brings everyone to ruin.

From Lahore the company traveled to Amritsar, but the Victoria and Elphinstone companies had already drawn all the wealth from that city. It was the hot season, and Amritsar was like a furnace. Most of the actors left for Bombay. The only ones who remained were Mary Fenton, Khatau, Naslu Sarkari, and three or four other actors. Taking them, Khambata reached Delhi. First he entrusted the company's luggage to Lala Lalsingh. In Delhi they stayed right at Lalsingh's hotel. This hotel too had been closed for some time. But Jahangir was completely destitute; he had not a single cowrie. Lalaji had to loan him money even for his meals. The company was shut down.

According to Dhanjibhai Patel, Rustam and Dorab Sachinvala were two brothers who were originally in the Empress and later joined the Victoria. Edu Sailani, who later became a famous actor in the Alfred Company, also worked in the Empress. The well-known Sohrabji Ogra was another product of Khambata's company. The Empress included other actors like Ardeshar Chinai and Mehrji N. Surveyor. Surveyor left the company and founded his own group, the

Parsi Ripon Theatrical Company. Surveyor travelled to about fifty Indian cities to perform his dramas.

Khambata's plays were performed in the Tivoli Theatre. In the days when Kavasji Khatau was performing *Khun-e Nahaq* in the Novelty, Khambata was busy performing *Zulm-e Narvan* in the Tivoli. *Zulm-e Narvan* was probably an adaptation of Shakespeare's *Othello* or *Cymbeline*.

Khambata's company and his actors' artistry so impressed Dadabhai Thunthi that he expressed an interest in becoming a partner. Debt-ridden though he was, however, Khambata would not agree to it.

Alfred Theatrical Company

It was 1868. The famous Parsi gentleman Framji Gustadji Dalal (aka Phalughus) was running a club named Gentlemen Amateurs. Its most well-known drama was the Gujarati translation of the English play *The Lady of Lyons,* in which Framji Joshi played the female part. One day Phalughus heard that some actors were leaving his club to establish a new company. Phalughus was a short-tempered individual. He blew up in the rehearsal room and shouted at Framji Joshi. As a result Framji left the Gentlemen Amateurs, his resolve heightened to form a new company.

In 1871 Framji Joshi established the Alfred Theatrical Company. In this regard Dhanjibhai Patel says, 'In 1871 the Alfred Theatrical Company emerged and presented several spectacles.'[12] According to Patel, another of its founders was Khurshedji Bapa Sola, who was not a very good actor himself but had a well-built body, good height, and wore a long Parsi coat and turban. He played the jinn role in *Jahanbakhsh ane Gulrukhsar,* which was well suited to his physique.

The company performed *Shahzada Shyabakhsh* in 1871. The plot was related to the history of Persia. Framji Joshi played the part of a woman named Firangis. The drama became very popular and created such a stir that the Alfred, although a new company, entered the ranks of its contemporaries, the Victoria and Zoroastrian companies. In *Jahanbakhsh ane Gulrukhsar*,[13] Framji Joshi came onto the stage as Gulrukhsar. In this play, mechanical scenes were employed for the first time. The eruption of a volcano, the emergence of a giant from the earth, and the descent onto the stage of flying fairies and other scenes were shown to good effect. The propensity towards spectacle was of great assistance in earning the Alfred its fame.

The director of the company, Hirji Khambata, was a respected artist of his time. It was unfortunate that in 1871 Framji Joshi was appointed Superintendent of the Central Press and left the company. The same year, Hirji Khambata directed and produced his own play, *Ab-e Iblis*, and then bid farewell to the company. In addition to these two plays, the company performed a Gujarati translation of Shakespeare's *The Taming of the Shrew*, and then it shut down.

It is not known how many years the Alfred existed. From another source we learn that in 1876 it performed *Shahzada Shyabakhsh*, but there is no firm proof.[14]

Around 1881 Nanabhai Rustamji Ranina, who had been a partner in the Parsi Theatrical Company, took steps to revive the Alfred. He was joined by Kavasji Palanji Khatau, Manakji Master, and Muhammad Ali Ibrahim. To stabilize the company, these owners purchased all the properties of the Natak Uttejak Company. Rehearsals began and after preparations were complete, the company went out on tour. In 1881 they successfully performed *Chandravali* in Delhi. Thereafter the company stayed sometimes in Bombay and sometimes outside of Bombay. In 1883 they performed *Harishchandra* in Bombay, and the same play was repeated with great fanfare in Lahore in 1884. Up until this time, the company had the services of the famous actor and director Sohrabji Ogra. Perhaps both *Chandravali* and *Harishchandra* were written by Murad Ali Murad, but there is no definite account available.

For three years the Alfred kept accumulating wealth and fame, and in 1886 it again folded. Thus, the second life span of the Alfred was only five years long.

In the third period, the reins were taken up by Kavasji Palanji Khatau, but because of his penury he faced innumerable difficulties. Once more Muhammad Ali Ibrahim helped him with funds and rescued the company. Sohrabji Ogra was the director, Amritlal the lead actor, and Mary Fenton the leading actress. Mary Fenton's arrival created a new trend on the Parsi stage. Previously the Alfred had not allowed any woman to join the company, but Khatau insisted and no one could object. Nonetheless a wave of protest spread among the actors and partners. The general audience was opposed to the advent of women.

In this period Murad Ali Murad was the company's chief playwright, and his plays dominated. However, Betab's *Mahabharat* was performed by this company in 1913. The company toured Poona, Hyderabad, and Ahmedabad, and when it returned to Bombay it began performing in the Royal Theatre, now known as the Royal Cinema.

Manakshah Balsara says that it was on account of Mary Fenton that the partners fell out. When the company was about to go from Quetta to Lahore (1889–90), Muhammad Ali Ibrahim turned the Alfred over to Khatau and left. The Lahore season proved to be very favourable for the company.

It is learned from the autobiography of the playwright, Narayan Prasad Betab, that he went to Calcutta with the Alfred Company in 1909. At that time, he was a company employee on a salary of Rs 175 per month. Thus the company continued operating under Khatau's ownership.[15] When the company was in Lahore in 1916, Khatau died there. His son Jahangir Khatau tried to run the company to the best of his ability, but in 1927 it was sold to the Madan Theatres. Its final drama was *Patni Pratap* written by Betab.

This is the story of the Alfred Theatrical Company. From 1871 to 1927–32 it had its ups and downs, for at least 56 years. The ownership changed, the actors changed, and who knows what all went on.

New Alfred Theatrical Company

Muhammad Ali Ibrahim quit the Alfred Company in 1890–91, as noted above. The Alfred or the original Alfred went into Khatau's hands, and Ali together with Manakji Master started another company called the New Alfred. It was an independent branch of the old Alfred. Ali began mounting his plays in the Royal Theatre in Bombay (now the Royal Cinema).

Sohrabji Ogra, who was staunchly opposed to allowing women on stage, became the director of the New Alfred. Jagannath Mahashankar, Bhagvan Amritlal, Abdul Rahman Kabuli, Elaizar, Nisar, and Purushottam, plus the comic actors Nasharvanji Jivaji Dadar and Ratanshah Jivaji Dadar, two brothers, were included in the New Alfred. The female parts were performed by Amritlal, Narmada Shankar, Nisar, and Motilal.

The company began its life with Murad's *Alauddin*, and continued to stage a number of plays by Murad. In 1910–11 there was a terrible fire in the New Alfred Theatre, and the company closed down. According to Manakshah Balsara, in 1914 the company was revived. Ardeshar Ghariyali had resigned his partnership and Muhammad Ali Ibrahim had died, perhaps of the shock of the fire and the loss to the company. Therefore the ownership was solely with Manakji Master. This time he began the programme with *Achhuta Daman*. After six months of rehearsals, the company went on tour and arrived in Bareli. Three years later after an extensive tour, the company returned to Bombay in full glory.

In 1918 there was another change of partners. Now Manakji Master, Manakshah Balsara, and Mehrvanji Kapadia became its owners. In 1920 the company went to Surat, Ahmedabad, and Muradabad for an exhibition. In Muradabad this author saw the company perform the dramas *Abhimanyu* and *Chalta Purza* for the first time. Director Ogra's acting in the farce *Raja Bahadur* was something to see. His signature phrase was *tarif to yahi hai*. When the spectators spotted Sohrabji on the stage, they would begin to repeat this phrase; such was his reputation as an actor. After five years the company returned to Bombay.

The New Alfred performed plays for a number of years and remained very successful in Bombay. In 1932 the company set up camp in Jaipur at the request of Maharaja Savai Mansingh. The theatre hall built earlier by Maharaja Ram Singh was located there, and the company exhibited several plays with great enthusiasm.

When the company was in Lahore, the owners Balsara and Kapadia received a telegram from Manakji Master, reporting that he had taken ill. They returned to Bombay from Lahore in 1932. Manak sold half of his share to the two surviving partners and was left with only Rs 500 per month to live on. In 1937 when the company was in Delhi, it was shut down for various reasons. The owners turned over the curtains and costumes and other properties to Lala Mukund Lal. In spite of promising to provide compensation, Lal never paid even a penny.

Among the company's directors, Sohrabji Ogra made great strides in preserving the fame of the company. Today he is remembered with much affection and respect by the 86-year old Balsara. 'We were in Sohrabji's hands. He did whatever he wanted, and we never interfered in his affairs. To fulfil Sohrabji's wishes, if we had to order something from somewhere, then we had no choice but to get it for him.'

When Sohrabji had to leave the company because of a stroke, Bhogilal became its director. Later Pandit Radheshyam worked there as an assistant. Radheshyam indulged in many exaggerations in his book *My Time in the Theatre*. Balsara reports that Radheshyam was never given the position of sole director. Balsara's daughter seems to have been extremely unhappy with Radheshyam's behaviour, although Balsara tried to placate her saying, 'Whatever happened, why refer to it.' These words indicate his generosity and greatness. Whether in regard to Radheshyam or Lala Mukund Lal, Balsara harboured no anger towards anyone. He cloaked himself in detachment, over-looking the harm done to him.

In the beginning the New Alfred performed plays by Murad, Dil, Hashr, and Ahsan, but later Radheshyam's Hindi dramas predominated. Dr Nami in his *Urdu Theatre* writes that Muhammad Ali Ibrahim donated money to the New Alfred on the condition that it perform Urdu dramas. When Balsara, who was manager of the Alfred and also closely connected with the New Alfred, was queried on this, he said that no such condition was placed on any partner. Each was responsible for the profit and loss of the company in proportion to the number of his shares. All the owners divided the work among themselves.

The chief actors of the New Alfred were Sohrabji Ogra, Bhogilal, Amritlal (Ambu), Umar Bhai, Qadar Bhai, Elaizar (Bhaduri), Nisar, Purushottam, and Narmada Shankar. According to Balsara, a very amusing incident occurred concerning Amritlal. When the company was performing in Lucknow, Amritlal became stricken by fever. His temperature was very high, and the doctor forbade him to move. It was natural that someone else play his part, but when Ambu heard this he couldn't accept it. Running to the performance site, he stubbornly insisted on playing his own role, even resisting the protests of the owners, who had to bend to his will. The surprising thing was that the fever left him and he felt no pain after that.

The company employed a scene painter named Miyan Husain Khan Anguthachhap. He was very skilled in his work, for which he received Rs 1500 per month. Later he became an associate of Dinshah Irani.

The following were the most well-known plays of the Alfred and New Alfred companies: Murad Ali's *Harishchandra* and *Chandravali*; Dil's *Laila Majnun* and *Nadir Shah*; Iftakhar Husain's *Shirin Farhad*, *Gulru Zarina*, *Mustafa Benazir*; Abbas Ali's *Shrimati Manjari*, *Nurani Moti*, *Nur-e Islam*, *Shahi Farman*; Naiyar Ambalavi's *Dehli Darbar*, *Mustafa Kamal Pasha*, *Alam Ara*, *Sultana Daku*, *Bangal ka Jadu*, *Zahar-e Ishq*, *Mashuq Arab*, *Id ka Chand*; Betab's *Mahabharat*; Hashr's *Sita Banvas*, *Bandevi*, *Surdas*, *Ankh ka Nasha*; Amanat's *Indar Sabha*; Mahshar Ambalavi's *Jallad Ashiq*, *Dard-e Jigar*, *Muhabbat ka Phul*, *Bavafa Qatil*; Rahat Muradabadi's *Roman Dilruba*, *Nur ki Putli*, *Chalta Purza*, *Khubsurat Bala*, *Achhuta Daman*, *Masharqi Hur*, *Yahudi ki Larki*; Radheshyam's *Abhimanyu*, *Bhakt Prahlad*, *Parivartan*.

A few points are worth mentioning in regard to the Alfred and New Alfred companies. Dr Nami in his unpublished volume says that the Alfred Company was founded in 1854, mixing it up with the Parsi Theatrical Company, and he calls this the Alfred Company No. 1. This is incorrect, because the Parsi Theatrical Company was founded in 1853.[16] Dhanjibhai Patel clearly fixes the founding of the Alfred in 1871.[17]

According to Ramnik Shripatray Desai's essay, 'List of Gujarati Theatrical Companies', in the 1952 commemorative volume for the Gujarati Drama Centenary, there are various notices for the Alfred Company. However, the sources for these are unknown, and all that is certain is that such lists spread errors. If further authentic material were to become available, these controversies could be sorted out.

Natak Uttejak Company

After Kaikhushro N. Kabra resigned as secretary of the Victoria, he still had boundless enthusiasm for the promotion of arts like drama. Therefore in 1875–76, approximately six years after leaving the Victoria, he founded the Natak Uttejak Company. Its original owner was Framji Gustadji Dalal (Phalughus).

Several factors were behind the company's founding. The first was the change in ownership of the Victoria. The second was that there was great excitement in the Shankar Seth Theatre on Grant Road, and the spectators' desire to see dramas was becoming very intense. The third was that actresses had begun to take parts on stage, and there was much resistance to this practice. The fourth was that the excess of mechanical scenes had turned dramatic art into magic shows. A major part of the audience had started to attend just for these wondrous scenes. Their attention could not be focused on the excellence of the performative art. Thus Kabraji wanted to found a company that would be free of these defects and safeguard both the arts of drama and acting. He had a separate theatre built for the Natak Uttejak Company, deciding on a site in front of Crawford Market instead of on Grant Road. Before it was completed, however, the company performed every Saturday night in the Framji Kavasji Hall in Dhobi Talao.

The language of this company's plays was Gujarati. The first play it performed was Kabraji's *Sudi Vache Sopari* (Betelnut between the Scissorblades). Their most famous play was *Harishchandra* written by Ranchhodbhai Udayram, which ran for about 100 nights. At the same time that the Natak Uttejak Company was performing *Harishchandra*, the Elphinstone was putting on *Aladdin* in the Shankar Seth Theatre, and Dadi Patel was engaged with his Hyderabadi ladies in the *Indar Sabha*. *Harishchandra*'s cast included all of the partners and actors of the company: Hormasji Dhanjibhai Modi (Harishchandra), Framji

Gustadji Dalal (Vishvamitra), and Kavasji Gurgin (Nakshatra). Taramati's part was played by Ardeshar Hiramanik.

The owners accumulated a goodly profit from *Harishchandra*. Framji Kavasji Hall had been taken on lease for one year only. When this period ended, the company had the Esplanade Theatre constructed in the field in front of Crawford Market. It was here that Ranchhodbhai's second drama *Nal Damayanti* was performed. Large numbers of Hindus came to see this play, women in particular. The company set up creches for their children and appointed some attendants to take care of them so that the women would be free. If any child cried, the doorman would go into the theatre to inform the mother, and she would come outside to quiet her child.

Kabraji's mind was full of all these schemes, and the pockets of the owners were filling up. But the owners were so ungrateful that they did not give even a portion of their earnings to him.

The company operated for sixteen years. One of the company members was an attractive boy who played the female role of Manijeh in *Sudi Vache Sopari*. He was first lured away by the Zoroastrian Company and later joined the Victoria; his name was Mehrvanji Pestanji Mehta.

The Natak Uttejak's third play was *Faredun*. This was the same drama that Kabra had written for Dadi Thunthi's Hindi Theatrical Company. But Thunthi had not been able to compensate him for it, thus Kabra after making some changes gave it to the Natak Uttejak. For some months this play too ran successfully.

After this the fourth play, *Sitaharan* by Narmada Shankar, was performed. Shankar himself was a very famous actor. Damodar Ratanji Shomani had written another drama called *Sitaharan*. Although it was published in 1884, according to the author's notice it was performed in 1877 by the Nitidarshak Drama Company under Pandit Gatulal

Ghanshyam's direction. Thus it is clear that Narmada Shankar had a model in front of him. One thing to remember in the context of *Sitaharan* is that when Ram and Sita first entered the stage, the entire Hindu audience arose from their seats and joined their hands in salutation. This was the expression of the religious sentiment of that age.

The Natak Uttejak Company commissioned and performed dramas based on both Parsi and Hindu legends. Most of these were written by Kabraji, who had also turned towards Hindu stories, e.g. *Nand Batrisi, Lav Kush*. In 1883, Kabraji wrote *Ninda Khanun*, based on Sheridan's *The School for Scandal* but adapted to contemporary Parsi society. The play became extremely successful and earned good money for the company. Darashah N. Patel was praised by the news-papers for his brilliant performance. This actor also did a great job playing the part of Shirin in the Parsi social drama *Kala Mendha*. The great fame Darashah Patel earned for his female roles is apparent from his popular performances of Damayanti in *Nal Damayanti*, Subhadra in *Subhadraharan*, Urika in *Ab-e Iblis*, and Tahmina in *Rustam Sohrab*.

Some other famous actors of the company were Manchershah Rustam Karamna, Dorabji Bajan, Navrojji Ditiya, Sohrabji Rustamji Vachha, Pesu Hatsena (Pesu Dhedi).

Although this company ran for a full sixteen years, it also had some ups and downs. At one time, Framji Gustadji Dalal was the sole owner of the company. The other partners had left the company because of his bitter, sharp temperament. Under these circumstances, Dalal abandoned Kabra and got hold of a Hindu writer named Shokar Bapaji Trilokekar. He was a good Gujarati writer and an interpreter in the Bombay High Court. Some of his dramas were performed by the Natak Uttejak such as *Damayanti Svayamvar, Vikramcharitra, Subhadraharan*, and *Chitrasen Gandharv*. A poet, he also wrote the songs himself.

In those days Dadi Thunthi had left the Victoria Company, and Dalal somehow or another made him a partner of the Natak Uttejak. The company's rehearsals had been held at night, but slowly Thunthi changed it into a day club. Instead of Gujarati, Hindustani plays began to be commissioned and went into rehearsal. Seeing this Dalal became very angry, but Thunthi kept him under his thumb. He even gave him a small role. However, the play *Paristan ki Pariyan* was a flop. Framji became very displeased at the failure of this opera, and the two partners separated. The company broke up, its properties being purchased by Nanabhai Ranina for his Alfred Company.

The company that had once witnessed governors in attendance, been supported by prominent householders of the city, and achieved unprecedented success, finally gave up the ghost. Dalal sold his sixteen-year old enterprise, taking his lifetime of theatrical experiences and entering the share market.

Elphinstone Dramatic Club

This club was founded in Elphinstone College by its students. In 1863 when Kunvarji Sohrabji Nazir passed his matriculation and entered the college, he laid the foundation for this club. He was assisted in this by several of his colleagues, particularly Dr Nasharvanji Navrojji Parakh (now of Rangoon) and Lieutenant Colonel Dr Dhanjishah Navrojji Parakh (of Poona); the two were brothers.

Dhanjibhai Patel says, 'Nazir's interest in drama was sparked during his college days, and from there it slowly increased.' This was an amateurs' club whose chief members were Dhanjishah Navrojji Parakh, Kunvarji Sohrabji Nazir, Dhanji C. Master (Palkhivala), Manakji Surti, Pestanji Nasharvanji Wadia, Mehrvanji Nasharvanji Wadia, D. N. Wadia, Nasharvanji Navrojji Parakh, and K. H. Kanga.

All of the above were Parsi youths and amateur artists from respectable, highly placed families who were involved in their own occupations. They had no cares about money. Whatever costumes they needed they had made out of their own funds. Their main purpose was to perform English drama. Shakespeare especially interested them. Jahangir Khambata's list of the dramas they performed includes *Bengal Tiger, Love's Quarrels, Living Too Fast, Village Lawyer, Mock Doctor, Bombastes Furioso, The Taming of the Shrew, Thumping Legacy, Othello, Lying Valet, Illustrious Stranger, Our Wife, Two Gentlemen of Verona, Sham Doctor*.

A prologue and epilogue were used in the presentation of English dramas in those days. The author and reader of these statements was usually Nazir or the Wadia brothers. In 1869 a newspaper published a notice, 'An original Prologue composed by Mr C. S. Nazir.' Another time a newspaper published, 'An original Prologue by Mr P. N. Wadia.'

On Sunday, 24 May 1869, this club performed a three-hour tragedy on the occasion of Queen Victoria's birthday. After that *The Taming of the Shrew* was performed. In 1889 Pestanji Wadia performed a comedy in the Novelty Theatre under the auspices of this club. Included among the spectators was the then governor's wife. The entire revenue was donated to the Countess of Dufferin Fund. Among the actors, Lt Col Parakh cannot be forgotten. As Portia in *The Merchant of Venice* and Zamora in *The Honeymoon*, he was so brilliant that spectators remembered him for years after.

The club went on expanding as new members joined, and slowly it was converted into a commercial club with Kunvarji Nazir as its owner. The new club became famous under the banner of the Elphinstone Theatrical Company, and the original club was renamed the Old Elphinstone Club. The Wadia brothers became the managers of the Old Elphinstone. The new Elphinstone under Nazir at first performed Gujarati plays, and then it began to perform plays in Urdu.

One of the Gujarati plays worth mentioning was *Alauddin ane Jadui Fanas* (Aladdin and the Magic Lamp), by Framji Sohrabji

Bharucha. Various mechanical scenes were used in this drama, and the plot itself was miraculous. The spectators were very pleased by such wondrous scenes. The most talented actor in it was Dhanjibhai C. Master.

Another drama that Nazir had the company perform was *Indar Sabha*. As is known, this was a poetic drama or opera. The lines between the dialogues that were needed to carry the story forward were also written in poetry. The original edition is unknown, but the *Indar Sabha* that was played by the Victoria Company was prepared by an Urdu poet. It is possible that Urdu *munshis* had not yet entered the Parsi companies by the time that the Elphinstone performed *Indar Sabha*. In any event, the specialty of the production was that as soon as each singing fairy entered the stage wearing the dress of her chosen colour, the entire court of King Indar was lit up in that colour. In this drama the hero Gulfam's part was played by N. N. Parakh and the heroine Sabz Pari's part by Shyavaksh Rustamji Master. Khurshedji Behramji Hathiram, who played Shirin in *Khushro Shirin*, performed the role of King Indar. It is not known whether the drama was performed in Urdu or Gujarati.

The third play to be performed was N. N. Parakh's *Sulemani Shamshir* (The Sword of Solomon), a five-act drama. Nurani's part was played by an actor named Pestanji whom people liked so much that they called him Pestan Nurani. A farce was also performed, entitled *Asman Challi* (The Sparrow). The hero's part was played by Nasharvanji Edalji Vachha and the heroine by Jamshedji Framji Madan.

In 1874 N. N. Parakh's second play, *Phalkasur Salim*, was performed in the Shankar Seth Theatre. This was a Gujarati play. The fifth play was Khurshedji Bahmanji Framroz's *Pakdaman Gulnar*. This time N. N. Parakh played the part of Gulnar and Shyavaksh Master came on stage as a tiny fairy. The play was in Gujarati and was very successful. Shyavaksh Master sang a song which in those days was sung in every household. Its lines went like this:

sabar re saburi, tun pakar gulnar,
khanch manne, khyal karo, khunni katar.

Patience, my Gulnar, have patience.
Be strong of heart, and remember the bloody dagger.

At the time that the Elphinstone Dramatic Club was gaining such fame, Nazir was the owner of both the Victoria and the Elphinstone companies, but one day he decided to leave the Victoria. He called a meeting of the actors and turned the Victoria over to Balivala, Apu, Mangol, and Ghariyali. He became the owner of the Elphinstone Theatrical Company, into which the Elphinstone Dramatic Club had already been absorbed.

After this, he was joined in the Elphinstone by N. N. Parakh, J. F. Madan, Framji Saklat, and Nasharvanji Vachha. N. N. Parakh was generally the leading actor in the Elphinstone plays. Parakh's voice was very sweet, and he was so successful and attractive that other companies tried to imitate him. It has even been said that Khatau and Khambata were followers of his acting style. But Dadabhai Thunthi was not in agreement with Parakh's method of acting. He always prevented his actors from copying Parakh. In 1874, when Nazir took the Victoria to north India on tour, Thunthi was made the director of the Elphinstone, but by then Parakh had left the company and gone into the medical profession.

Upon Thunthi's becoming director, he seized upon Edalji Khori and had him write a new drama, *Sitamgar*. The part of Sitamgar was played by Thunthi himself. This too was a Gujarati drama, and its costumes and sets were all in Iranian style. The famous actors in this play were Master Ratanji Navrojji Minvala, Mehrvanji Munshi, and Ratanji Thunthi. The part of the gang leader was played by Thunthi.

Finally after various ups and downs the Elphinstone was sold to J. F. Madan of Calcutta. He made the company as commercial as possible and admitted new actors. There is no record of any Urdu or Hindi play performed by this company.

Parsi Theatrical Company (No. 1)

According to a 1854 newspaper advertisement, the first drama company to begin performing dramas was the Hindu Dramatic Corps established in 1853. In that year the Parsi Dramatic Corps was also established. According to Dhanjibhai Patel, 'Parsis in Bombay made the first attempts at presenting drama in October 1853, and the pioneers in this field were Parsis themselves. They gave their club the name Parsi Theatrical Company. Its owner at that time was a lively, bohemian Parsi.'[18]

The Parsi Theatrical Company was founded in the home of Pestanji Dhanjibhai Master, who was himself an actor in it. At the time of the founding, the participants (who were also partners) were Pestanji Master, Nanabhai Rustamji Ranina, Dadabhai Eliot, Manchershah B. Mehrhomji, Bhikhaji K. Mus, Kavasji H. Bilimoriya, Rustamji H. Hathiram, and Kavasji Nasharvanji Kohidaru (later famous as Kavasji Gurgin; also a partner in the Victoria Company).

A managing committee was simultaneously established to run the company efficiently. This committee was made up of influential, respectable Parsi householders. Its members were Prof. Dadabhai Naoroji, Khurshedji N. Kama, Ardeshar F. Mus, Jahangir Barjorji Vachha, and Dr Bhau Daji Lad. Dr Lad, although a Maharastrian, was very fond of dramatics and was an extremely helpful individual.

Dr D. G. Vyas says that this company's first play was Edalji Khori's *Rustam ane Sohrab* (1870)[19] and Shyavaksha Darashah Sharof[20] says the same.

From an 1855 issue of *Rast Goftar*, it is apparent that this company performed *Faredun* and a farce, *Uthaugir Surati* (The Thief from Surat), in the same year. The notice read as follows:

PARSI THEATRE

For the benefit of the Patriotic Fund

The Parsi Theatrical Company wishes to inform the public

that its twelfth show will take place

on February 27th in the Grant Road Theatre

during which the following plays will be performed:

The Tale of Padshah Faredun

and an amusing farce entitled *Uthaugir Surati*.

The question worth considering is whether this company had any relation to the Parsi Dramatic Corps. The evidence is unclear. It also must be remembered that the *Faredun* written for the Victoria Company by Kaikhushro Kabraji was different from the Parsi Theatrical Company's *Faredun*.

Aside from *Rustam ane Sohrab*, *Rustam Jabuli* and *Rustam ane Ekdast* were performed here. From other sources we learn that the company was disbanded in 1856.

Parsi Theatrical Company (No. 2)

When the Victoria Company came under its five new partners and embarked on tour, the Victoria Theatre was lying empty. Dhanjibhai Patel says: 'Performers associated with the theatre along with some courageous young people and prominent citizens decided that they should not lose the opportunity of performing on balmy Saturday nights during the earning season. They sat down and had long discussions, and some of the colourful Zoroastrian brethren created a new drama company, which they called the Parsi Theatrical Company.'[21]

This second Parsi Theatrical Company, aside from having the same name, had no connection with the first. It based its activities in the Victoria Theatre. At first it was apparently not a professional company. Three or four good souls got together and founded it, chief among whom was Framji Dadabhai Apu's younger brother, Dinshah Dadabhai Apu. Through craftiness and sweet-talking he rounded up a few people. Some of these were third-rate actors, and some were Parsis who wanted to join the stage.

As the Victoria Company had gone outside of Bombay, this company's members decided that actresses should be brought onto the stage. The first actress was Latifa Begam, who was presented on stage in the *Indar Sabha*. From the standpoint of the art of acting Latifa was ignorant, but she was proficient in song and dance. Her voice had a natural sweetness and her footwork was unusually forceful. Her blandishments were also accomplished, such that she created a strong impression on her viewers. A surprising thing happened at the close of the performance of the *Indar Sabha*. Just as the play concluded, Latifa, still in costume, was draped in an overcoat by a Parsi, thrown into his Victoria carriage, and whisked away by the back door. The company owners were too cowardly to confront the abductor. Latifa's sudden disappearance did not stop the advent of women onto the stage. However, there was substantial discussion of the matter in the newspapers, and most of the opinions expressed were in opposition to the admission of actresses. Kaikhushro Kabra himself was against the policy.

A few months after Latifa's departure, Amir Jan and Moti Jan, two Punjabi sisters, entered the theatre company. Amir Jan was very accomplished in singing Sufi-style *ghazals*. A number of Muslims were captivated by her talents and were desirous of meeting her. From the day the sisters joined the company, its finances soared, but on the other hand, half the company went on leave because of the women's presence. Amir Jan married a Muslim and left to establish a home, taking Moti Jan with her. The Parsi company's rudder broke in two.

The following actors worked in the Parsi Theatrical Company: Navrojji D. Mazgaonvala (Ditiya), Kavasji Mistri (Kau Hando), Dhanjibhai Photographer (Dhanju Lambo), Manakji Mistri (Maku Dhansakh), Pesu Pukhraj, Khashru Jek, Dadabhai Mehta (Dadi Ba), Dinshah Dadabhai Apu, Bapu Tharthari, Mobed Shehriyarji, Kunvarji Buchia (owner of the London Hotel). Aside from these, there was a Parsi mechanic and a painter.[22]

This company also travelled outside of Bombay. They went to Bharuch, according to references in several places. Their famous plays were *Indar Sabha, Laila Majnun, Benazir Badremunir, Padmavat, Shakuntala, Jahangir Shah aur Gauhar, Chhail Batau Mohana Rani*. All these were written by the poet Aram, were in verse, and were performed by various companies, because although protected by copyright, no one observed it. It is not known when this second Parsi company folded.

Parsi Theatrical Company (No. 3)

When Dadi Thunthi's Mumbai Theatrical Company was disbanded, Navlu Mazgaonvala, Dorab Bajan, Dinshah Apu, and Framji Apu founded this company. The name was old but the owners were new. With great enthusiasm the old company was revived, and there is no doubt that in its time this company succeeded in achieving a great deal of fame. This was also a partnership company.

Unfortunately there is no lengthy description of this third Parsi company, and there is no information as to which plays it performed. Dhanjibhai Patel does not seem very well acquainted with the activities of this company. He has described with great interest the acting of Dadabhai Mistri and said that he played the part of Prince Tusho in Sanjana's *Shahzada Erich* with expertise. Mistri also was fond of singing, and he had systematically studied music with an *ustad*. He played the female part of an ogress in *Jahanbakhsh ane Gulrukhsar*.

Nasharvanji Virji was also a great actor of the Parsi Theatrical. Two of this company's playwrights were very famous: Bahmanji N. Kabra and Jahangir Nasharvanji Patel. Patel's *Phakdo Phituri* was very well known.

The Parsi Theatrical Company No. 3 toured Sri Lanka in 1898 and performed the following plays: *Aladdin, Indar Sabha, Khushru Hasina, Khudadad, Qamaruzzaman, Gulva Sanovar, Gul Rukhsar, Gul Bakavali, Gulistan-e Khandan-e Haman, Gopichand, Chatra Bakavali, Jahangir Shah, Tabdil-e Qismat, Chow Chow, Laila Majnun, Zulm-e Vahashi.*

The company partner Framji Dadabhai Apu died in Bombay, and his brother Dinshah Apu died during a trip to Madras. As a result, all of the company's properties, including its dramas, were bought by J. F. Madan's company in Calcutta, and the Parsi Theatrical Company ended. *Kasauti, Husn Ara, Amrit* (by Betab) and *Azam Shah* were also performed by this company.

Shakespeare Theatrical Company [23]

A few young men became partners and founded this company in 1876. They decided to have Shakespeare's plays translated into Gujarati and perform them in costumes of Shakespeare's era. Some of the actors were matriculates and college students, and they gathered others engaged in office jobs and business. The owner of this company was Manchershah Navrojji Mehta. Now they needed a playwright. The famous authors Edalji Khori and K. N. Kabra were already attached to the Victorian and Zoroastrian companies, so they did not have the courage to ask them. They began to look for a new playwright and found him in Dosabhai Framji Randeliya, who promised to write a Shakespearean play. Finally after great difficulty he produced a version of *Romeo and Juliet*. But later it was learned that the same play had already been performed in 1858 by the Students' Amateur Club. The author of that play was not known. The high quality of the play was praised in the *Parsi Mitra*. Dosabhai was wise not to publish his whole name with the drama, using his pseudonym 'Delta' instead.

Romeo and Juliet was performed under Hirji Khambata's direction, with Hormasji Jamshedji Antiya playing the role of Romeo. His mannerisms and acting astonished the spectators. Two or three times the drama was performed and then the company slacked off. The owners took the costumes and properties home, and the actors went elsewhere or thought of opening another company. An inspiring thought had arisen, something was done about it, and then it was over.

Shah-e Alam Theatrical Company [24]

Its founder was Dorabji Rustamji Dhabhar. He wanted to have a theatrical company whose name was unique. Dadi Patel had named his company after Queen Victoria, whereas Dhabhar named his after an emperor of Hindustan. He chose the Elphinstone Theatre for the performance of his dramas. Dolu Dhabhar's brother Sohrab Dhabhar assisted him a great deal.

The first play they performed was the Urdu drama *Jan-e Alam aur Anjuman Ara*. Jan-e Alam's part was played by Dolu Dhabhar himself. He did his own make-up, and it was so good that people mistakenly thought that Dadi Patel was playing the role. However, his identity was revealed from his voice and gait. The second play's name was very strange: *Jabuli Selam ane Aflatun Jin*.

Dolu Dhabhar was an all-round actor and was prepared to tackle any role. In one Urdu drama he performed the role of a *hijra* very well. He was also a good singer, and he wrote about half a dozen plays. The Victoria Company had these dramas corrected by their *munshi* and performed them.

Although Dolu Dhabhar founded the Shah-e Alam Company on a challenge from Dadi Patel, employing all new actors, in the course of time some of them became very famous in the Parsi theatre. The first such was Kavasji Palanji Khatau. The second was Jamsu Gullala, who was excellent in the female roles and stayed with Balivala's Victoria for quite a long time. The third was Pestanji Jijibhai Batlivala who was known as Pesu Pukhraj. His female impersonation was worth seeing. His voice, angle of the neck, and eye gestures were the most prominent aspects of his acting. He had been given this name after the fine job he did as the Pukhraj Pari in the *Indar Sabha*. His dancing made him look as if he were made of rubber. At Balivala's insistence he stayed in Jaipur in the palace theatre of Ram Singh, the maharaja. Later he abandoned female roles, and in *Insaf-e Mahmud Shah Ghaznavi* he played the watchman. Pesu traveled with Balivala to Burma on the first tour, but he was unable to go to England in 1885. Jahangir Khambata has also mentioned this company.[25]

Irani Theatre Companies[26]

The Parsis and the Iranis are two separate castes. In the late nineteenth century when theatre plays were popular, the Bombay Iranis were a relatively poor community. Their business was to sell soda water, lemonade, ice cream, and so on. Thus it was natural for them to come into contact with the Parsi theatre companies. They also wanted to form their own company and perform plays in Persian, their language. Seeing Parsi plays based on the *Shahnama*, they were moved by the memory of the heroes of their motherland and their enthusiasm increased. Thus in 1870 the Iranis established a club, known as the Irani Theatrical Company or the Persian Zoroastrian Club.

The first drama they performed was *Rustam Barjor*, and it was in Farsi. Every actor was Irani. The songs were also in Farsi although the tunes were Hindustani. The costumes and scenes were all Irani.

Actually this company and its activities were a surprising and unusual achievement of 1870. In *Rustam Barjor* the part of Gurgin was played by Pestanji Belati. Dadi Patel was especially involved in these events. The Iranis wanted to present a living picture of the ancient period through their drama. In their acting and stagecraft, they were eager to show each and every item in its naturalistic form. In this play, the two warriors entered the stage seated on actual horses and challenged each other to a fight. Once when they were attacking each other with maces, Barjor's horse broke through the stage platform and sank into the ground. With great difficulty he was lifted out. Although the horse was seriously injured, the actor playing Barjor leaped off and kept coming at Rustam with his mace. The curtain was lowered, and the horse was rescued eventually.

This company's second drama was *Faredun Zohak*. Its plot was also based on the *Shahnama*.

Among the unusual scenes of this company was one in which Barjor was seen working in a field, the peculiarity being that the entire stage was transformed into a field of green grass. The rising sun was shown coming up over this field. This scene marked the first use of magnesium wire, which was later adopted by other companies.

Some Parsi actors were also included in the Irani Theatre Company, namely Rustam Fiddler, Pestanji Belati, Kau Rodabe, and Ardeshar Hiramanik. Rustam Fiddler worked in a solicitor's office; some called him Rustam Bukuji. He was known for making strange sounds in his throat and playing the fiddle. There was a difference between his speaking and singing voice. He was especially fond of song genres such as *rekhta* and *ghazal* and was not interested in classical *thumri* and *khyal*. He sang the opening prayer in *Faredun Zohak*.

Pestanji Belati's full name was Pestanji Framji Belati. Later he turned the Irani into the Irani Zoroastrian Theatre Company and became its owner. The third Parsi actor was Kau Rodabe, or Kavasji

Nasharvanji Daruvala. He played the part of Rodabe, from which he acquired the name Kau Rodabe. He entered the world of theatre because of his friendship with Naslu Tahmina. Later he shifted to the Victoria Company and stayed there, although when Dadi Patel formed his Original Victoria Theatrical Company, he joined Patel along with his friend Naslu Tahmina.

After exhibiting the above two dramas, this company folded. There was a second Irani company started by Pestanji Belati called the Persian Zoroastrian Club. It was established in 1871. It performed Bandekhuda's *Barjor ane Mehrsimin Ozar*. Dosabhai Mangol played a Negro named Ekdast with great success and was called Dosu Ekdast because of this. The Irani companies did not run for many days. Their plays could not become popular because they were written in Farsi. This was so, even though before each scene a person stood behind the curtain and explained the action and the songs to the audience in Parsi Gujarati. There is no doubt that the enthusiasm and success of the Iranis owed a great deal to Dadi Patel, who was their clandestine director.

Parsi Ripon Theatrical Company[27]

The founder of this company was Mehrji N. Surveyor, who had been an actor in Jahangir's Khambata's company and played a comic part in *Zulm-e Narvan*. He took his company to approximately fifty cities, traveling as far as Burma and the Straits Settlements. While in Khambata's company, he obtained expertise in applying make-up. Surveyor is credited with performing 50–60 dramas, and his theatrical life included numerous ups and downs. Aside from this, little is known about this company.

Gentlemen Amateurs

This club was established by Framji Gustadji Dalal (Phalughus).[28] Sharof says that it was founded in partnership with Kavasji Kohidaru (Kavasji Gurgin).[29] It performed *The Lady of Lyons* in Gujarati, in which Framji Joshi played the leading female role. Joshi passed his matriculation in 1868, took up government service, and slowly advanced to become Superintendent of the Central Press. He was an excellent singer, and other companies admired his work as a female impersonator also. Phalughus was always suspicious of Joshi, fearful lest some other company lure him away. One day Phalughus heard that Joshi wanted to form his own company. Being hot-tempered by nature, he exploded at Joshi in the rehearsal room, 'Listen, *shetia*, we all perform plays out of passion, yet you do it only for the complimentary tickets. I've taken on a lot of risk running this company. If some other club tries to deceive you into joining their company, just think about the risk I'm bearing. My rivals may not know that when I show my true colours, I can force them to drink from a leaf-plate.' Shortly thereafter the two had an argument and they split up. This incident occurred around 1868. Thereafter it seems the company dissolved. Joshi joined K. N. Kabra's Victoria Company and left the Gentlemen Amateurs. Patel states that he saw Joshi playing the part of Firangis in the Alfred Company's *Shahzada Shyabakhsh* in 1871.

The Gentlemen Amateurs perhaps folded because of the split between Joshi and Phalughus. Its performances were held at the Victoria Theatre on Grant Road. The company performed *The Comedy of Errors* in which Dhanjibhai Keravala and Framroz Joshi both played female roles.

Khoja Dramatic Club [30]

Darashah Sohrabji Tarapurvala was an employee of an Italian steamship company named Rubetino Steam Navigation Company. He was a manager in this concern, having slowly advanced to this position. But he was very fond of drama. He also was practised at writing plays, and on the basis of the *Shahnama* he composed *Rustam ane Safed Dev* (Rustam and the White Devil). After his tour to Hyderabad, Dadi Patel entrusted the performance of this play to a good cast, but it was not successful in Bombay. To make the drama more popular, Darashah himself played the part of the white devil. In spite of the involvement of some well-known actors like Kavasji Gurgin, Hormasji Kakaval, and Framji Gustadji, the success achieved was not up to expectations. This play did not receive much popularity until it was performed at a benefit night for Darashah.

Darashah had already performed the role of Afrasiyab successfully in *Bejan ane Manijeh*. After the successful benefit night, he was infected with the disease of making money. He quit his job and formed a new drama group called the Khoja Dramatic Club. The financial liability for the club rested on other Khojas. Darashah wrote another play based on the *Shahnama* for this club called *Kaikaus ane Saudaba*. He attempted to give the part of Saudaba to a Khoja boy, but his wishes were not always fulfilled. One day Kavasji Khatau and Darashah happened to meet on Grant Road, and Darashah presented his difficulty to Khatau. Khatau appeared on the stage of the Khoja Club to play the part of Saudaba. Several times he performed for this company but finally he gave it up. Darashah again became depressed.

Next he thought of setting up a lottery, produced in association with the upcoming exhibition in Turin. Fine prizes were announced for the winners: advertised were a piano, organ, horse, carriage, sofa, etc. A lot of money was collected but no prizes were awarded. The ticket buyers were deceived, and Darashah's status suffered a severe blow.

Kavasji Khatau assembled some old actors and performed a play by Kabra in the Gaiety Theatre. In this too Darashah's role was not well received. As a result he lost his reputation completely and went off to Rangoon or Singapore to open a bakery. Finally he died in the Parsi General Hospital in Bombay.

Parsi Stage Players

According to Sharof, a schoolmaster named Fardunji Kavasji Sanjana started this company. Its first play was *Sir Bertrand* in Gujarati. Patel says that the company was managed by Nasharvanji Dorabji Apakhtyar.[31] He was an author, journalist, and singer who composed his own songs and performed them. Slowly his songs took the form of drama and other companies started to adopt them. Apakhtyar's troupe began to perform 'sketches'. For example, in *Kajora no Skech* (The Unfit Match), an aged bridegroom gets married to a ten- or twelve-year-old bride. This sketch contained a song by Apakhtyar, and it was well liked by the spectators. Various reform-oriented sketches like this were performed. A number of singing boys were needed for this task. When Apakhtyar found out about Manakji Barbhaya's expertise in vocal music, he took him into his company. Now a new thought occurred to Nasharvanji. He himself was a poet, a singer, and a music teacher. In those days the playwrights Dalpatram and Bandekhuda were constantly approached by other companies to write songs, but Apakhtyar himself composed the songs for his plays using the tunes of his favourite *ragas* and *raginis*.

Apakhtyar was a very respected Parsi individual of his time. Thus the whole Parsi community would generally go to see his plays, which were held in the Shankar Seth Theatre. One day he decided to take up the story of Sohrab and Rustam and set it to music. The news of this 'opera' created a sensation as soon as it hit the newspapers. Kabraji also found out about it. He laughed when he heard the news and sat down with paper and pencil.

In the opera *Sohrab Rustam*, Manakji Barbhaya played Sohrab. He entered the stage wearing a suit of armour, brandishing a sword, accompanied by his Turani army. With restless energy he began to sing: '(courageously) Who dares to confront the mighty Sohrab? This roar, this sword! Who will take up the challenge?'

The spectators, hearing this voice, became dumbfounded. The entire house became silent, as all began to gaze attentively at what was to happen next. Meanwhile from the other camp, a tall, well-built youth named Apakhtyar, holding a mace began to declaim loudly: 'Be not proud, oh foolish, heedless young man. I'll thrash you in a trice!'

Seeing this scene all the Parsis were wrenched by the history of the old warriors of their homeland. For some days Manakji played Sohrab's part, then one day Dadabhai Pavari took his place on stage. He had been one of the chief actors of the Zoroastrian Club, was one of its partners, and played the part of Khushru in *Khushru Shirin*.

This opera of *Sohrab Rustam* was written and performed in competition with the Victoria Company's plays, *Bejan ane Manijeh* and *Rustam ane Sohrab*. Edalji Khori's *Rustam ane Sohrab* contained songs, to be sure, but only as many as were common in dramas of the time. The reason for the popularity of Apakhtyar's opera was that he composed his own music and used musically talented actors. The entire credit for the conception can doubtless be given to Apakhtyar.

The Parsi Stage Players were famous only for their sketches. Their outlines set to music were the antecedents of later dramas.

Parsi Baronet Club

This company was established in 1875.[32] Its founder was Nasharvanji Forbes, and he received much help from his brother Edalji Forbes. He had previously worked in the Zoroastrian Club. The Zoroastrian had started the practice of singing a salaam, and Forbes was the one who used to perform it. At that time the entire band used to play along. Forbes quit the Zoroastrian Club and founded the Parsi Baronet Club. He consolidated the entire management of the company in his hands.

The director's job was turned over to Pestanji Kavasji Sanjana, a teacher at the Elphinstone School. Other respected Parsi actors also were attached to this company.

The company performed a play called *Mehrsimin Ozar.* Nasharvanji had a special drop scene made for the company, showing a portrait of Sir Jijibhai (Jejeebhoy) and beneath him the Sir J. J. Hospital, a memorial to his generous spirit that still exists today. At the beginning of every drama, Nasharvanji came out from behind this curtain and sang a song of praise to Jijibhai, of which two lines were: 'This colourful curtain instructs you to achieve fame. He who achieves fame will never die.' The author of this song was Bandekhuda.

Although this company performed various plays, the unfortunate thing is that even Patel does not recall any of them.

Nasharvanji was closely associated with the Gentlemen Amateurs and the Zoroastrian Club. His personality was of a very high order. He was the secretary of Sir Dinshah Petit for a long time. He had complete command over English and was also a successful actor.

Albert Theatrical Company

Manakji Master was its founder. He was known as 'Maku Jeria'. He dreamed of destroying the Zoroastrian Club. Why? Only he knew the answer. But when he found out that the government had honoured Seth Behramji Jijibhai by making him a legislative councillor, he immediately booked the Shankar Seth Theatre for his own company. He went directly to Seth Behramji's bungalow in order to obtain his protection and began running around to offer his respects. The Zoroastrian stage was left behind. By way of felicitation, he sang this *ghazal* by Bandekhuda:

The skies have showered mercy, our happiness is boundless.
Seth Behramji has become councillor for the second time.
The government and the people are joyful, as is all Bombay.

The Albert Company extends its blessings. May you live long!
Education and encouragement, law and reform,
Benefactor of the public, source of hope for all!

Nothing is known in detail about the performance history of this company.

New Parsi Victoria Theatrical Company

The owner of this company was Kavasha Dinshah Engineer. The preface to the opera *Har Jit* (Win or Lose), a translation into Urdu of *King Lear* by Murad Ali, indicates that the director of the New Parsi Victoria Company at the time was K. M. Bilimoriya. Engineer writes in the preface: 'God has bestowed his favour on this company, so that within a short duration it has been able to perform two new dramas on the Bombay stage. This new Urdu play *Win or Lose* (*Har Jit*), based on *King Lear* by famous poet and master dramatist Shakespeare, will be performed today, Dec. 28, 1904, before the devoted public by this fortunate company.'

From this introduction it is also known that the company's first play was *Dhup Chhaon* (Light and Shade), which was performed approximately 100 times. Its plot was based on Bulwer Lytton's *The Lady of Lyons*, and the author was Murad Ali Murad. Actually Edalji Khori had written a drama entitled *The Lady of Lyons* in 1868. In 1892 Murad Ali rewrote it under the name *Dhup Chhaon*.[33] As with *Har Jit*, the name of Joseph David is also written on the title page of *Dhup Chhaon*, from which it can be presumed that David assisted Murad by telling him the English story.

In *Dhup Chhaon* a landowner's daughter, Mahru, is seen walking in her garden. Just then a youth named Muhabbat Khan approaches her with a proposal of marriage, but Mahru has him ejected from there. After Muhabbat Khan's departure, a gardener named Banke Khan comes along and presents her with some flowers. Mahru accepts them. When Muhabbat Khan hears about this, he becomes very angry. With the help of his friend Dilavar Khan, he causes much trouble to befall Mahru's lover.

Dr Nami has said that the owner of the New Parsi Victoria Company was Navrojji Rustamji Sanjana.[34] But as has been stated above, the preface to *Har Jit* says that the company's owner was K.D. Engineer. Dr Nami has given no proof of his statement.

This company used to perform its dramas in Bombay's Royal Theatre. Two dramas before *Har Jit* are mentioned in the introduction. One is *Dhup Chhaon*, the other is unknown. Ramnik Desai in his list does not give the name of the New Parsi Victoria.

Hindi Theatrical Company

There was a time when both Dadi Patel and Dadibhai Thunthi were partners in the Victoria Theatrical Company, but Dadi Patel always wanted to dominate. Thus a mutually antagonistic relationship developed between the two. Dadi Patel did not want Dadibhai Thunthi to be pleased by the situation. Finally the two split up.

The hostility grew to the point where one day they exchanged heated words in regard to the opera *Benazir Badremunir*. In this drama, the fairy Mahrukh is shown as being enamoured of Benazir. Hence she takes the sleeping Benazir along with his cot and flies off to fairyland. Dadi Patel had prepared this mechanical scene with the help of Dadi Ratanji Dalal of the Alfred Company. After he saw it, Dadi Thunthi said to Dadi Patel, 'For God's sake, change this business. It looks like child's play.' Dadi Patel did not appreciate the criticism, and he immediately retorted, 'I'm going to make Benazir's cot fly just like this, in this excellent way. You go and try it in your own theatre company.'

Dadi Thunthi was provoked, and he began to think of ways to prove his point. He got up and went to his own rehearsal room. The matter died down for a while. When Thunthi left the Victoria Company, he adopted a new philosophy. He found a vacant lot he liked on Grant Road in front of the Coronation Theatre. He had a new theatre of the 'American type' built there, which he named the Hindi Theatre. Possibly Dadi Thunthi used the word 'Hindi' in opposition to Dadi Patel's reputed 'love of Urdu'.

While this theatre was being built, Dadi Thunthi formed a new club, named the Hindi Theatrical Company. It began rehearsing *Benazir Badremunir* even as the theatre was under construction. This drama was different from its predecessor of the same name, being written by a *munshi* who worked for Thunthi. It was in Urdu but the language was not easy. Every morning until 10.30 at night Dadi Thunthi worked supervising all the projects. The following were with the company at the time: Dadi Ratanji Thunthi (company owner, actor, and director), Dadi Aspandiyarji Mistri (Dadi Jadubaz), Ardeshar Sharaf (a business-man, but fond of drama), Jahangir Pestanji Khambata (Jahangir Lambo), Kavasji Kalingar (Kau Kalingar), Kavasji Palanji Khatau, Kavasji Mistri (Kau Hando), Framji Gustadji Dalal (a partner in the Victoria), Jamshedji K. Daji (Jamsu Manijeh), and others.[35]

Remembering the business from the opera *Benazir Badremunir*, Thunthi searched for someone who could make mechanical scenery according to his specifications. Eventually, he found a Marathi named Bhauji. Bhauji built a mechanical scene in which Kala Dev (Kau Kalingar) with both hands lifts the cot up with the sleeping Benazir (Ardeshar Sharaf) and flies through the air to Mahrukh's palace. As soon as Benazir flies off, his reception hall vanishes. Kala Dev is revealed flying through a deserted jungle at a height of fifty feet above the stage. The scene was prepared with great difficulty. Both actors in the scene had placed their lives at risk, but Kau Kalingar was a strong and courageous youth. Ardeshar was much afraid, but Kau said, 'You're completely safe in my hands.' Nonetheless Dadi Thunthi made arrangements to have pillows stuffed with cotton spread across the stage so that if suddenly there was an accident and one of them fell, the least injury would be sustained. Upon viewing this scene, applause echoed throughout the theatre. Thunthi had done what he told Dadi Patel he would do and showed him. Later he called Dadi Dalal and taunted, 'You too showed Benazir's cot flying, now come and see how I make Benazir fly.' Dadi Dalal replied, 'Fine, I'll come see it. But who constructed this scene? Bhauji must have made it.'

Dadi Thunthi added new curtains and new costumes to the play, but it had no songs. This was a big deficiency, and perhaps that was why the play was not very successful. But Dadi Thunthi was not distressed. He went to K. N. Kabra for help, and Kabra offered him the drama *Faredun* without asking for any payment. Kabra stipulated that when Thunthi paid him Rs 100, he would get the rights to the drama.

Faredun was not yet on the boards of the Hindi Theatre when Dadi Thunthi was invited to Bhavnagar by the Thakur Saheb. He arrived there without any preparation and performed *Bejan Manijeh* together with the farce *Zafar aur Kesar*, along with *Benazir* and the farce *Le Parun Gale Parun*. The Hindi Company in this fashion ended the season in Bhavnagar and returned to Bombay. On arriving, they performed *Faredun*, but it was not successful.

Finally a businessman took control of all the company's property as payment on a debt. Dadi Thunthi was deprived of the chance to produce another drama, and the company shut down. Thunthi never gave any money to Kabra, but still he received the rights to *Faredun*.

Indian Theatrical Company

This company performed the drama *Nana Sahab* in 1868. Written by Framji Kondrad, it portrayed Nana Sahab, the famous leader of 1857, as a rebel not a patriot, thus expressing the Parsis' loyalty to the British. The drama was in Hindustani and can easily be included within the tradition of Hindi plays that were staged.

Parsi Imperial Theatrical Company

It is not known who founded this company or who its owners were. But it existed in 1913, because there is a notice that the company performed Ghulam Muhiuddin Nazan's *Hur-e Arab* that year under Joseph David's direction. Then in 1914 Nazan's next play, *Khaki Putla*, was also performed by the company under David. Nazan's *Matlabi Duniya* was performed by the same company. Although this play was in existence in 1916, the third edition of its songs was published in 1917. It too was directed by Joseph David. After this, *Nur-e Vatan* and *Bagh-e Iran* were performed, in 1919 and 1920 respectively.

Ramnik Desai considers the first phase of this company as lasting until 1919–20.[36] Aside from the above dramas, he lists the following as performed by the company in this period: *Eshiyai Sitara, Ghafil Musafir, Qaumi Diler, Virat Parv*. In addition to Urdu, the Gujarati plays *Jauhar Gadh* and *Sansar Nauka* are mentioned.

Nami says *Qaumi Diler* was composed in 1923.[37] If this play was written in 1923, how could it have been performed before 1920? One of these statements is incorrect. In my estimation, the date of composition should be 1913. The edition Nami received must have been published in 1920, and that is why he gave that date.

The second phase of the Parsi Imperial according to Desai was from 1920 to 1924, during which the owner was Seth Ramdas Kalyandas.[38] In these four years the only performed dramas listed are *Sansar Nauka* (in Gujarati) and *Nur-e Vatan*. Nami says that *Nur-e Vatan* was written in 1919 for this very company. I also have seen *Nur-e Vatan's* songbook of 1919. Thus it was surely performed in the first phase. In the second phase it may have been revived, for which reason Desai gives it a place here. In addition, Nazan according to Nami wrote the dramas *Sher-e Kabul, Rukhi Lutera, Ghazi Salahuddin Fateh, Khuni Sharab*, and *Nur men Nar* and *Krishna Kumari*, in 1921, 1922, 1923, and 1924 respectively. Nami has not said which company the last three were written for. The rest were undoubtedly written for the above company and must have been performed by it. Desai too is silent about their performance.

Desai dates the third phase from 1926. The owner in this year is not given but there is a notice of a performance of *Sharif Khun*. In 1927 Daniel David became the company's owner and in that year *Asmat ka Daku*, *Vir Garajna*, *Vir Amar Singh*, and *Payam-e Haq* were performed. Nazan wrote *Bolta Hans* in 1927 but there is no mention of it being performed. His play *Sultana Chand Bibi* was performed in 1928. From Desai's description it seems that either the company ownership changed or that the song collections did not publish the owner's name. He has mentioned *Sacho Sevak* in 1928. Perhaps it was in Gujarati, as the name implies.

Finally this company was bought by Madan Theatres. Only the play *Talvar ki Dhani* is listed by Desai as being performed then. But until 1929 Nazan continued to write for this company. In 1928 he wrote *Phulon ka Har* and in 1929 *Lal-e Chaman*.

It is clear from the above description that the Imperial Theatrical Company made a contribution by performing plays for quite a long time.

Notes

1 PNTT, p. 192.

2 [*Dakhmu* is the commonly used word for the Parsi 'tower of silence.']

3 *Parsi Prakash*, Vol. 2, p. 452.

4 (a) *Rast Goftar*, Dec. 4, 1870; (b) *Parsi Prakash*, Vol. 2, p. 352.

5 PNTT, pp. 261–63.

6 PNTT, pp. 267–74.

7 PNTT, p. 87, Section 37; in *Parsi Prakash*, Vol. 2, the date is given as 16 May 1868.

8 This is an error. The Colonial and Indian Exhibition was held in summer 1886. The Victoria Company arrived in London on 7 December 1885 and returned to Bombay on 21 June 1886.

9 This word was used for professional artists, including courtesans.

10 *Parsi Prakash*, Vol. 2, p. 253.

11 Sharof, p. 113.

12 PNTT, p. 206.

13 Its author was Khurshedji Bahmanji Framroz, and it was a four-act drama published 25 April 1871.

14 (a) Nami, *Urdu Thetar* (unpublished section); (b) Manakshah Balsara in an interview also stated that the founding happened in 1876.

15 Betab, *Atmacharit*, p. 83. The director of this Alfred was Amritlal Keshavlal Nayak. [The correct title is *Betab Charit*. First published in Patiala by Ramrakkha Ram, 1937, the autobiography was reprinted by Rashtriya Natya Vidyalaya (National School of Drama), New Delhi, in 2002.]

16 PNTT, p. 2.

17 PNTT, p. 206.

18 PNTT, p. 2.

19 *Gujarati Natya Patrika*, October 1959, p. 5.

20 Sharof, p. 19.

21 [PNTT, p. 358.]

22 [Names corrected against PNTT, p. 360.]

23 [PNTT, pp. 263–67.]

24 [PNTT, pp. 316–18.]

25 Jahangir Pestanji Khambata, *Maro Nataki Anubhav* (Fort Bombay: The Parsi Ltd. Press, 1914), p. 102.

26 [PNTT, pp. 114–21.]

27 [PNTT, pp. 311–12.]

28 PNTT, p. 39.

29 Sharof, p. 17.

30 [PNTT, pp. 337–40.]

31 PNTT, p. 48.

32 PNTT, p. 103. [See also PNTT, pp. 195–96.]

33 Nami, Vol. 2, p. 318.

34 Nami, Vol. 2, p. 314.

35 [PNTT, p. 278.]

36 Ramnik Desai, *Gujarati Natya Shatabdi Mahotsav Sangrah*, p. 120.

37 Nami, Vol. 2, p. 330.

38 Ibid. [Gupt refers in the text to Desai; the reference to Nami by means of *ibid.* must be erroneous.]

CHAPTER 6

Parsi Actors[1]

Khurshedji Mehrvanji Balivala

Balivala's father was not well off. After imparting some practical knowledge to his son, he sent him to apprentice as a compositor in a printing press. In those days, the Victoria Theatrical Company was performing *Robinson Crusoe* in the Royal Theatre on Grant Road. Once, when Khurshedji chanced to see this drama, he memorized a few of its better lines. Later, he displayed his knowledge to some of the actors, and they were very impressed. They wanted to attract him to the Victoria Company. They went to his father to obtain his permission, and in this fashion Balivala joined the theatre world.

The Victoria was rehearsing its new play, *Bejan ane Manijeh*, and Balivala got the role of Kobad. He performed it with such artistry that the public began to call him 'Khushru Kobad'. After that he played Gorda Farid in *Rustam ane Sohrab* in an appealing way. Jahangir Khambata helped him improve his acting and also noticed that he had considerable directorial ability. Their partnership continued for a long time and earned them much fame.

When the Victoria Company presented the first Urdu drama, *Sone ke Mul ki Khurshed*, Balivala played the part of Firoz. His sweet voice and musical renditions were very appealing. He earned fame as Benazir in *Benazir Badremunir*. In *Bholi Jan* he played Hijo Tarivala, and his singing caused throngs to gather in the Novelty Theatre.

By then, Balivala had left his job as compositor and become a regular employee of the Victoria Company. When the company was turned over to Dadi Patel, he was receiving a salary of forty rupees, the amount generally given to the better actors. But he was still so poor that when he left for Hyderabad with the company, he carried only a shawl and blanket against the piercing cold.

After the tour to Hyderabad, Thunthi, Apu, Mangol, and Ghariyali became the Victoria Company owners, but Kunvarji Nazir entrusted the responsibility of day-to-day management to Balivala. Under the new management team, the company went first to Calcutta, and from there all over India. On this tour, Dadabhai Thunthi was contracted by the Maharaja of Jaipur and remained there with a group of actors. But Balivala prepared some new dramas: *Alauddin, Humayun Nasir, Puran Bhagat, Hir Ranjha,* and *Sitam-e Haman.* He gained the reputation of being a capable director and became the sole proprietor of the company.

In 1878, the Victoria toured Rangoon and Singapore with Balivala. In 1881, he led the troupe to Mandalay at the invitation of King Theebaw. There they were received with great honour. The company performed thirty-five dramas in Mandalay, for which the king paid Rs 43,000 in cash. Balivala committed a daring feat by going to Mandalay, because it was outside of the protection of the British Raj.

In 1885 Balivala took his company to London for the Colonial Exhibition.[2] Here they performed *Saif us-Suleman,* in which Balivala played the part of Pagal Khan. Pleased with his acting, the Gaiety and Drury Lane Theatre owners offered him a salary of forty pounds per month. In London, Balivala produced *Harishchandra, Insaf-e Mahmud Shah Ghaznavi, Humayun Nasir, Ashiq ka Khun* and other dramas, but they were not very successful. The earnings from Burma were squandered in England. The major reason for the company's failure was not language, because a translator summarized each scene for the

FIGURE 18. Daya Shankar, famous actor in the Gaiety Theatre.
Courtesy: Indira Gandhi National Centre for the Arts.

spectators. Rather, the company incurred a heavy fine when they failed to obtain a government license due to ignorance of local regulations. Balivala's biggest attainment from the London trip was the felicitation bestowed upon him when he performed *Harishchandra* and *Aladin* before Queen Victoria and Edward VII.

Balivala was honoured for his acting with two gold medals from the king of Burma, two medals and a gold watch from the citizens of Lahore, and a silver watch from the Parsis of Colombo. In September 1913, Balivala suffered a stroke and expired.

Dorabji Rustamji Dhabhar

He was known by the name of Dolu Dhabhar. He was a singer of Turra Khyal, a skilled actor, a poet, and a playwright. He established the Shah-e Alam Theatrical Company. To compete with Dadi Patel, he chose a theatre near the Victoria Theatre, and his brother Sohrab Dhabhar helped him gather together some Parsi boys to perform. Dolu Dhabhar's first production was *Jan-e Alam aur Anjuman Ara*. The plot was taken from *Afsana-e Ajayab*. Dolu played the part of Alam. The make-up job was so outstanding that people thought it was Dadi Patel on stage. Then they learned the truth when Dolu began to speak.

Dolu was a successful actor, playing everything from the role of a eunuch or *hijra* to that of emperor with equal ease. In one drama, he impersonated an opium addict. He also knew how to dance, and he had particular command over Urdu. He wrote a number of Urdu dramas which the Victoria Company had revised by their own authors.

Framroz Rustamji Joshi

He passed his Matriculation Examination in 1868. Among his friends were Dhanjishah N. Parakh (Lieutenant Colonel) and Jahangirji Behramji Marzban (author and owner of the newspaper, *Jam-e Jamshed*). Framroz spent his life as a government servant. He was the superintendent of the Government Central Press and was also a Freemason.

Framroz Joshi played the main female role in *The Lady of Lyons*, which was performed in Gujarati in the Grant Road Theatre by the Gentlemen Amateurs Club under Framji Gustadji Phalughus. Because he was not connected to the Elphinstone Theatrical Company, Framroz did not come into contact with its female impersonators, Nasharvanji N. Parakh and D. N. Wadia. Some company might have stolen Framroz on account of his artistry, but due to Phalughus's sharp temper no one dared raid his company for actors.

FIGURE 19 (LEFT). Framroz Rustamji Joshi, well-known female impersonator. Source: Daru-khanawala.

FIGURE 20 (RIGHT). Jamshedji Framji Madan, actor and entrepreneur. Source: Daru-khanawala.

Framroz was also very fond of singing, and although he was no Tansen, he attracted the spectators with his ability to render the songs connected to his roles with considerable sweetness.

After *The Lady of Lyons*, Phalughus was immersed in thoughts of mounting another play when the news reached his ears that Framroz wanted to establish a new company. His anger exploded and he went straight to the rehearsal room, where he berated Framroz. After a heated argument, Joshi left and began to think about his future plans.

Framroz Joshi's decision to leave the Gentlemen Amateurs hurt Phalughus deeply, but the bird had escaped from his hand. The Gentlemen Amateurs broke up in 1868. Phalughus wanted to join another good drama company, and his wishes were fulfilled. Kabraji established the Victoria Company in 1867, and in 1868 Phalughus became a member in it.

Framji was concerned for himself because he had a unique appetite for drama. Thus he joined the Alfred Theatrical Company which was running at that time. In 1871 he played the role of Firangis in the drama *Shahzada Shyabakhsh* for the Alfred. The company's second play was *Jahanbakhsh ane Gulrukhsar*, in which Framroz Joshi played Gulrukhsar.

In April of 1871, Framroz Joshi separated himself from the world of theatre.

Kaikhushro Navrojji Kabra

Kaikhushro Kabraji was born on 21 August 1842, and died on 25 April 1904. In the sixty-two years of his life, he educated Parsi society and made important contributions to it. He remained active his entire life in various plans for the uplift and advancement of his community. At a very young age, he became the editor and presiding officer of the newspaper *Rast Goftar*, and for as long as he was at the helm, he performed his responsibilities with great honesty, impartiality, and fearlessness.

In 1867 he established a Parsi gymnasium. To give it a firm foundation, he gathered all the existing Parsi theatre companies and had them present a benefit performance. The play chosen was *The Comedy of Errors*. The proceeds collected over the two nights of performance were placed in a permanent fund for the gymnasium, to be held as compensation against damages.

Then Kabraji was faced with the question, what to do with the actors he had assembled? Should he allow them to scatter or organize them into a company of significant stature? He decided on the latter course, and with his counsel, the Victoria Theatrical Company was founded. In the early stages of the company, Kabraji wrote three dramas for it and directed them himself.

In one of his plays, *Bejan ane Manijeh*, Jamshedji Daji played his part so well that Kabraji decided to have a benefit night for the actor. But certain people forbade Jamsu Manijeh's participation in this effort. As a result, Kabraji himself took on the role of Manijeh. All were astounded to see his acting. This was his first and last appearance as an actor.

Kaikhushro Kabra was a brave, erudite critic and reformer. The Parsis rightly consider him the father of the Parsi stage.

Jahangir Pestan Khambata

He was a boy of restless temper and mischievous nature. He attended school but had no inclination towards studies. He abandoned his classes to follow his interest in drama. Rather than sitting idly, he began to attend rehearsals wherever he found them. Once he demonstrated to an actor how he thought his part should be performed. Seeing his acting, the other actors were impressed with his abilities, and at their recommendation he was taken into the Victoria Theatrical Company. Initially Jahangir handled the female roles, but he was not very good at them. He was too tall to create a charming impression as a woman. There was also too much haste in his voice. Dadabhai Thunthi scolded him repeatedly for his habit of speaking too rapidly. Sometimes he beat him too.

Jahangir performed the role of Arunavaz in the play *Jamshed* for the Victoria Theatrical Company. Jahangir had one shortcoming: he never stuck to a single place for long. He left the Victoria to join the Alfred Company. He didn't stay there either. Proceeding to Delhi, he started his own company. Dhanjibhai Patel used to call him a *bhamta bhut*, a wandering spirit.

Jahangir stayed for a while in Dadabhai Thunthi's Hindi Theatrical Company. In this company, he played the part of the fairy Mahrukh in *Benazir Badremunir*. At that time, Jahangir was at the height of his powers as an actor. One time he expressed a strong desire to go to England and learn the art of performing, and just like that, he did it too. But he did not return enriched by what he had obtained, although there may have been some slight influence of an indirect sort on him.

Jahangir generally performed in the Tivoli Theatre. He also acted in the Urdu drama *Zulm-e Narvan*, an adaptation of Shakespeare's *Cymbeline* or *Othello*. He was very fond of pantomime as well and took part in it with Nasharvan Sarkari, himself appearing as a doctor and Nasharvan as his compounder.

Jahangir was an able and worthy disciple of his maternal uncle, Hirji Khambata, in the art of acting and make-up. Kavasji Khatau learned how to act in the same company and then started his own Alfred Company.

Jahangir Khambata also wrote some dramas, such as the popular Gujarati play *Juddin Jhagro*, along with *Dharti Kamp* and *Kohiyar Confusion*. Jahangir penned another book which has proved very useful and interesting, entitled *My Experiences in the Theatre*.

Kavasji Palanji Khatau

He was from a poor family and lived in a side street in Dhobi Talao in a small house with his brothers. His life as an actor began in 1875, when he first performed in the Shah-e Alam Company of Dolu Dhabhar. Later, he joined Jahangir Khambata's Empress Victoria Theatrical Company. He was taught the art of acting by his guru Khambata. Khatau was fortunate to find such a teacher, and Khambata was lucky to get such a talented student. With his artistic gifts, Khatau became Khambata's right-hand man.

Kavasji achieved fame in *Gorakhdhandha*, *Mahabharat*, *Khun-e Nahaq,* and *Asir-e Hirs*. Being an accomplished singer, his art reached a high level. He was also interested in writing dramas. Together with Khambata, he adapted the first performance of the *Indar Sabha* for the

Victoria Theatrical Company. He is also credited with turning *Ali Baba aur Chalis Chor* into an opera.

Kavasji Khatau was very fond of tragic roles. He played the part of Hamlet with such panache that people began to call him 'Henry Irving'. Enchanted with Khatau's histrionics, Miss Mary Fenton left her father and joined forces with him. For some time she lived with Khatau, becoming the queen of the stage. It is said that Jahangir Khatau was their son.

In 1916, when Khatau's Alfred Theatrical Company was in Lahore, he fell ill and died of diabetes. His popularity was so great that people would not let his body be placed in the cart for removal to the final resting place. The actors carried the body on their shoulders, and thousands of spectators joined the funeral procession.

Pestanji Framji Madan (Pesu Avan)

Pestanji Framji Madan was among those actors whom Dadi Patel loved and trusted. In addition to acting in Gujarati plays, he made a very important contribution to virtually every Urdu play that was produced during Dadi Patel's lifetime.

Pestanji Madan was very beautiful and his speech was sweet. Spectators were smitten by his looks and voice. Shakespeare's *Pericles* had been translated into Gujarati as *Dad-e Dariyav*. The Victoria Company produced this play in Iranian costumes. Pestanji played the part of the young woman, Avan, with such talent that people started calling him 'Pesu Avan' as a pet name. He also performed in *Sunana Mulni Khurshed*. After these two plays, Dadi Patel gave Pesu Avan a part in *Benazir Badremunir*, an opera in verse, an original idea of Dadi Patel's. In this play Pestanji Madan's elder bother Nasharvanji Framji Madan, who was famous as 'Naslu Tahmina', played the part of the fairy Mahru. This was Naslu Tahmina's first occasion to appear onstage in a singing part.

When Dadi Patel formed the Original Victoria Theatrical Company, both brothers were performing in it. They were also partner-owners of the company. After his death, they left Bombay and went to settle in Calcutta. One of their brothers was Jamshedji Framji Madan. He performed with Dr Nasharvanji N. Parakh in Parakh's play *Sulemani Shamshir*. The Madan Theatres belonged to these brothers.

Kunvarji Sohrabji Nazir

Kunvarji Sohrabji passed his Matriculation Exam in 1863 and in the same year entered Elphinstone College.[3] His classmates included Dadabhai Sohrabji Patel, Rustamji Mehrvanji Patel, and Hormasji Ardeshar Wadia. Due to Nazirji's industry, the Elphinstone Dramatic Club was established in this college. The club used to perform English dramas in Western costumes. Nazirji was always in the forefront of these plays.

The passion for theatre that he developed in his college days persisted until the end. The Elphinstone Dramatic Club was an amateur group, and its performances took place in the old Shankar Seth Playhouse. By 1863, a number of theatrical companies had been established in Bombay.

The Elphinstone Dramatic Club began to change, little by little. Plays started being performed in Gujarati, and later the turn to performance in Urdu and Hindi occurred. Along with these changes, the organization and form of the club evolved from amateur to professional. Nazir had a large hand in these developments. There came a time when the sole proprietor of the Elphinstone Theatrical Company was Kunvarji Sohrabji Nazir.

The first drama performed in Gujarati was entitled *Raja Karan Ghela*. After that, *Indar Sabha* was performed, in which Nazirji made very favourable use of limelight. *Alauddin ane Jadui Fanas* was also a popular play, thanks almost entirely to Nazir's efforts.

In 1885 Nazir went to London with Balivala's Victoria Theatrical Company as its agent and interpreter. He had an excellent command of the English language. He wrote a book in English entitled *The First Parsi Baronet*, and he also composed a number of the prologues that were featured before English-language plays.

Nazir was also a partner in the Victoria Theatrical Company. But due to its losses and his disagreements with Dadabhai Patel, he abandoned this position. Later he joined up again, and then once more split away. This game of hide and seek continued for some time.

In those days, there was no playhouse in the Court district, now better known as Churchgate, so Nazir decided to build one along the lines of the Grant Road Theatre in front of the Victoria Terminus. It was called the Gaiety Theatre. English companies often performed there. Sometimes Nazir also participated in their rehearsals and contributed his own direction. This stuck in the craw of the British, especially the white women. Nevertheless on one occasion Nazir appeared on stage, playing the lead opposite Miss Birchenough in the play *The Honeymoon*. Miss Darling also sang an English song written by Nazir in the Shankar Seth Theatre.

In 1885, Nazir founded the Jubilee Theatrical Club and began to perform plays in Urdu. This company mostly toured outside of Bombay. It is difficult to say what Nazir's acting was like. It can only be imagined that his entrances and exits in Urdu plays were as colourful as they were in English plays.

With this new company, Nazir toured primarily in the princely states. During the hot season, he fell ill with fever one time while on a trip to Tonk, and there he died. His body was transported to Jaipur and interred in the Parsi tower of silence in the presence of his son, Rustamji Kunvarji Nazir.

Sohrabji Framji Ogra

Sohrabji Ogra began his study of acting under the tutelage of Dadi Patel. He was a comedian of a very high order. Most of his life was spent in the New Alfred Company.

Ogra was jovial, gregarious, and of a fun-loving nature. His robust physique and melodious voice both lent additional charm to his personality. However, as a director he was a firm believer in discipline. None of his actors had the nerve to show up even one minute late for rehearsal. There was never the least complaint about him in this regard, even from the company managers. Ogra placed a lot of trust in Pandit Radheshyam and relied on him to take over rehearsals in his absence.

I witnessed Ogra's acting myself in the farce *Raja Bahadur* performed with the play *Abhimanyu*. This was a satire on the type of individual who is easily swayed by flattery. The British in those times awarded the titles of 'Raja Bahadur' and 'Ray Bahadur' to such individuals. Sohrabji's physical movement and manner, vocal inflection, purity of pronunciation, and facial expressions were all very natural and pleasing. In this farce, his signature line was *tarif to yahi hai*. These words became synonymous with his image. As soon as the spectators saw him, they would burst out with *tarif to yahi hai*, indicating the great rapport between the actor and his public. From this standpoint, Sohrabji was extremely fortunate.

Sohrabji was offended by the presence of actresses on the stage. While he was in charge, no female performer was given admission to the New Alfred Company.

Sohrabji died as the result of a stroke.

Dadabhai Sohrabji Framji Patel

In August 1869, Kaikhushro Kabraji resigned from his post as secretary of the Victoria Theatrical Company, which he had founded in May 1868. After a search, the management chose Dadabhai Sohrabji Patel, MA, as the new secretary. Dadi Patel was an amateur actor in the Elphinstone Theatrical Company who for several years had been taking part in dramas. He was from a wealthy family and received an allowance of two thousand rupees a month. Because of his passion for drama, however, he became estranged from his father.

Upon becoming secretary, Patel consolidated his control such that the managing committee virtually came to an end. Patel emerged, in effect, as the overall chief. To fulfil his dramatic ambitions, he also secretly became the director of the Irani Theatrical Company.

In 1872, Dadi Patel was the director of the Victoria, and he was at the same time a partner in the Elphinstone Club with Kunvarji Nazir. In that year, he produced the Urdu drama *Nurjahan* with the Elphinstone at the Shankar Seth Playhouse. In fact, the inspiration to introduce drama in Urdu sprang from Dadi Patel's brain. He had a Gujarati play by Edalji Khori, *Sunana Mulni Khurshed*, translated into Urdu, and then he produced it in 1871. This play, now entitled *Sone ke Mul ki Khurshed*, was the first staged Parsi drama in Urdu. The performance was by the Victoria Theatrical Company at the Victoria Theatre. In 1874, Patel handed the Victoria Company over to Nazir and left. On the one hand he had inaugurated Urdu drama; on the other, he abandoned prose and introduced the poetic musical form, opera. At his instigation, Nasharvanji Mehrvan Khansahab wrote the opera *Benazir Badremunir*, which earned Patel measurable success.

Dadi Patel performed another important task, namely to speak with the actors and get them to agree to rehearse in the day instead of at night, increasing their monthly pay accordingly. The intent of this move was to make the performers twenty-four hour salaried employees. No doubt there were some actors who did other jobs during the day and could come to the theatre only at night, and they opposed him, but Dadi Patel was not very concerned. He was especially attentive towards two actors: Khushru Kobad (Khurshedji Balivala) and Pesu Avan (Pestanji Madan). His fame rested on these two, and both of them were willing to join the 'day club'.

Dadi Patel accepted the invitation of Sir Salar Jang, prime minister of Hyderabad, and with great difficulty and risk reached there. The Hyderabad tour was extremely successful.

While he was the director of the Irani Theatrical Company, Dadi Patel produced a magical and wondrous atmosphere by combining various mechanical scenes. Fields of green filled the entire stage and the sun rose over them. Live horses were ridden onto the stage by Rustam and Barjor and challenged to fight against each other. Not only was he a proven director, Dadi Patel played the part of Hatim in *Hatim Bin Tai* so artistically that it was remembered for years afterward. This was one of the most successful and outstanding of his plays for the Victoria Company.

Dadi Patel's acting was very lively, attractive, and natural. Several actors imitated the special costume he had made for his part as Hatim. Two scenes were particularly powerful, one in which Hatim is transformed into a rock, and a later one in which he is changed into water. In the same manner, he was very successful as an actor in *Alamgir*. How a man stands on the earth in conscious and unconscious states, how he falls, what the condition of his body and soul are, and other mental and physical conditions were displayed to great effect.

It was a misfortune for the Parsi theatre that at the age of thirty-two this Parsi youth took ill in Bangalore. He died in March 1876 in the arms of his friends, leaving behind the immortal fame of his art.

Dadabhai Ratanji Thunthi

Dadabhai Thunthi was among the most famous actors, directors, and managing partners of the Parsi theatre. It is not known when he began his work with the theatrical companies, but in 1874 when Kunvarji Nazir took his Victoria Theatrical Company and left on tour, the reins of the Elphinstone Company were entrusted to Dadabhai Thunthi. At that time, Thunthi had Edalji Khori compose the play *Sitamgar* in Gujarati, following which he directed its performance. Dadabhai himself played the role of Sitamgar, and his finesse in acting won the hearts of the spectators. This drama was performed in Iranian costumes. In the play, a group of bandits pursuing a boy enter a jungle, at which point the chorus was supposed to sing a song. In those days, there was not an established practice of singing in stage plays. Music education for Parsi boys and girls was viewed with suspicion. In the absence of singers in the company, Thunthi himself changed costume, appeared as a member of the bandit gang, and led the chorus himself.

When the Victoria Company went to Calcutta, Nazir summoned Thunthi to perform there in his production of the *Indar Sabha*. After finishing the job of playing the role of Indar, Thunthi went to Bombay and began to run the Elphinstone Company. He received one hundred rupees per month as salary for his directorship of the Elphinstone.

Thunthi was the inventor of the *jalsa* or preliminary concert at the start of a performance. All the singers in the company would come together before the main drama and sing in chorus. With this innovation, Thunthi attracted the attention of the public from the very beginning. Later other companies imitated this practice of his.

After the season in Poona, when the Victoria Company returned to Bombay, Nazir spurred the actors to take over the company management, and in 1876 a committee of four actors headed by Khurshedji Balivala became joint partners. But without Thunthi's help, they had no hope of success. The actors approached Thunthi, who was already the salaried director of the Elphinstone, and he thus became a partner in and director of the Victoria as well. His first move was to order the preparation of a whole wardrobe of new costumes and new curtains. In 1877, Thunthi quit as a partner in the Victoria. He may have been unwilling to undertake the trip across the seas to Rangoon and Singapore that the other managers were proposing.

Thunthi acted with great success in the Victoria's production of *Aladin*, an opera in which Thunthi captivated the listeners just as he had in *Sohrab Rustam*.

It is a well-known fact that Dadi Patel and Dadi Thunthi did not get along, and therefore Thunthi eventually freed himself from the Victoria Company. Immediately, he founded a new club known as the Hindi Theatrical Company, which performed in the Hindi Theatre. The scene that Thunthi presented in *Benazir Badremunir* was extraordinary. Dadi Patel had shown the fairy Mahrukh transporting Benazir on a flying cot, but Thunthi, improving upon the scene, had Benazir at Mahrukh's command holding the Kala Dev captive as he flew through the skies. The creator of this mechanical scene was the Marathi technician, Bhave.[4]

Early Actresses in the Parsi Theatre

At first, the Parsi public was strongly opposed to women acting on the stage. Even Kaikhushro Kabraji, an advocate of independence for women, was opposed to bringing actresses on stage, and the pages of *Rast Goftar* and other journals were full of these debates. Dadi Patel is said to have been the first to take the bold step of bringing two Muslim women with him from Hyderabad. One of them, Latifa Begam, was expert in dance. In the *Indar Sabha*, she made the playhouse on Grant Road reverberate, and spectators came just to see her. She would dance for so long that her socks began to tear. One day she was abducted from the wings by a spectator who wrapped her in his overcoat, seated her in his carriage, and whisked her away.

FIGURE 21. Miss Munni Bai, actress of the twentieth-century Parsi theatre. Source: Namra.

Two other early actresses were Amir Jan and Moti Jan, both Punjabi women who were good singers. Amir Jan was especially accomplished at Sufi *ghazals*, and many Muslim businessmen tried to court her. Finally one of them married her, and she left the stage. Her sister Moti Jan also abandoned the company, and in this manner, amidst much controversy, the Parsi Theatrical Company came to an end.

Miss Gauhar first worked in Balivala's Victoria Company, but later she worked for several other companies. Miss Fatima was also in Balivala's company. It is said that once she entered his room while he was sleeping. Suddenly he woke up and, seeing her unexpectedly, suffered an attack of paralysis. Miss Malika too worked in the Victoria and other companies. Miss Khatun was said to be Miss Gauhar's sister. One of her lovers allegedly cut off her nose. Miss Gulnar ran a paan shop in Rangoon and later joined the theatre. Miss Jamila was a Jewish girl. Other early actresses were Miss Bijli, Miss Kamali, Miss Gulab, Miss Ganga, and Miss Umda Jan.

But among all of these, Miss Mary Fenton was the most famous. Her father was an Irish soldier who after retirement presented magic lantern shows around Delhi for a living. She met Kavas Khatau while he was rehearsing for a performance with Jahangir Khambata's troupe. Mary came to the theatre every night, and they fell in love. She then went with him to Bombay and began to perform. As her competence in Gujarati, Urdu, and Hindi improved and she took to wearing Parsi dress, she became a successful actress. She also adopted the name of Mehrbai.

Mary played the part of the Jogin in Talib's *Harishchandra*, a role which was as popular as her Bholi Gul in the Gujarati play of that title. Kavasji Khatau and Mary got married, but later they separated. She then worked for various companies until her death. She was undoubtedly one of the most successful, attractive, and popular actresses of her time.

Although most theatre companies began hiring actresses after this, the New Alfred held out and resisted admitting women as long as Sohrabji Ogra was in charge. In the beginning of the twentieth century, many women worked on stage: Miss Kajjan, Miss Gauhar, Miss Munni Bai, and others.

Notes

1 [Most of the major actors were also company directors or managers. The most important male performers are listed alphabetically by surname, followed by Gupt's separate section on female performers. Many minor actors have been omitted.]

2 [See note 8, p. 178 above.]

3 PNTT, p. 8.

4 [In the previous account of the incident, Gupt gives the Marathi technician's name as 'Bhauji'. See pp. 174–75.]

Other Elements of the Parsi Theatre[1]

THE AUDIENCE

From the beginning of the Parsi theatre until about 1870, the audience consisted mainly of Parsis and Iranis. In those days the Parsis lived in Dhobi Talao in the Court area, in Boribandar (Churchgate), and near Grant Road and Charni Cross Road. That is why the first Parsi theatre houses were built in those areas. The Iranis also formed their own companies and performed in Persian, but because spectators were few and the revenue insufficient, they did not meet with much success.

In 1870, when Dadi Patel thought of performing dramas in Urdu instead of Gujarati, Hindu and Muslim spectators began to come to the theatre. The English also came to the Grant Road Theatre to watch 'Hindu drama', although they were more interested in English plays. Thus, while the majority of the Parsi theatre audience consisted of Parsis, the theatre was also frequented by Iranis, Muslims, Hindus, and high-ranking British officials and their families.

At the start, it was not considered proper for Parsi women to go to the theatre, but Kaikhushro Kabraji promoted women's independence, and finally Parsi women accompanied by their husbands or brothers began to attend plays. Sometimes the companies put on shows expressly for women. The Natak Uttejak Company's performance of *Harishchandra* attracted so many women that the company arranged creches for their children outside the theatre hall.

There were several classes of spectators. The ticket prices for English dramas were as follows: stalls or box Rs 6, upper box Rs 4, pit Rs 3. Gradually the prices came down to Rs 2–4. When Vishnudas Bhave produced his play *Raja Gopichand* in 1853 in the Grant Road Theatre, the tickets ranged from three rupees for the dress circle to one rupee for the pit. When the Parsi companies toured outside Bombay, they charged between five rupees and eight annas, with free passes for specially invited officials. From these prices, it can readily be imagined what the composition of the audience was. Women in purdah were seated in a separate section, with a single ticket price. The prostitutes of the town also sat in that section.

The most convenient method of advertising a show was by proclamation. Handbills were distributed from horse carts, announcing the subject of the play to be performed that night, its spectacular scenes, sets, and the names of the actors. When women began appearing on the stage, their names, and sometimes their photographs were included. Before the conclusion of the play each night, an individual appeared in front of the drop scene and announced the next day's play.

The audience, when pleased with the actors' songs, would shout 'Once more!' Sometimes, 'once more' was demanded even after the drop scene had fallen. If 'once more' was declared two or three times, the manager would satisfy the audience's desire by having the scene repeated. Sometimes this created the ridiculous effect of slain characters, recently killed in combat, rising from the floor and beginning to fight all over again.

Audiences were especially thrilled by spectacular mechanical scenes. Deities descending from the heavens, gods and demons rising from a rift in the earth, a sleeping prince carried off through the air and delivered to a fairy, a railway train falling from a broken bridge into a river: these were the kinds of trick scenes that audiences loved.

Although every company announced that entry to the theatre was by ticket only, sometimes louts and drunkards would create trouble. The play would be suspended until order was restored, inconveniencing the gentlemen among the viewers. Such undesirable incidents also happened during English dramas, which were attended by soldiers and sailors seeking entertainment.

In every drama there were one or two intervals, during which vendors sold peanuts, soda, and snacks. These were also times when commotion filled the lower-class sections. Basically, the Parsi theatre audience represented the middle and lower working classes. They responded to anything new or unusual with vocal demonstrations. The Parsi companies sometimes performed in prose, sometimes in verse, sometimes in a mixture of both. The lyrics of the songs were metrical and rhythmic, but not truly poetic. Still, the audience enjoyed them, clapping and shouting their appreciation.

THE PLAYWRIGHT AND THE SPECTATORS

In the absence of spectators, the creation of drama is an impossibility. The playwright not only expresses himself, he also expresses the interests and desires of the society of which he himself is a part. In the early stages of the theatre, Parsis were drawn to their history and religion. Kaikhushro Kabraji recognized this craving and in consequence created the plays *Bejan ane Manijeh, Jamshed* and *Faredun*. The Parsi public welcomed his brave move. His farces, which were performed on the same stage after the main drama, satirized elements of contemporary society.

Together with the revival of feelings towards their community, elite Parsi families were increasingly affected by contact with the English and their culture. The Parsis had come from outside India and settled here. They were better suited to adopting English ways of living than Indian ones. Many adaptations of English plays were performed on the Parsi stage. Some dramas took their plots from English novels. In order to please the spectators, several versions of *Hamlet* were enacted. Then fairies, princes, devils and wizards from Muslim tales became more attractive than English spirits and ghosts, and the Parsi stage presented its patrons with such highly successful plays as *Indar Sabha, Khurshed Sabha, Farrukh Sabha, Havai Majlis* and *Benazir Badremunir*.

When the Parsi theatrical companies turned their attention towards the Hindu spectators, they had plays written on such stories as *Harishchandra, Gopichand, Mahabharat, Ramlila* and *Bhakt Prahlad*, which they subsequently performed. Very fine plays were also written on patriotic and devotional themes, for example the Alexandria Company's powerful production of *Vatan* (Homeland). *Zakhm-e Panjab* (The Wounds of the Punjab) was prevented from being performed by the government for a number of years. The democratic nature of theatre is evident from the heterogeneity of its spectators. If a play is written only for the aristocratic class, then its failure is certain. The playwright through his endeavours meets the ordinary people face to face. How then can he ally himself to only one class? As Samuel Johnson said, 'The drama's laws the drama's patrons give. For we that live to please must please to live.'

PERFORMANCE SPACE OR STAGE

It cannot be disputed that the stage is as important as the script to the creation of drama, for the stage is where the presentation occurs. No description is available of the shape of the earliest stage of the Parsi theatre. But Dhanjibhai Patel has written that when the Irani Theatrical Company performed *Rustam ane Barjor* in the Grant Road Theatre, both warriors made their entrances seated on the backs of actual horses, challenging each other to do battle.[2] This gives some sense of the likely width and depth of the stage. Regarding the theatre

FIGURE 22. Cowasjee Patel and a young actor before a painted curtain. Courtesy: Indira Gandhi National Centre for the Arts.

used by the New Alfred Company, its width including wings was seventy feet, with a depth of sixty feet, excluding the dressing room. The seating area was 115 feet by sixty feet, or 6,900 square feet. The stage proper included the central space with curtains and wings, a subterranean layer with trapdoor, and a revolving platform that was used for box sets.

FIGURE 23. Scene from *Romeo and Juliet*. Source: C. J. Sisson, *Shakespeare in India* (1926).

STAGE SCENERY

Painted curtains which dropped from pulleys according to the action were used in every play. The one closest to the front was called the drop scene, and behind it the curtains were changed in accordance with the drama. Usually the street scene was the one most used after the drop scene. The actors assembled in front of it for the invocatory prayer as soon as the drop scene was raised. It was also used in farces. Unless some special scene was required, the dialogue scenes of the farces were enacted before it. Other curtains commonly used were the jungle scene, the 'cut' curtain, palace, garden, and camp scenes.

At first these curtains were painted by foreigners, among whom the German Kraus and the Italians Ceroni and Rua were famous.[3] Among the Parsi painters, Pestanji Madan was well known. The

FIGURE 24. The drop scene from a mythological play. Source: Sisson.

Maharashtrian Hindu, Anand Rao, was made a partner in the Zoroastrian Theatrical Company on the basis of his painting. Another known painter from Maharashtra was Divakar. The New Alfred Company's painter, Husain Khan, was also well known. He was illiterate, but his monthly salary was Rs 1500, according to Manakshah Balsara. His co-worker was Dinshah Irani, but he wasn't considered to be as good.

Some dramatists indicated the order of curtains together with the scenes of their plays, as seen in the text of Abdullah's play, *Sakhavat Khudadost Badshah*. Abdullah was the owner of the Indian Imperial Theatrical Company, and this play was written and performed in April 1890. The first scene took place in the court of the king of Yaman, and the script indicated curtain number 13. Altogether there were fourteen curtains plus the drop scene, totalling fifteen. Abdullah's disciple Nazir Beg also adopted this system. The first scene of *Sat Harishchandra* is set at the river bank, shown by curtain number 9. This play too had fourteen curtains; it was written in 1888.

The chief Parsi companies had their own drop scenes made according to their special interests. The Zoroastrian Theatrical Company's drop scene had a religious orientation. It depicted the court of King Gustasp. The messenger of God, Zarathustra, is shown standing in court with a ball of fire in his hand. Near him the hakim Jamasp, Prince Asfandiyar, Pishotan, the warrior Zarir and others are standing respectfully.

On the Victoria Company's drop scene, the throne of King Jamshed was painted under the direction of S. S. Bangali. When Kaikhushro Kabra's *Jamshed* was performed, the Parsi spectators were especially attracted to this drop scene.

The Paris Exhibition was featured on the Elphinstone Company's drop scene. This company mainly performed English plays, so the idea was not inappropriate.

The manager of the Original Victoria Theatrical Company, Dadi Patel, was at odds with Kunvarji Nazir, who had been his partner in the old Victoria before they split up. Patel had a drop scene made that showed a powerful serpent, which was supposed to be Nazir. A beautiful prince, Patel himself, sat above on a balcony looking at the hissing snake as it tried unsuccessfully to bite him.

The Baronet Theatrical Company depicted J. J. Hospital on a portion of its drop scene, and a picture of Sir Jamshedji Jijibhai was painted above it. The hospital was the sign of his charity and munificence. Every night at the start of the performance the company manager, Nasharvanji Forbes, used to sing a *ghazal* by Bandekhuda in praise of Jijibhai.

Dadi Thunthi founded the Hindi Theatrical Company and had a drop scene painted with a Hindu woman praying in a temple. This author saw a similar curtain painted by Divakar in the possession of Manak Lal, the manager of the Shah Jahan Theatrical Company. Maybe this was the drop scene of the Hindi Theatrical Company.

LIGHTING

In the early period, there was no electricity. The stage was lit by candles, clay lamps filled with oil, or torches. There were no footlights at that time. Gradually, gas lights were introduced. Gas or carbide was first used by Kunvarji Nazir in his production of the *Indar Sabha*, when he bathed the stage in different colours according to the dress of the fairies. When electricity was later invented, there was a great increase in the appeal of the scenes, and various fantastic effects could be shown.

The lights were raised and dimmed for the entrances and exits of the characters. The lights were put out completely for a moment when a deity descended from heaven or entered the earth. Sometimes the lights would be reduced suddenly to allow the entrance of dancers from behind columns. To create the illusion of a sunset, Dadi Patel first made use of magnesium in a Persian play. The Parsi theatre companies were quite aware of the importance of the use of lighting. Many non-Parsi troupes were influenced by them.

COSTUMES

Ordinarily, stage dress was sparkling and gaudy, although historical dramas were performed in appropriate costumes. The crowns of kings and queens were studded with glass bits that glittered brightly. The female characters wore many kinds of costume jewellery; necklaces, bracelets, and anklets were all of artificial materials. When a dancer wore a particular costume for a dance, she was not supposed to wear it again later in the play. This resulted in dancers appearing sometimes

FIGURE 25. Master Nainuram. Courtesy: Natya Shodh Sansthan.

in English frocks, sometimes in Punjabi salwar-kameez, and sometimes in sari and blouse. Hindu characters wore dhotis and wooden sandals, with sages displaying white beards and matted hair. Muslims generally wore beards, of a shape and size consonant with the character's social role. Three colours were commonly used: white, black, and brown or reddish.

The make-up of today was not available, and although Parsis are usually fair-skinned, they would apply zinc oxide to lighten their

FIGURE 26. Typical costumes used in Shakespeare adaptations. Source: Sisson.

complexions. Vermilion was used to redden the cheeks and collyrium for accenting the eyes. The actors as a rule applied their own make-up. Wigs were made of hair, and crafted to represent women, bald men, old men, and youngsters with curly locks. Fairies wore velvet pantaloons, and their wings were constructed of lace and silver work. Devils had black complexions and sprouted horns.

MUSIC

Aside from a few *ghazals*, the music of the Parsi theatre was classical: *thumri, dadra, jhinjhoti, kalingara,* and so on. Sometimes the influence of Western music was apparent. The only defect was that the song lyrics lacked deep feeling. In the beginning, dramas were written only in prose. Dadi Patel introduced the notion of opera with *Benazir Badremunir,* and the addiction to songs grew to such an extent that occasions of joy, deaths, wars, and dialogues were all accompanied by singing. These songs did nothing to advance the plot or characterization. The demand for singers increased accordingly, and their commercial value soared.

Notes

1 [The following five sections occur not as a separate chapter but under a heading, 'Other Accessories of the Parsi Theatre', Gupt, pp. 212–26.]

2 PNTT, pp. 117–18.

3 [PNTT, p. 412.]

The *Indar Sabha* and Its Influence

The original *Indar Sabha* was written by Saiyad Agha Hasan, whose pseudonym was 'Amanat'. According to Amanat's son Saiyad Hasan Latafat, 'Friends made the request that the story of Raja Indar be cast in verse replete with metrical varieties such as *ghazal, masnavi, nazm, thumri, holi, basant, savan, dadra*, and *chhand*, to display in language [the author's] munificence of sensibility and brilliance of mind.'[1] From this it is clear that the *Indar Sabha* had no connection to Wajid Ali Shah, although the common opinion is that he commissioned the drama and played the part of Indar in it.

Amanat himself said, 'Because of my state, I did not go much into society. Due to a speech defect, I sat at home and grew anxious. One day, one of my well-wishers, Haji Mirza Abid Ali Ibadat, suggested affectionately that I should compose a poetic entertainment in the manner of a *rahas*, and thereby earn fame in the world.'[2]

The question then arises, what is meant by *rahas*? *Rahas* is the Urdu translation of the Hindi word *ras*, meaning 'circle-dance'. Later *rahas* was applied to those plays based on the amours of Krishna and the *gopis*. The word was also used for the performances of professional *ras* players or *rasdharis*. These plays took up religious themes. According to Dr Rizvi, 'Wajid Ali Shah, after composing the *Rahas of Radha and Kanhaiya*, wrote plays based on other tales, and he gave them all the name *rahas*, expanding the meaning of the word. Now

FIGURE 27. Cover of Amanat's *Indar Sabha*, published in
1853. Courtesy: The British Library.

every play regardless of its subject was called a *rahas*.' On this basis, the
Indar Sabha was also considered a *rahas* in the beginning. On the title
page of the third edition, the following was written: *jalsa rahas parilafa
maruf be indar sabha*. On the title page of the Altaf Press edition,
Kanpur, the words are: *jalsa rahas madan husan va safa musammi be indar
sabha*. Amanat himself stated, 'This book, a *rahas*, published for the
second time,' and 'Published for the third time, this book, a *rahas*.'[3]

FIGURE 28. Ramdulari playing the Sabz Pari, or Emerald Fairy, in the *Indar Sabha*. Courtesy: Natya Shodh Sansthan.

In its time, the *Indar Sabha* earned a degree of fame scarcely imaginable. It was translated into Indian and non-Indian languages. Its lyrics and tunes inhabited the tongues of singers. Through it, forgotten classical music received an elixir of new life. It was translated into Marathi and German. Its influence in Sri Lanka is found in plays in the Sinhala language. It became so influential that some dramatic companies performed portions of it before the main item in order to entice spectators. With its widespread impact, romantic tales about demons, fairies, Indar, and princes, and their dramatic presentation, became famous under the name of the *Indar Sabha*. The Muslim author Nazir Beg in his play *Harishchandra* sent Vishvamitra to the Caucasus mountains, considered the home of the fairies, so that he could get support in his attempts to lure Harishchandra away from the truth. This episode, while on the one hand inappropriate to the plot, on the other hand proves the influence of the *Indar Sabha*.

Due to the influence of the *Indar Sabha*, several *sabhas* and *jalsas* were written. Some famous compositions are the following:

(1) *Pariyon ki Havai Majlis*. *Majlis* and *sabha* are synonyms, meaning 'assembly' or 'gathering'. This play was written by Khansahab Nasharvanji Mehrvanji Aram. Qamar uz-Zaman, while sleeping, sees Mahlaqa in a dream and falls in love with her. Upon awakening, he sets off in search of his beloved, and in the end he finds her.

(2) Taking the same plot and title, Munshi Muhammad Miyan Manzur wrote a play for the Victoria Theatrical Company. It is in three acts with rhymed verse.

Qamar uz-Zaman, son of Raja Jahandar Shah in the town of Halab, sees Mahlaqa, daughter of Shah-e Jin, king of the Caucasus mountains, in a dream and falls in love with her. While he is dreaming, it turns morning and his servant enters and awakens him. The prince, whose dream is interrupted, is so angry that he raises his sword to kill the servant. Just then his minister enters. The minister too is threatened, but he promises to find the princess Mahlaqa, and with that the prince is consoled. Then the minister and prince set off to find Mahlaqa together.

As daughter of the king of fairyland, Mahlaqa lives in a palace guarded by devils (*devs*), which can only be reached by means of magic and charms. While Qamar is on his love-mission, he meets an ascetic on the road who gives him a special club and tells him that it will help him in his difficulties. And this is what happens. Qamar reaches Mahlaqa's palace only after defeating the *devs* with his magic and charms.

An assembly of fairies is taking place in Paristan. The fairies are singing *ghazals* for princess Mahlaqa, and the princess appears in midair. She also explains her sadness to them in a *ghazal*. At this her maid announces that Qamar has arrived, but she remains immersed

FIGURE 29. Handbill for a Calcutta performance of the *Indra Sabha* in 1938. Courtesy: Natya Shodh Sansthan.

in her song of separation. The maid still consoles her and says to consider herself married to him.

Meanwhile the *dev* is very startled to see Qamar there, but he becomes humble when he views the magical club. The prince tells him of his love for Mahlaqa in a *ghazal*.

At this, the *dev* claps and the princess suddenly appears. Qamar and Mahlaqa look at each other and declare their mutual love. In the midst of this, Shah-e Jin arrives and seeing the whole scene, is startled.

He interrogates the prince, who replies with a declaration of love. Joining voice with him, the princess expresses her desire that they be married. This is enough for Shah-e Jin to give Mahlaqa's hand to Qamar. After further song and dance, the play ends.

(3) Taking the same story, Haji Abdullah wrote a play called *Havai Majlis va Hataf Nairang Tilasm* for his drama company, the Indian Imperial Theatrical Company.

(4) It is said that Munshi Raunaq also wrote a play by the name of *Pariyon ki Havai Majlis*. Maulvi Mohammad Abdul Vahid Qais wrote a play *Jalsa-e Paristan*. Qais was a disciple of Haji Abdullah and wrote the play at his direction. His play was also performed by the Indian Imperial Theatrical Company.

(5) Aram wrote a play called *Farrukh Sabha*. This too is a play in verse. Another name for it is *Qamar uz-Zaman va Vazm Ara*. It is said to have been written in 1883, and it too was written for the Victoria Company. The plot is almost the same. Qamar is the son of King Alam Shah of Husainabad. Just like the Qamar of *Havai Majlis*, this prince also sees Vazm in a dream and falls in love with her. Vazm seeing Qamar in a dream likewise falls in love with him and sends a *dev* to bring him to her. The prince narrates his dream and expresses his uneasiness before his father. Astrologers and magicians are called to determine the meaning of the dream. They recommend that a Negro (*habshi*) be put to sleep in the prince's bed. The Negro, mistaken for the prince, is carried off, but Vazm is distressed at not finding her beloved. Her guru advises her to take on the guise of a maid-servant and go to Qamar. When the opportunity arises, she should carry him off. Vazm finds the right moment and with the aid of Simtan Pari carries off the prince. But the prince rejects her overtures of love. The princess imprisons him. The ruler of Paristan, Shah Farrukh, finds out about this and marries Vazm to Qamar and Simtan Pari to the Negro. The

play ends happily. This play is sometimes confused with the afore-mentioned *Qamar uz-Zaman*.

(6) *Khurshed Sabha* or *Sani Indarsabha* was written by the famous Urdu author Shamsul Ulama Muhammad Husain 'Azad' Dehlavi.

(7) *Ishrat Sabha* or *Lajjat-e Ishq*. No author is listed; only the publisher's name is given. But some lines at the end of the play indicate that the book's author is one Amiruddin.

(8) *Nagar Sabha*, written by Kali Prasad Ji. It is said to have been published in 1874, but no description is available.

(9) Another drama by the same name, written by Bakhsh Ilahi 'Nami'. It also is not described. Another composition by the same author is *Ashiq Sabha*, but it is not available anywhere either.

(10) *Bandar Sabha*, written by Bharatendu Harischandra and actually a parody of the eponymous dramas. In this *Indar Sabha* there is a Shuturmurg (Ostrich) Fairy. The whole composition is so beautiful that one wonders why the writer only parodied a portion of the original. If the whole of the *Indar Sabha* had been cast in this form, it would have been a contribution to Hindi literature.

(11) Husaini Miyan Zarif also wrote an *Indar Sabha*, named *Nai Janakvati Indar Sabha*, *urf Gulshan Pur Fiza*. Aside from a few parts at the beginning, it is entirely the *Indar Sabha* of Amanat.

The following characteristics are found from examining the above *sabha* and *jalsa* plays.

(1) All of the plays are in verse, with different prosodic forms and *raga-raganis* included.

(2) The language of them all is Urdu mixed with Hindi. This is the language understood by most spectators. In the places where difficult Urdu is used, it must have been beyond the comprehension

of most spectators, but the abundance of music and the context would have ameliorated the difficulties.

(3) All plays have at the most three acts, and at the least two. In comparison with prose plays, they are short because of the predominance of music.

(4) All the plays' plots are in the same stream of thought. Either a fairy falls in love with a mortal and then the mortal falls in love with her, or it happens the opposite way, but in the end both are surely united. The objective is completed through the help of the *devs*. All *devs* and *paris* are subjects of some king or another. The place is generally Paristan or Koh-e Kaf (the Caucasus Mountains). The kings' names are various. The introduction of flying beds, *devs*, and fairies into literature is a contribution of the Muslims.

(5) The atmosphere of all the plays is filled with magic and the marvellous. The hero obtains the heroine only by overcoming magic, and the reason for his success is a mantra or *asa* that he gets from a sannyasi.

(6) Magic and charms create a visible spectacle, to convey which on stage the Parsi theatrical companies spent thousands of rupees. Because of this element of wonderment, large numbers of spectators came to see these plays. These scenes were also featured in advertisements.

In conclusion, one must acknowledge that Amanat's *Indar Sabha* gave rise to innumerable spectacular musical dramas. The fame of the *Indar Sabha* spread through its many adaptations as various dramatic companies travelled around performing it. A number of dramas were influenced by it, featuring the same cast of divine characters. These writers were not unethical in their borrowings, they were simply under the *Indar Sabha*'s sway. Its songs and melodies were popular through-out the land. Even the island of Ceylon was affected, where the first Sinhala playwright, Mr Fernandes, was greatly influenced by it.[4]

Notes

1   Saiyad Masud Hasan Rizvi, *Lakhnau ka Avami Istej* (Lucknow: Kitab Ghar, 1957), p. 44.

2   Ibid., p. 44.

3   Ibid., pp. 45–46.

4   [The first Sinhala playwright is generally considered to be C. Don Bastian. No 'Mr Fernandes' appears in the commonly available histories of Sinhala drama.]

CHAPTER 8

Impact of the Parsi Theatrical Companies

From this brief outline, it is apparent how many companies were established by the Parsis in Bombay, and among them which could stand in the competition. These companies also toured outside Bombay and earned great profit and fame in various parts of India. Some even went to foreign countries and made a name for themselves there.

In this country, their influence extended in all directions. Southeast of Bombay in Hyderabad and in Madras, theatrical companies were established that performed numerous plays in Urdu. Several theatre houses and troupes were formed in Maharashtra that show the clear influence of the Parsi companies. In the distant north, a number of companies were started in imitation of Parsi companies in Peshawar, Lahore, Amritsar, and Ludhiana. Many theatrical companies were also established in Uttar Pradesh. In addition, non-commercial companies were also formed in the United Provinces that performed plays in *shuddh* or chaste Hindi. Among the actors in these companies were Pandit Madan Mohan Malviya, Pandit Madhav Shukla and Pandit Pratap Narayan Mishra.

At the end of the theatre era when the talkies arrived, films like *Alam Ara* and *Khun-e Nahaq* were taken directly from the Parsi stage. Later the drama and the cinema diverged on account of their separate techniques. The spectatorship succumbed to cheap entertainment, and theatre came to a virtual halt.

OTHER THEATRE COMPANIES

Parsi Amateurs Dramatic Club. This club appears to be very old. Its monogram was found on a copy of Talib's *Harishchandra* in the author's possession, on which is written: 'not for sale, rehearsal copy'.

Diamond Jubilee Theatrical Company. Among its leaders was Dhanjibhai Patel. Rustam Fiddler first attained fame here.

Parsi Jubilee Theatrical Company. Its founder was Kunvarji Nazir. After he separated from the Victoria and Elphinstone companies, he created this company. He toured with this company among the princely states outside of Bombay. When they were performing in Tonk, he fell ill; he died and his final rites were carried out at a Parsi resting place in Jaipur.

Bombay Parsi Original Opera Company. As is apparent from the name, this company was known for its operas.

Arya Bhushan. This was a famous company of Poona whose main purpose was to perform Marathi plays, though they also performed in Hindustani. *Harun Rashid* was performed by them.

Arya Subodh. This was also established in Poona. Among its managers was Rustam Modi, Sohrab Modi's elder brother.[1] Joseph David directed for this company. David performed Hamlet in *Khun-e Nahaq*, and later this role was performed by Sohrab Modi. Marathi plays and their Hindi adaptations were also performed. The company didn't last long.

National. Its director was Joseph David. They performed *Aftab-e Dakkin*.

New Parsi Theatrical Company. They performed *Dhup Chhaon, Har Jit, Kali Nagin, Dukhtar Farosh,* all under Joseph David's direction.

Imperial. This was a famous company, but little is known about it except that Joseph David directed for them *Naqli Shahzada, Andaz-e Jafa, Bhola Shikar, Tir-e Havis, Hur-e Arab, Khaki Putla, Matlabi Duniya,*

FIGURE 30. Plaque commemorating the opening of the playhouse in Jaipur in 1878. Courtesy: Natya Shodh Sansthan.

Ghafil Musafir, Eshiyai Sitara, Nur-e Vatan, Sansar Nauka, Bagh-e Iran, Karm Prabhav, Sher-e Kabul, Qaumi Diler, and *Nur men Nar.*

Aside from the above-mentioned companies, the following were established outside of Bombay:

Nizami Company, Hyderabad. Performed *Adha Nikah* and *Ajib Ishq,* both written by Muhammad Shamsuddin Amir Hamza 'Amir'.

Mahbub Shahi Natak Company, Hyderabad. Performed Amir's *Sahir Sabha.*

Deccan Dramatic Company performed Amir's *Sahar Khamri* and *Zauhar Khanjar.*

Ballroom Company performed Amir's *Lalvi ki Naqal.*

Albert Natak Company, established in Madras. Performed Amir's *Tilasm Ishq, Namuna Asmat, Zohra Mushtari.*

FIGURE 31. The old theatre of Jaipur, now the Ramprakash Cinema. Courtesy: Natya Shodh Sansthan.

From north India the following companies are known:

Ripon Indian Club, Peshawar.

Civilized Theatrical Company, Lahore.

Original Opera and Dramatic Company, Lahore. Saiyid Buzurg Shah Manager performed a translation of a Gujarati play entitled *Tilasmat Sulemani* in 1887.

Victoria Theatrical Company, Amritsar.

New Indian Opera Theatrical Company, Sakkar, Sindh. They performed *Afsun-e Ishq*.

Alexandria Theatrical Company

Its founders were Mohammad Seth and Zeb Seth. In 1908 its managing proprietor was Joseph David, a fact known from the preface to two plays, *Sunhari Khanjar* and *Ah-e Mazlum*. Its first play was *Intaqam* written by Suleman 'Asif'. After that, *Ah-e Mazlum* written by Khali-ul Rahman 'Khalil' Muradabadi was performed. Their third play was *Sunhari Khanjar* by Ibrahim 'Mahshar' Ambalavi. Later plays included *Khuni Sherni*, by Ishrat Husain Taiyyar, and *Vatan*, which this author saw in Muradabad in 1919–20. This was a drama full of nationalist sentiment, and those were the days of the Non-Cooperation Movement. Thus *Vatan's* popularity was completely natural. Among its songs was a very inspiring *ghazal*: *jo aye mehman hamare hokar lage hakumat hamin pe karne/ makan se bahar makan vale pare hue hain.* Several times the company had to suffer the wrath of the British because of its political tendencies. This company used to perform in Bombay in the Ripon Theatre.

The plot of *Sunhari Khanjar* was based on the novel *Vendetta* by Marie Corelli. It also includes a French farce, *Le Bourgeois Gentilhomme* (originally by Moliere). *Ah-e Mazlum* was an adaption from the English writer George W. M. Reynolds.

New Elphinstone Natak Mandali

The name appears on the cover of a book published in 1894, *Gulzar-e Neki, namna Urdu Natak man Gavatam Gayano*, a Gujarati collection of Urdu theatre songs.

Parsi Curzon Natak Mandali

Its manager and director was Mehrji Nasharvanji Surveyor, according to the preface to *Kordil. Kordil* was written by the Calcutta author Zahin. It was performed in Calcutta, in Burma, and in other Indian cities.

Orpheus Theatrical Company

It is not known whose company this was, but they performed *Legion of Yunan* by Ibrahim 'Mahshar'. Mahshar was a good writer, so perhaps this was a good company.

Indian Dilpazir Theatrical Company of Itawah

According to Nami, they performed *Gul Bakavali* by 'Nami', a versified composition published in 1893.

Rajputana-Malwa Theatrical Company of Jhalawar

All that is known is that its managing director was the famous author and actor Nazir Beg Nazir.

Indian Imperial Theatrical Company of Agra

Its owner was Hafiz Mohammad Abdullah, and its patron was the Maharaja of Dhaulpur, L.B.R. Nihal Singh. All of Abdullah's plays were performed by this company, in Dhaulpur, Agra, Kanpur, Gwalior, etc. Nazir Beg Nazir, who later became an independent company owner, was first an actor here.

Moon of India Theatrical Company

Its manager was Muhammad Vazir Khan. Nazir wrote two plays for him, *Sitam Ishq Marufbe Natija Muhabbat* and *Tamasha Gardish-e Taqdir Marufbe Sat Harishchandra Natak*.

New Star of India Theatrical Company of Agra

Its owner in 1904 was Nazir Beg Nazir. The company performed several plays of his.

Lightning of India Theatrical Company

Its managing director was Nazir Beg.

Parsi Jubilee Theatrical Company of Bombay

Managing director was Nazir. Chief actress was Shirin Jan, for whom Nazir wrote several plays. The author thinks this was a United Provinces company that added 'of Bombay' to its name for glamour.

Students' Amateur Club

A non-commercial company that performed a Gujarati adaptation of *Romeo and Juliet* in 1858. The same play was published in 1876 by Dosabhai Randeliya 'Delta'.

The Indian Theatrical Club

Existed in 1868. Performed a Hindustani-language play *Nana Sahab*. Nana Sahab is shown as an enemy of the nation, and the British Raj is praised.

Bharat Vyakul Company

Founded in Meerut by Vishvambar Sahay Vyakul. He authored *Gautam Buddh*, its most famous play. They also performed several plays by 'Mayal'. The company was very popular for some years, but then Vyakulji developed tongue cancer, and after his death the company broke up.

Corinthian Theatrical Company

Founded in Calcutta by the Madan brothers. Slowly it absorbed Betab, Hashr, and all the good playwrights, drawing them to Calcutta. The Alfred and smaller companies were merged into it. Betab's *Patni Pratap* was one of their better plays.

CONCLUSION

Research shows that the first theatre in Bombay was the Bombay Theatre, established in 1776 in front of the present Central Library. It was built by Englishmen, and English plays were performed there. It is natural, therefore, that it imitated the theatre of England. The stage, hall, costumes, and plots were all English, as were the actors and spectators. Gradually this theatre went into debt, and finally it was sold off. In 1846, a new theatre was built on Grant Road to take its place. Here too English plays were performed at first. In 1853, this theatre began to be used for Marathi and then Hindi and Gujarati plays.

Thus all the virtues and vices of the English theatre were inherited by the Parsi theatre. The English mainly worked in service and as businessmen. Drama was a favoured form of entertainment for them. But because of the dearth of actors and lack of resources, theatrical activity was considerably constrained. Only those plays found a place on the stage which were not too serious and had few characters, especially few women characters. Little attention was paid to costuming because of the lack of funds. Farces also became popular, usually occurring at the end of the main drama. The orchestra would perform in between. The sets would not necessarily be appropriate to each play; furniture such as chairs and tables were commonly used. Painting was featured on the curtains, and foreign artists were employed. This was the kind of amateur stage that the Parsis adopted.

This does not mean, however, that only English influence was felt on the theatre of the new playhouses. The Indian folk traditions were also prevalent, and forms like Nautanki and Bhavai had many adherents. The Khetvadi Theatre was a popular venue for the performance of translations from Sanskrit drama. Vishnudas Bhave of Sangli brought his troupe to Bombay in 1853 and created a rage for musical folk theatre. These musical plays were the basis for the later turn towards 'opera'.

The Parsi companies first presented theatrical renditions of historical legends from their homeland, Persia. The plays of Kaikhushro Kabraji were important in this connection. Parsi youths from Elphinstone College were active in establishing drama clubs, and they primarily performed Shakespeare's plays in English. Musical 'sketches' were also popular in the early stages. The practice of including a farce seems to have followed the English example. At first, these were different from the main drama, and usually satirized Parsi customs and society. Later, they were joined to the main drama and added a subplot to it, and gradually became more closely integrated.

The language of the dramas was Gujarati in the beginning. Then Urdu became popular, but this is not to say that the whole audience preferred Urdu. Urdu was well understood in the United Provinces and the Punjab. The playwrights who found employment in the Parsi theatre were all conversant with Urdu, but the introduction of Urdu did not solve the whole problem from the standpoint of business. As Narayan Prasad Betab said in the introduction to his *Mahabharat*, 'Neither pure Urdu, nor chaste Hindi, the language is mixed; the sugar does not stay separate from the milk, it all blends together.'

The influence of the Parsi theatrical companies extended beyond the Parsi community. Non-Parsis also established their companies. In several princely states such as Jaipur and Patiala, theatre houses were built. The subject of the dramatic literature of the princely states requires a separate volume in itself.

Today, certainly, the Indian theatre is searching for its identity anew. But the Parsi theatre cannot be neglected in moulding either the present or future form of theatre. The Parsi theatre was experimental theatre of a sort. Its experiments are visible in the dramas of its time. Let us hope that our theatre directors and patrons do not forget the past in the search for the new theatre.

Note

1 According to an interview with the famous film actor Sohrab Modi.

The Beginnings of Hindi Drama in Bombay and Maharashtra

HINDU THEATRE

The plays performed in the Bombay Theatre (1776-1846) were always in English. Even in the newly established Grant Road Theatre, plays were primarily performed in English. The Maharashtra State Archives and Antiquities Department contains two editions of *Theatre Diaries* in which a list of dramas performed between 1816 and 1819 is included. In these daily listings, no Indian language play is mentioned.

From the 16 February 1846 issue of the daily newspaper, *The Bombay Times and Journal of Commerce*, it is learned that attempts to revive 'Hindu drama' had been made before February 1846 and that they had been successful. But what those attempts were and which plays were performed is not illuminated. Only this, that a theatrical committee was formed to arrange for performances. This committee announced that on the following Sunday a play would be performed in Khetvadi. The editor notes that this was a translation of a Sanskrit drama by a Brahmin. The same Brahmin was present on stage in the role of the jester (*vidushak*) and directed the play.

It seems that there is particular significance attached to the terms 'Hindu drama' and 'Hindu theatre'. Ordinarily this terminology indicates that some concrete object such as a 'Hindu playhouse' or 'Hindu drama' exists. But my guess is that 'Hindu theatre' was used to designate the entire Hindu art of theatre. This phrase was the invention of Mr Horace Wilson, who translated certain Sanskrit plays under the rubric of 'Hindu theatre' and published their synopses.[1] He called the Sanskrit plays 'Hindu drama' because they were written by Hindu playwrights. The contemporary newspapers use these words to refer to plays written by Hindus or performed by them, rather than referring to any specific playhouse or particular play. This view is supported by the item from *The Bombay Times*, which is on page 316. Hemendra Nath Das Gupta has also used the phrase 'Hindu theatre'.[2] Thus those scholars who consider 1853 to be the start of Indian language dramas—whereas in Sangli, Vishnudas Bhave presented *Sita Svayamvar* in 1843 in Marathi—will have to rethink their position.

The same newspaper item also provides information about the stage, acting, and costumes in 1846. The stage was not a raised platform or *chabutra*. There were no chairs at the ground level for spectators to sit on. Benches were arranged in ascending rows on all four sides like bleachers, and hundreds of viewers including rich, poor, high, and low sat there to watch the play. No distinctions were made according to class or caste. It can be assumed that the site was like an open-air theatre.

Before the beginning of the play, the jester entered and acquainted the audience with the entire plot of the drama. Then the actors entered the stage wearing sparkling and unusual costumes, and in this way the performance got under way. The jester was present in every scene, entertaining the audience with his pithy sayings from time to time.

How long these plays in Khetvadi went on and which dramas were performed is not known. Another point to remember is that there is no indication of the language of the dramas. Possibly they were in Marathi, but there is no reference to this in the history by Professor Banhatti.[3] It may be that they were written in Hindustani.

My opinion is that these plays of 1846 should be considered a link in the chain that began in 1843 with Vishnudas Bhave's *Sita Svayamvar* in Sangli. There is some difference of approach in the Marathi dramas performed by the Bhave troupe from 1843 to 1851. It is certain that in the translated dramas, Sanskrit prose must have been used in the dialogues. This prose portion does not appear in the text of the *Natyakavitasangrah* composed by Bhave.[4]

The second stage of Marathi drama began when Vishnudas Bhave's theatre troupe came to Bombay. This was Bhave's first trip to Bombay, although the company had toured beyond Sangli previously, ending their tour in Poona. The Bombay tour is thought to have occurred between February and April of 1853. Based on *The Bombay Times*, 16 February 1853, Professor Banhatti considers the first performance of Bhave's plays to have taken place on 14 February 1853. This performance occurred in the garden of Vishvanath Atmaram Shimpi. The dramas performed were *Indrajit Vadh, Sulochana Sahagaman, Ashvamedh Yajna*, and *Lav-Kush Akhyan*.[5] The newspaper says that the performance began at precisely seven in the evening. Although the arrangements were not exemplary, nonetheless the local gentlemen who took on the burden of organization deserved praise. The attendance was very large. The accomplished actors performed *Sulochana* until a quarter of ten, and the remainder of the time was devoted to *Lav-Kush Akhyan*. The acting of the boys was particularly notable. Among them was a big man who called himself Mahadev and took every opportunity to regale the audience with jokes. The performance ended at two in the morning.

The same dramas by Bhave were performed again in the Grant Road Theatre on Thursday, 9 March 1853.[6]

Professor Banhatti makes no mention of any performance by the Bhave troupe between 14 February and 9 March 1853. In fact, the Bhave troupe performed in the Muledhar temple on Saturday, 18 February, as well. The patron of this performance was Mr Atmaram Kesho Bhandari.[7] The arrangements were deplorable. Neither were there chairs, nor pit, nor stage, although the venue was given the designation of *rangmanch*. Carpets were spread on the ground and the spectators sat on them. The noise of the women and men folk made it impossible for the actors to entertain the spectators. The drama *Ram Vanvas* was performed, lasting from 9 p.m. to 2 a.m.

These notices create a certain confusion. Were 'The Hindu Dramatic Corps' and 'The Hindu Dramatic Corps of Sangli' two names for the same troupe, or were there two separate companies? According to the notice in *The Bombay Times* of 16 February 1853, the Bhave troupe was called 'The Hindu Theatre'. This phrase could also have been used for Bhave's dramas. The notice of 8 March 1853 refers to 'The Hindu Dramatic Corps, recently arrived from the Deccan.' Again, in the 11 March 1853 issue, 'The Hindu Dramatic Corps, recently arrived from Sangli' is named. The remaining notices refer only to 'The Hindu Dramatic Corps'.

From all of these notices, it can be concluded that 'The Hindu Dramatic Corps' and 'The Hindu Dramatic Corps of Sangli' were both names for Bhave's theatrical troupe, and that after coming to Bombay, this troupe changed its name because of other theatrical companies which must have been performing under caste-specific names. If only to distinguish themselves from the theatricals of the English, which took place in the Bombay Theatre, this name seemed appropriate. To inform the English spectators, the 'Hindu Dramatic Corps' may be considered to have been founded in contradistinction to the English companies.

The Bhave company had been called 'The Sanglikar Hindu Players' (*sanglikar hindu natakkar*), according to the Marathi newspaper, *Jnanprakash*, 21 January 1853.[8] On 15 May 1862, *Jnanprakash* called this company 'The Old Sanglikar Players' (*kadimi sanglikar natakkar*), from which it appears that some new company called 'The Sanglikar Players' had arisen.

To sum up, around 1846 Indian-language dramas began to be performed in Bombay, and up to 1853 there is ample description of them in the newspapers. But these dramas were probably in the Marathi language.

HINDI PLAYS

Now the question arises, when was the first Hindi play performed in Bombay? A notice in *The Bombay Telegraph and Courier*, 24 November 1853, announced, 'The Hindu Dramatic corps most respectfully beg to acquaint the Bombay public, Native and European, that they will have the honour to appear on the boards of the Grant Road Theatre, on Saturday the 26th instant, when the interesting play of Raja Gopichund and Jalunder will be performed in Hindoostanee.' On 3 January 1854, *The Bombay Times* ran a notice saying that both parts of *Raja Gopichand and Jalandhar* would be performed. The ticket prices had been reduced to attract more spectators. A synopsis of the play and a review were published in the same paper on 9 January 1854.

AUTHOR OF THE PLAY

Who was the author of *Raja Gopichand and Jalandhar*? In the foreword to his book *Natyakavitasangrah*, Vishnudas Bhave writes, '*mi ek navincha natak vasavun te prayog kela* (I read and experimented with a new play.)' This new play was *Gopichand* and it was written in Hindustani. In this connection, Professor Banhatti cites the author of Vishnudas Bhave's biography, Vasudev Ganesh Bhave.[9]

From these two references, no doubt remains that the author of *Raja Gopichand and Jalandhar* was Vishnudas Bhave himself, and that the *Gopichand Akhyan* printed in the *Natyakavitasangrah* and the *Raja Gopichand and Jalandhar* performed in the Grant Road Theatre were one and the same. Dr Nami's opinion, that Dr Bhau Daji Lad composed *Raja Gopichand and Jalandhar*, is incorrect.[10] He has given no evidence for his claim. Dr Lad was among those who encouraged Bhave to perform his play in the Grant Road Theatre.

In conclusion, if the 1846 Khetvadi Theatre performances of dramas translated from Sanskrit were not in Hindustani, then the first play to be performed in Hindi in Bombay was Bhave's *Raja Gopichand and Jalandhar*, which had its debut in 1853 in the Grant Road Theatre.

CHARACTERISTICS OF THE PLAY *RAJA GOPICHAND AND JALANDHAR*

It appears that Bhave originally titled the drama *Gopichand Akhyan*, but it was changed to *Raja Gopichand and Jalandhar* for the advertisement. This was a musical drama written in folk style. It had no prose sections. At the time of performance, the actors would interpolate prose passages whenever and wherever needed. This showed their skills in improvisation and helped knit together the various parts of the story. Sometimes a spectator would utter a witticism and the actor would immediately satisfy him with a response.

In this drama, the first two lines form the invocation (*mangala-charan*), but this invocation was used as a *nandi*, as was the practice in other dramas. The author could extend it in any fashion at the time of performance, although in the printed text it was short. After this invocation, a short synopsis of the plot follows in fifteen lines. After that, Mainavati enters with her sixteen female companions. She travels to Jalandhar Jogi's place, touches his feet, and tells him her purpose. After a dialogue between the two, the director takes the audience back to the story-line by means of the verse-form *samya*. The entire drama follows this pattern, with passages of dialogue and *samya* sections alternating to stitch the narrative together.

There is no novelty in the play's story. The popular story of King Gopichand, who purifies his mortal body by taking up yoga, is told here in dramatic form. The main characters are Mainavati, Gopichand, and Jalandhar Nath.

THE AUTHOR OF THE COMPOSITION

Basically, it was Vishnudas Bhave, even though his name is only given in the last stanza. Some of the poems in the play are by previous poets, among them Vishvambharnath, Gurunath, and Kabir, and the rest are by him. All the stanzas are meant to be sung and are written in *ragas* and *raginis*.

The language of the play is Hindustani. This is the language which was current at that time in the southern section of the country. It lacks any literary touches. One characteristic of this play is that it shows how far Hindi had spread as a national language and what its form was at that time. There are numerous defects from the standpoint of present-day grammar, but those should not be made the focus of attention. The point is that this language was spoken more than a hundred years ago, insofar as the notice of its performance was first published in *The Bombay Telegraph and Courier* in 1853.

PERFORMANCE OF *GOPICHAND*

When Vishnudas Bhave first came to Bombay, he practised the traditional style of performance familiar to his actors and himself, which he had adapted from the Kannada Yakshagana. The performances of the

Sanglikar Players on 18 February 1853 in the Shri Muledhar temple sponsored by Atmaram Kesho Bhandari and on 14 February in Vishvanath Atmaram Shimpi's garden were in accordance with this traditional practice.

But the performance of *Gopichand* took place in the days when Bhave had already witnessed dramatic performances at the Grant Road Theatre and had become familiar with its European tradition. Certainly he was influenced by these performances and must have thought it would be good if he could perform his play in the same theatre with its tradition of scenery and other European conventions. He expressed this desire, but the daily rent of the theatre seemed to be beyond his means. In the foreword to his *Natyakavitasangrah*, he says the tariff for one night was five hundred rupees. In fact, it was about fifty rupees. It seems that an extra zero was added by the printers in some editions.

It can be imagined how changes were necessary in order to adapt the original text to the conditions of the stage in the Grant Road Theatre. There must have been a special attempt to divide the stanzas into appropriate acts and scenes in order to give it a modern shape. The performance copy of the script must have been different from the original text. Moreover, when the play was performed again, it was divided into two parts. Thus it should be considered Hindi's good fortune that among its earliest dramas *Gopichand* obtained the shelter of an entirely modern stage.

CONTEMPORARY AUDIENCE

It is sufficient to mention that the audience that took an interest in the English plays at the Bombay Theatre was made up of respectable, upstanding Englishmen, as well as youth in the navy and army who often made noise and prevented others from hearing. But the audience for Hindu dramas mainly sat on carpets spread on the floor to watch the plays. There was no raised stage in front of them. The tickets to these shows were sold relatively cheaply. Thus the number of spectators must have been fairly large. Among them men, women, and children were all present. Noise would have been a natural result. Nonetheless there was no lewdness or violence in their behaviour. Because the stories of Hindu dramas were from the Puranas, the attitude of the viewers was full of devotion. For this reason they maintained self-control.

No particular attention was given to the costumes. Although there is no detailed description available of the Hindu Dramatic Corps, still it can be assumed that male and female characters used whatever dresses were available. There was no thought as to their historicity.

CONCLUSION

From the above it is clear that the first known drama to be played in Bombay in Hindi was Bhave's *Gopichand* or *Gopichand and Jalandhar*.

Bharatendu's assertion that the first performed Hindi play was *Janaki Mangal*, which played in the Banaras Theatre in 1868, is false.

There is another reference to a drama performed by the Marathi companies. It too was called *Gopichand*, and its author was Annaji Govind Inamdar.

The famous Marathi dramatic company of Ichalkaranji was praised at different times for its achievements. Various favourable reviews of the company are listed by Professor Banhatti in Appendix 10 of his book.[11] Among those praising the company is the name of Annaji Govind Inamdar. All that can be concluded from this reference is that he was fond of drama. He was a connoisseur of the dramatic art and was not far behind in encouraging it.

The same Inamdar composed a play called *Gopichand*. The date of composition is not known, but it is certain that the play was published in three editions. The first edition was published in Solapur in 1869, a copy of which is in the India Office Library in London.[12] The second edition was printed in 1877 in Bombay by Bhau Govind, and the third on 22 February 1887 in Poona by Jnan Chakshu Press in Budhwar Peth. It is surprising for a book to go into three editions in Hindi. This shows how popular the play was. It appears from the prologue to the third edition that the drama was improved in each edition. Where the author felt the connections in the plot were weak, he made great attempts to strengthen them.

Notes

1 [Horace Hayman Wilson, *Select Specimens of the Theatre of the Hindus, Translated from the Original Sanskrit*, 2 vols. 3rd edn, London: Trübner, 1871.]

2 Hemendra Nath Das Gupta, *The Indian Stage*, Vol. 1 (Calcutta: M. K. Das Gupta, 1946), p. 280.

3 Shrinivas Narayan Banhatti, *Marathi Rangbhumi cha Itihas* (Pune: Venus Prakashan, 1957).

4 [Vishnu Amrit Bhave, *Natyakavitasangrah*, Adya Maharashtra Natakakarte, 1885, cited in Banhatti, p. 20.]

5 Banhatti, Appendix no. 7 [p. 391].

6 [Banhatti, p. 392.]

7 *The Bombay Times*, 22 February 1853, pp. 358–59.

8 Banhatti, pp. 108–09, 212.

9 Banhatti, pp. 104–05. [Vasudev Ganesh Bhave, *Vishnudas urf Vishnu Amrit Bhave yanche Charitra*, 1943. Banhatti, p. 20.]

10 Nami, *Urdu Thetar*, Vol. 1, p. 192.

11 Banhatti, pp. 417–20.

12 Krishnacharya, *Hindi ke Adi Mudrit Granth* (Varanasi: Bharatiya Jnanpith Prakashan, 1966), p. 5.

Index